The Colonial Virginia Register

A List of Governors, Councillors and Other Higher Officials, and Also of Members of the House of Burgesses, and the Revolutionary Conventions of the Colony of Virginia

Compiled by
William G. Stanard
and
Mary Newton Stanard

HERITAGE BOOKS
2011

HERITAGE BOOKS
AN IMPRINT OF HERITAGE BOOKS, INC.

Books, CDs, and more—Worldwide

For our listing of thousands of titles see our website
at
www.HeritageBooks.com

A Facsimile Reprint
Published 2011 by
HERITAGE BOOKS, INC.
Publishing Division
100 Railroad Ave. #104
Westminster, Maryland 21157

Originally published
Albany
1902

Library of Congress Catalog Card Number: 65-21922

— Publisher's Notice —
In reprints such as this, it is often not possible to remove blemishes from the original. We feel the contents of this book warrant its reissue despite these blemishes and hope you will agree and read it with pleasure.

International Standard Book Numbers
Paperbound: 978-0-7884-2395-6
Clothbound: 978-0-7884-8618-0

TABLE OF CONTENTS

Preface	5
Governor	13
Secretary of State	21
Auditor General	22
Receiver General	23
Treasurer	24
Attorney General	25
Surveyor General	26
The Council	27
The House of Burgesses	51
The Conventions of 1775 and 1776	201

PREFACE

The compilers of this *Register* trust that it may prove useful to students of Virginia History and Genealogy.

They have been at pains, through diligent research and faithful citation, to secure for it that accuracy which is the only merit of a book of its character, and have exhausted all American sources known to them, though they believe it possible that there may be some few lists of the House of Burgesses which, in spite of every effort, they have failed to bring to light. They are well aware that many lists could be added from the unpublished journals of the House of Burgesses in the British Public Record Office, which they hope may some day be copied for the Virginia Historical Society, or the Virginia State Library, and the information contained in them be made accessible.

There will be found below, a very brief account of the various offices of the Colonial Government, and some notice of the sources from whence the lists are derived.

GOVERNOR.—The Colony of Virginia was from 1607 to 1624, under the control of the Virginia Company, of London. At the first settlement, in 1607, the governing body consisted of a council of seven, with a president whom they were to select out of their own number. This system lasted until 1609, when the Company chose a Governor and Lieutenant-Governor (Lord Delaware and Sir Thomas Gates) who were the first to bear those titles, and whose successors were, like themselves, appointed by the Company, until the revocation of its charter.

Throughout the remainder of the Colonial period the executives of Virginia were appointed by the King. Their titles varied, some being styled "Governor and Captain-General," others "Lieutenant Governor," or "Deputy Governor." From 1704 to 1768 the higher title was borne by sinecures in England, while the actual power was in the hands of "Lieutenant Governors," resident in Virginia.

Vacancies were occasionally supplied, until an appointment could be made in England, by the election of a governor, by the Council, but this was only the case during the earlier years of the Royal Government. Later, the office was filled by the succession of the member of the Council senior in point in service, under the title President of the Council, or sometimes, President of Virginia.

From 1652 to 1660 the Governors were elected by the House of Burgesses, though there is some reason to believe that their choice may have been influenced by the wishes of the Parliamentary authorities, or of Cromwell.

SECRETARY OF STATE.—Lord Culpeper, writing in 1683, said, "The Secretary is a patent officer, from the first seating of the country, the very next in dignity to the Governor, or Commander-in-Chief." The office was one which conferred much power and influence on the occupant. He had the right to appoint all county clerks, and as these were men of weight in their respective communities, it was frequently charged that through them the Secretary exercised too much influence in the House of Burgesses. He was keeper of the colonial seal and ex-officio clerk of the Council and General Court, though the duties of these offices were actually performed by the titular clerks of the respective bodies.

All patents and other papers from the executive were issued from the Secretary's office, and all of the executive records, as well as those of the General Court were in his custody.

An important part of the Secretary's duties was to keep the English government constantly informed in regard to affairs in Virginia, and send home copies of all public papers.

AUDITOR GENERAL.—As the name of this office indicates, the duty of the incumbent was to examine and audit all accounts of collectors and receivers of the public revenue in Virginia. During a considerable period the place was held by persons who were nominally deputies, while the chief title was borne by an Auditor General of the Colonies in England.

THE RECEIVER GENERAL was the custodian of the revenues of the Colony, particularly of quit rents. There were certain taxes, however, raised under acts of the General Assembly which were in charge of a treasurer elected by that body and which did not go into the hands of the Receiver General.

THE TREASURER at an early period seems to have had the duties afterwards assigned to the Receiver General, and was appointed by the Company, or the King. But from 1693 he was elected by the General Assembly, and had charge of the revenues raised under the laws enacted by that body. Practically he was the agent of the House of Burgesses, and the representatives of the people were so jealous of keeping entire control over this office, that through a long period of years the Speaker of the House was chosen Treasurer.

THE ATTORNEY GENERAL'S office requires no explanation. There were in each county deputy king's attorneys corresponding to our modern commonwealth's attorneys.

THE SURVEYOR GENERAL appointed, and had general supervision over the county surveyors, and it is believed could be appealed to in case of dispute. William and Mary College was granted the office of Surveyor General, but frequently the visitors of the college chose an individual to execute it.

THE COUNCIL.—From 1607 to 1624 the members of the Council were chosen by the Virginia Company, and during the Royal Government, which succeeded, were appointed by the Crown on the recommendation of the Governor. As a rule, when a vacancy occurred, the Governor made a temporary appointment, which was usually confirmed by the King.

The Councillors were the Governor's advisers in executive matters, and patents, etc., are stated to be issued with their "advice and consent." They constituted the General Court —the supreme court of the Colony—and also had legislative functions as members of the upper house of the Assembly, corresponding somewhat to our senate. The same persons, therefore, held executive, legislative, and judicial offices.

Among those slightly acquainted with our colonial history there seems to be a common impression that the House of Burgesses alone constituted the colonial legislature. This, of course, is a mistake, for though the Council did not have the power to originate money bills, yet their concurrence was necessary to all laws, as was also the Governor's consent, and ultimately, the King's.

In addition to the powers already named the members of the Council almost uniformly held the higher offices, such as secretary, auditor, etc., and were also, as a rule, the county lieutenants or commanders in chief in their own and neighboring counties.

Theoretically this accumulation of offices in a few hands was entirely wrong, but it seems, in practice, to have worked fairly well, as the members of the Council, who in general were men whose estates and interests lay entirely in Virginia, do not appear to have had views at variance with those commonly entertained in the Colony.

The House of Burgesses.—This was the popular portion of the Government composed of the representatives of the people. The members were elected upon a suffrage basis which varied at times, but which during all the latter part of the colonial era was a freehold.

After some variation during the first part of the Seventeenth Century the number of Burgesses became fixed at two for each county, with one each for the City of Williamsburg, Borough of Norfolk, Jamestown and William and Mary College. For a time Virginia included one "pocket" or "rotten" borough, for after the population at Jamestown had dwindled away and the island had come into the possession of the Ambler and Travis families, the Burgesses appear to have been practically appointed by these two families.

An assembly could be called, prorogued, or dissolved by the Governor, and very frequently the same assembly would continue in existence for many years, but of course with changes of membership as vacancies occurred.

When a member of the House of Burgesses accepted any

office of profit he vacated his seat in the House by so doing, but was always eligible for re-election except when he became a sheriff or coroner. In the first case it was doubtless thought that the duties of his office would require his presence in his county. There does not seem to be the same objection in the last named case, but at any rate, accepting the office of coroner seems to have been a favorite device for getting out of the House of Burgesses.

Sources of Information

For the lists of Governors, Councillors, Secretaries of State, Auditor, Receiver, Surveyor and Attorney Generals, and Treasurers, the principal sources have been: Of books in print, Alexander Brown's Genesis of the United States and First Republic of America; the various works of E. D. Neill; Hening's Statutes at Large of Virginia; Campbell's History of Virginia; The Calendar of Virginia State Papers; Hotten's Emigrants; The "Collections" of the Virginia Historical Society; The Virginia Magazine of History and Biography; The William and Mary Quarterly; the Lower Norfolk Antiquary; Water's "Gleanings;" the Virginia Colonial Almanacs; the printed journals of the House of Burgesses, and the Virginia Gazette newspaper. Of records in manuscript, information has been chiefly derived from the abstracts of English State Papers made by W. N. Sainsbury for the State of Virginia; the journals of the Council, in the Virginia State Library; the records of the Virginia Company of London (from the copy in the Virginia Historical Society collections); the "Randolph Manuscripts," and "Robinson's Notes," both consisting of extracts from the Virginia colonial records, and both part of the Virginia Historical Society Collections, and various manuscripts relating to the early history of Virginia now in the Congressional Library. Occasional assistance was obtained from the Virginia county records, where not infrequently an order of Council or of the General Court is found recorded with the names of the Councillors present when it was made.

The sources from whence the lists of Burgesses are derived are given under each session, but some little additional explanation may be useful here. It was the rule during most of the Seventeenth Century, and not infrequently in the early years of the Eighteenth, for the salaries of the Burgesses to be paid by their respective counties, and in the levy laid next after the session, these items would appear. In this way the names of many members are found in the county records.

The printed journals of the House of Burgesses in the Virginia State Library and the Congressional Library also afforded most valuable information, for though the names of the members are rarely given in full (except when there are two persons of the same surname) yet in the appointment of committees practically all of the surnames of members appear, and a comparison of these with other lists, together with an acquaintance with Virginia family history and with the county records, enables one to supply with certainty the Christian names. The journals, too, show what vacancies occurred during the existence of the Assembly, by the entry of requests from the House to the Governor to issue writs for new elections, and also furnish names in the action of that body on contested election cases.

The colonial almanacs (which were always published late in the year before that whose date they bear—as is the case now) contain lists which have in the main been found to be very accurate, of the members of the House in existence at the time when the almanac was printed.

The Journals of the Council, sitting as Upper House, also contain information, for they give the names of members of many committees which from time to time came up with bills passed by the Burgesses.

Of course all the remaining volumes of the Virginia Gazette are of much value for this purpose.

RICHMOND, VIRGINIA.
September 28, 1901.

GOVERNOR

1607, April —Captain Edward Maria Wingfield, President of the Council.

1607, Sept. 10.—Captain John Ratcliffe, President of the Council.

1608, Sept. 7.—Captain John Smith, President of the Council.

(1609, May 23.—Thomas West, Lord de la War, or Delaware, appointed "Governor and Captain General;" but did not reach Virginia until June 10, 1610.) Born in England, 1577; died at sea June 7, 1618.

1609 —Captain George Percy, President of the Council. Born in England, September 4, 1586; died in England, March, 1632.

1610, June 10.—Thomas West, Lord Delaware, Governor.

1611, Mar. 28.—Captain George Percy, Deputy Governor.

1611, May 19.—Sir Thomas Dale, "High Marshall," and Deputy Governor.

1611, Aug. —Sir Thomas Gates, Acting Governor.

1612, Mar. —Sir Thomas Dale, Acting Governor.

1616, April —Captain George Yeardley, Lieutenant or Deputy Governor.

Born in England; died in Virginia, November, 1627.

1617, April 9.—Captain Samuel Argall, Lieutenant or Deputy Governor.
Born in England, 1572; died in England, 1639.

1619, April 9.—Captain Nathaniel Powell, Senior Councillor, Acting Governor.
Born in England; killed by the Indians, March 22, 1622.

1619, April 19.—Sir George Yeardley, who had been knighted and appointed Governor and Captain General, November 18, 1618, arrived in the Colony.

1621, Nov. 18.—Sir Francis Wyatt, Governor.
Born in England, 1588; died in England, August, 1644.

1626 —Sir George Yeardley, Lieutenant Governor.

1626, April 19.—Sir George Yeardley, Governor (Commission dated April 19)

1627, Nov. 14.—Captain Francis West elected Governor by the Council.

1628, Mar. 5.—Dr. John Pott elected Governor by the Council.
Born in England; probably died in Virginia.

1629-30, Mar. —Sir John Harvey, Governor. He was deposed by the Council and sent to England.

1635, April 28 (?)—Captain John West elected Governor by the Council.
Born in England, December 14, 1590; died in Virginia, 1659.

1636, April 2.—Sir John Harvey, Governor, arrived in Virginia. (His commission was dated January 11, 1635.)
Born in England; died, it is believed, in Virginia.

1639, Nov. —Sir Francis Wyatt, Governor.

1641-42, Feb. —Sir William Berkeley, Governor.
Born in England, about 1606; died in England, July 19, 1677.

1644, June —Richard Kemp elected Governor by the Council during Sir William Berkeley's absence in England.
Born in England; died in Virginia, 1656.

1645, June —Sir William Berkeley, Governor.

1652, April 30.—Richard Bennett elected Governor by the General Assembly; but probably in accordance with a private intimation of the wishes of the Parliamentary authorities. Bennett, who was one of the commissioners sent by Parliament to subdue Virginia, brought with him sealed instructions, not to be opened until Virginia surrendered.
Born in England; died in Virginia, 1675.

1655, Mar. 31.—Edward Digges, elected Governor by the House of Burgesses.

Born in England, 1620; died in Virginia, March 15, 1675.

1657-8, Mar. 13.—Samuel Matthews, elected Governor by the House of Burgesses, "until the next Assembly, or until the further pleasure of the supreme power in England shall be known."
Born in England; died in Virginia, January, 1660.

1660, Mar. 23.—Sir William Berkeley, elected Governor by the General Assembly. But on March 9, 1659-60, Sir William Berkeley, as Governor, and his Council, appointed a sheriff for Lower Norfolk County. This was four days before his election by the Assembly, so there may be some truth in the old account that he was first made Governor by a popular uprising. His commission from the King was dated July 31, 1660.

1661, April 30.—Col. Francis Moryson, Deputy Governor, during the absence of Berkeley in England.
Born in England; died in England.

1662, Fall of.—Sir William Berkeley, Governor.

1677, April 27.—Herbert Jeffreys, who had been commissioned Lieutenant Governor, November 11, and Governor, October 9, 1676.
Born in England; died December 30, 1678.

1678, Dec. 30.—Sir Henry Chicheley, Deputy Governor, His commission was dated, February 28,

1673-4, and during Culpeper's administration he acted as Deputy Governor during the former's frequent absence from the Colony.

Born in England, 1615; died in Virginia, February 5, 1682-3.

1680, May 10.—Thomas, Lord Culpeper, Governor.

Born in England; died in England, 1719.

1683. Sept. —Nicholas Spencer, President of the Council.

Born in England; died in Virginia, Sept. 23, 1689.

1684, April 15.—Francis, Lord Howard of Effingham, Lieutenant Governor. His commission was dated, September 28, 1683.

Born in England; died in England, March 30, 1694.

1687, April —Nathaniel Bacon, President of the Council. (Though Lord Effingham did not sit in the General Court, he remained in Virginia and signed patents as late as October 20, 1688.)

Born in England, 1619; died in Virginia, March 16, 1692.

1690, Oct. 16.—Col. Francis Nicholson, Lieutenant Governor.

Died in England, March 5, 1728.

1692, Oct. 15.—Sir Edmund Andros, Governor.

Born in England, December 6, 1637; died in England, February 27, 1713-14.

1698, Dec. 9.—Col. Francis Nicholson, Lieutenant Governor (Commissioned July 20, 1698).

(1704 —George Hamilton Douglas, Earl of Orkney, was commissioned Governor-in-Chief for life; never came to Virginia; died July 29, 1737.)

1705, Aug. 15.—Edward Nott, Lieutenant Governor.
Born in England, 1634; died in Virginia, Aug. 23, 1705.

1706, Aug. —Edmund Jenings, President of the Council.
Born in England, 1659; died in Virginia, December 5, 1727.

(1707, Aug. 14.—Col. Robert Hunter, was commissioned Lieutenant Governor; but was captured on his voyage by the French and never came to Virginia.)

1710, June 23. —Col. Alexander Spotswood, Lieutenant Governor.
Born 1676 at Tangier, Africa, (where his father was surgeon to the English garrison); died June 7, 1740, at Annapolis, Md., when about to embark for the campaign against Carthagena.

1722, Sept. 8.—Hugh Drysdale, Lieutenant Governor.
Died July 22, 1726.

1726, July 11.—Robert Carter, President of the Council.
Born in Virginia, 1663, died in Virginia, August 4, 1732.

1727, Sept. 8.—William Gooch (subsequently knighted) Lieutenant Governor.
Born in England, Oct. 21, 1681; died in England, December 17, 1751.

(1737, Sept. 6.—William Anne Keppel, Earl of Albemarle, appointed Governor-in-Chief; died Dec. 23, 1754; never in Virginia.)

1740 —From between September and December, 1740, until July 25, 1741, or somewhat later, Rev. James Blair, D. D., President of the Council, was Acting Governor during the absence of Governor Gooch on the Carthagena expedition.

James Blair, born in Scotland, about 1655; died in Virginia, August 3, 1743.

1741 —Sir William Gooch, Governor.

1749, June 20.—John Robinson, President of the Council.

Born in Virginia, 1683; died in Virginia, September, 1749.

1749, Sept. 5.—Thomas Lee, President of the Council.

Born in Virginia, 1690; died in Virginia, Nov. 14, 1750.

1750, Nov. 14.—Lewis Burwell, President of the Council.

Born in Virginia, 1710; died in Virginia, 1752.

1751, Nov. 20.—Robert Dinwiddie, Lieutenant Governor.

Born in Scotland, 1673; died in England, July 27, 1770.

(1756, July —John Campbell, Earl of Loudon, appointed Governor General of all the American Colonies; never in Virginia.)

1758, Jan. —John Blair, President of the Council.

Born in Virginia, 1689; died in Virginia, November 5, 1771.

1758, June 7.—Francis Fauquier, Lieutenant Governor.

Born in England, 1703; died in Virginia, March 3, 1768.

(1763 —Sir Jeffrey Amherst, made Governor-in-Chief; never in Virginia.)

1768, Mar. 7.—John Blair, President of the Council.

1768, Oct. 28.—Norborne Berkeley, Baron de Botetourt, Governor-in-Chief.
Born in England, 1718; died in Virginia, October 15, 1770.

1770, Oct. 15.—William Nelson, President of the Council.
Born in Virginia, February 20, 1677; died in Virginia, November 19, 1772.

1771, Aug. —John Murray, Earl of Dunmore, Governor-in-Chief; appointed in July, 1771; fled from the seat of government in June, 1775.
Born in Scotland, 1732; died in England, May, 1789.

1775 —During the interregnum in 1775, many executive functions were exercised by the Committee of Safety, the members of which were elected by the Conventions, These members were: Edmund Pendleton, George Mason, John Page, Richard Bland, T. L. Lee, Paul Carrington, Dudley Digges, William Cabell, Carter Braxton, James Mercer, and John Tabb, elected August 17, 1775, and Joseph Jones, and Thomas Walker, added, December 16, 1775 in place of Braxton, elected to Congress, and Mason, declined.

SECRETARY OF STATE

Gabriel Archer *(Recorder)*	1607-1609
William Strachey	1610-1611
Ralph Hamor, Jr.,	1611-1614
John Rolfe	1614-1619
John Pory	1619-1621
Christopher Davison	1621-1623
William Claiborne	{ 1625-1635 { 1652-1660
Richard Kemp	1635-1649
Richard Lee	1649-1652
Thomas Ludwell	1661-1678
Philip Ludwell	1678-
Daniel Parke	1678-1679 (died that year)
Nicholas Spencer	1679-1689
William Cole	1689-1692
Christopher Robinson	1692-1693
Ralph Wormeley	1693-1701
Edmund Jenings	{ 1702-1712 { 1720-1722
William Cocke	1712-1720
John Carter	1722-1743
Thomas Nelson	1743-1776

AUDITOR GENERAL*

* From about 1705 there was a sinecure Auditor General of the Colonies resident in England, and those who held the office in Virginia, though practically Auditors General, were in name deputies.

THOMAS STEGG	1664-1670
EDWARD DIGGES	1670-1675
NATHANIEL BACON	1675-1687
WILLIAM BYRD	1687-1704
DUDLEY DIGGES	1705-1710
PHILIP LUDWELL	1711-1716
PETER BEVERLEY	1716-
JOHN GRYMES	1718-

John Grymes, was appointed to the position in 1718; but it cannot be certainly ascertained how long he held it.

NATHANIEL HARRISON   1724-1728
The date of his appointment does not appear. He was certainly in office in 1724, and at his death in 1728. Nor is it known who filled the place between 1728 and 1732.

JOHN BLAIR   1732-1771
It does not appear from any records consulted whether a successor was appointed to Auditor Blair.

RECEIVER GENERAL

EDWARD DIGGES	1672-1675
WILLIAM BYRD (1)	1687-1704
WILLIAM BYRD (2)	1705-1716
JAMES ROSCOW	1716-1723
JOHN GRYMES	1723-1748
PHILIP GRYMES	1749-1754
RICHARD CORBIN	1754-1776

TREASURER

Between 1607 and 1620, Thomas Studley, Daniel Tucker, and Abraham Persey or Piersey, under the titles of "keeper of the store," or "cape merchant," performed functions similar to those of a treasurer.

George Sandys	1621-1625
Jerome Hawley	1636-1639
Roger Wingate	1639-1641
William Claiborne	1642-1660
Henry Norwood	1660-1677
Henry Whiting	1692-1693
Edward Hill	1693-1699
Robert Carter	1699-1705
Benjamin Harrison	1705-1710
Peter Beverley	1710-1723
John Holloway	1723-1734
Sir John Randolph	1734-1736
Richard Randolph	1736-1738
John Robinson	1738-1766
Robert Carter Nicholas	1766-1776

ATTORNEY GENERAL

RICHARD LEE	1643-
GEORGE JORDAN	1670-
PETER JENINGS	1670-1671
WILLIAM SHERWOOD	1677-
EDWARD HILL	1679-
EDMUND JENINGS	1680-1691
EDWARD CHILTON	1692-
WILLIAM RANDOLPH	1696-

1696 is the only year in which it is known certainly that William Randolph was Attorney General. He may have held the office a few years earlier.

BARTHOLOMEW FOWLER	1699-
BENJAMIN HARRISON	1697-1702
STEVENS THOMSON	1704-1714
JOHN CLAYTON	1714-1737
EDWARD BARRADALL	1737-1743
WILLIAM BOWDEN	1743-1748
PEYTON RANDOLPH	1748-1766
JOHN RANDOLPH	1766-1776

SURVEYOR GENERAL*

*By the provisions of its Charter in 1692, William and Mary College was given the office of Surveyor General, and those who filled the place after that date were appointees of the College.

WILLIAM CLAIBORNE	1621-1625
ROBERT EVELYN	1637-
THOMAS LOVING	-1665
EDMUND SCARBOROUGH	1665-1671
ALEXANDER CULPEPER	1672-1692
MILES CARY	1692-1708
WILLIAM BUCKNER	1708-1716
PETER BEVERLEY	1716-1728

THE COUNCIL

(The dates opposite the names denote time of appointme..t or of first appearance in the extant records.)

BARTHOLOMEW GOSNOLD, 1607
  Born in England. Died Aug. 22, 1607, in Virginia.

EDWARD MARIA WINGFIELD, 1607
  Born in England about 1560. Died after May 23, 1613, in England.

CHRISTOPHER NEWPORT, 1607
  Born in England. Died 1617, in the East Indies.

JOHN SMITH, 1607
  Born in England, January, 1579. Died in England, June 21, 1631.

JOHN RATCLIFFE, 1607
  Born in England. Killed by Indians, October, 1609.

JOHN MARTIN, 1607
  Born in England. Died after March 8, 1626-7, in Virginia.

GEORGE KENDALL, 1607
  Born in England. Shot for mutiny in Virginia, 1607.

MATTHEW SCRIVENOR, 1608
  Born in England. Drowned in James River, 1609.

GABRIEL ARCHER, 1607
  Born in England. Died 1609-10, in Virginia.

RICHARD WALDOE, 1608
  Born in England.

PETER WYNNE, 1608
    Born in England. Died, 1609, in Virginia.
GEORGE PERCY, 1609
    Born, Sept. 4, 1580, in England. Died, 1632, in England.
FRANCIS WEST, 1609
    Born, Oct. 30, 1586, in England. Died, probably in Virginia, in 1633 or 1634.
SIR THOMAS GATES, 1610
    Born in England. Died, September, 1622, in Holland.
SIR GEORGE SOMERS, 1610
    Born in England, 1554. Died, July, 1611, at Bermuda.
SIR FERDINANDO WEYNMAN, 1610
    Born in England. Died, 1610, in Virginia.
WILLIAM STRACHEY, 1610
    Born in England. Died (probably) 1634.
SIR SAMUEL ARGALL, 1610
    Born before 1585, in England. Died, Jan. 24, 1625.
SIR THOMAS DALE, 1611
    Born in England. Died, Aug. 9, 1619, at Masulipatam, East Indies.
RALPH HAMOR, 1611
    Born in England. Died about March, 1627-8, in Virginia.
JOHN ROLFE, 1614
    Born, May 6, 1585, in England. Died, March, 1622, in Virginia.
SIR GEORGE YEARDLEY, 1616
    Born about 1579, in England. Died, November, 1627, in Virginia.

NATHANIEL POWELL, 1619
Born in England. Killed, March 22, 1622, in Indian Massacre.

JOHN PORY, 1619
Born about 1570, in England. Died, 1635-6, in England.

DANIEL TUCKER, 1619
Born in England. Died, February, 1624-5, at Bermuda.

REV. WILLIAM WICKHAM, 1619
Born in England.

REV. SAMUEL MACOCK, 1619
Born in England. Killed, March 22, 1622, in Indian Massacre.

THOMAS NEWCE, 1620
Born in England. Died, about April 1, 1623, in Virginia.

THOMAS HARWOOD, 1620
of Warwick County, Va.
Born in England. Died in Virginia.

JOHN POUNTIS, 1620
Born in England. Died, 1623-4, on ship-board.

WILLIAM TRACY, 1620
of Berkeley Hundred, Va.
Born in England. Killed, March 22, 1622, in Indian Massacre.

DAVID MIDDLETON, 1620
Born in England.

MR. BLEWITT, 1620
Born in England.

GEORGE THORPE, 1620
    of Berkeley Hundred, Va.
    Born, about 1576, in England. Killed, March 22, 1622, in Indian Massacre.

LAWRENCE BOHUN, M.D., 1620
    Born in England. Killed, March, 1621, in sea fight, in West Indies.

ROGER SMITH, 1621
    Born in England. Died, after 1629.

GEORGE SANDYS, 1621
    of Jamestown,
    Born, March 7, 1577, in England. Died March, 1643-1644, in England.

ROBERT PAULETT, 1621
    Born in England. Died before 1623, in Virginia.

SIR WILLIAM NEWCE, 1621
    Born in England. Died, about December, 1621, in Virginia.

MICHAEL LAPWORTH, 1621
    Born in England.

MR. LEECH, 1621
    Born in England.

JOHN POTT, M. D., 1621
    of "Harrop," James City County, Va.
    Born in England.

MR. OULDSWORTH, 1621
    of Berkeley Hundred, Va.
    Born in England. Died before July, 16, 1621.

JOHN BERKELEY, 1621
    Born in England. Killed, March, 22, 1622, in Indian Massacre.

CHRISTOPHER DAVISON, 1621
Born in England. Died, 1623, in Virginia.
WILLIAM FARRAR, 1623
of Henrico County, Va.
Born in England. Died in or before 1637, in Virginia.
WILLIAM TUCKER, 1623
of Elizabeth City County, Va.
Born, 1589, in England.
SAMUEL MATTHEWS, 1623
of "Matthews Mount," Warwick County, Va.
Born in England. Died in Virginia, 1659.
WILLIAM CLAIBORNE, 1623
of New Kent County, Va.
Born, about 1587, in England. Died, about 1677, in Virginia.
SIR JOHN HARVEY, 1624
Born in England. Died probably in Virginia.
ABRAHAM PIERCEY, 1624
Born in England. Died, October, 1628, in Virginia.
ISAAC MADISON, 1624
Born in England. Died, 1624, in Virginia.
JABEZ WHITAKER, 1626
Born in England.
EDWARD BLANEY, 1626
Born in England.
WILLIAM CAPPS, 1627
Born in England. Died, after 1630.
NATHANIEL BASSE, 1630
Born in England.

JOHN WEST, 1630
    Born, Dec. 14, 1590, in England. Died, about 1659, in Virginia.
RICHARD STEPHENS, 1630
    of James City County, Va.
    Born in England. Died, about 1636.
JOHN UTIE, 1630
    of "Utimaria," York County, Va.
    Born in England. Died, 1639, in Virginia.
HENRY FINCH, 1630
    Born in England. Died after 1633.
CHRISTOPHER COWLINGE, 1630
    Born in England.
THOMAS PUREFOY, 1631
    of "Drayton," Elizabeth City County, Va.
    Born in England. Died in Virginia.
WILLIAM PIERCE, 1631
    of James City County, Va.
    Born in England. Died in Virginia.
HUGH BULLOCK, 1631
    of York County, Va.
    Born in England. Died, after 1637, in England.
WILLIAM PERRY, 1632
    of Charles City County, Va.
    Born in England. Died, Aug. 6, 1637, in Virginia.
JOHN BREWER, 1632
    of Warwick County, Va.
    Born in England. Died, 1635, in Virginia.
RICHARD KEMP, 1634
    of James City County, Va.
    Born in England. Died, 1656, in Virginia.

JOHN STONER, 1634
 Born in England. Died, 1634, during voyage to Virginia.
THOMAS HINTON, 1634
 Born in England.
HENRY BROWNE, 1634
 of James City (Surry) County, Va.
 Born in England. Died, about 1652, in Virginia.
GEORGE MENIFIE, 1635
 of James City and Charles City Counties, Va.
 Born in England. Died about 1645 in Virginia.
WILLIAM BROCAS, 1637
 of York and Lancaster (Middlesex) Counties, Va.
 Born in England. Died 1655, in Virginia.
JOHN SIBSEY, 1637
 of Lower Norfolk (Princess Anne) County, Va.
 Born in England. Died 1652, in Virginia.
ADAM THOROUGHGOOD, 1637
 of Lower Norfolk County, Va.
 Born in England. Died 1640, in Virginia.
FRANCIS HOOKE, 1637
 of Elizabeth City County, Va.
 Born in England. Died 1637, in Virginia.
JOHN HOBSON, 1637
 Born in England.
JEROME HAWLEY, 1637
 Born in England. Died about August, 1638, in Maryland.
GEORGE DONNE, 1637
 Born about 1605, in England. Died after 1641, in Virginia.

RICHARD TOWNSEND, 1637
    of York County, Va.
    Born 1606, in England. Died after 1645, in Virginia.
CHRISTOPHER WORMELEY, 1637
    of York County, Va.
    Born in England. Died before October, 1649, in Virginia.
FRANCIS EPES, 1637
    of Charles City County, Va.
    Born in England. Died probably before 1655, in Virginia.
ROBERT EVELYN, 1637
    Born in England. Died after 1642.
AMBROSE HARMER, 1639
    of James City County, Va.
    Born in England.
RICHARD BENNETT, 1639
    of Nansemond County, Va.
    Born in England. Died in 1675, in Virginia.
ARGALL YEARDLEY, 1639
    of Northampton County, Va.
    Born 1605, in England. Died, 1655, in Virginia.
THOMAS WILLOUGHBY, 1639
    of Lower Norfolk County, Va.
    Born 1601, in England. Died in Virginia.
ROGER WINGATE, 1639
    Born in England. Died about 1641, in Virginia.
WILLIAM BROWN, 1640
    of James City (Surry) County, Va.
    Born in England.

HUMPHREY HIGGINSON, 1641
  of James City County, Va.
  Born in England. Died 1665, in England.
WILLIAM BERNARD, 1641
  of Nansemond County, Va.
  Born in England. Died March 31, 1665, in Virginia.
THOMAS PAWLETT, 1641
  of " Westover," Charles City County, Va.
  Born in England. Died January, 1643-4, in Virginia.
THOMAS PETTUS, 1641
  of " Littleton," James City County, Va.
  Born in England. Died after 1660, in Virginia.
RICHARD MORRISON, 1641
  of Elizabeth City County, Virginia.
  Born in England. Died before 1656.
SIR FRANCIS WYATT, 1641
  Born 1588, in England. Died 1644 in England.
GEORGE LUDLOW, 1642
  of York County, Va.
  Born September, 1596, in England. Died 1656, in Virginia.
THOMAS STEGG, I., 1642
  Born in England. Perished 1651-2, in shipwreck.
FRANCIS MORYSON, 1650
  Born in England. Died after 1678.
BRIDGES FREEMAN, 1650
  of James City County, Va.
  Born in England. Died after 1651.
RALPH WORMELEY, 1650
  of York Co., and of " Rosegill," Lancaster (Middlesex) County, Va.
  Born in England. Died 1651, in Virginia.

SIR WILLIAM DAVENANT, 1650
    Poet Laureate of England.
    Born in England. Died December 7, 1668, in England.
WALTER CHILES, 1651
    of James City County, Va.
    Born in England.
RICHARD LEE, I., 1651
    of Northumberland and Westmoreland Counties, Va.
    Born in England. Died about 1664, in Virginia.
WILLIAM TAYLOR or TAYLOE, 1651
    of York County, Va.
    Born in England. Died after 1655, in Virginia.
SIR THOMAS LUNSFORD, 1651
    of Rappahannock County, Va.
    Born about 1610, in England. Died about 1653, in Virginia.
EDWARD HILL, I., 1651
    of "Shirley," Charles City County, Va.
    Born in England. Died about 1663, in Virginia.
JOHN CHEESMAN, 1652
    of York County, Va.
    Born 1595, in England. Died before 1678, in England
EDWARD DIGGES, 1654
    of "Bellfield," York County, Va.
    Born about 1621, in England. Died March 15, 1675, in Virginia.
SAMUEL MATTHEWS, II., 1654-5
    of Warwick County, Va.
    Born in Virginia. Died 1670, in Virginia.
HENRY PERRY, 1655
    of James City County, Va.
    Born in Virginia. Died after 1661, in Virginia.

Thomas Dew, 1655
   of Nansemond County, Va.
   Born in England. Died after 1660, in Virginia.
William Gooch, 1655
   of York County, Va.
   Born 1626, in England. Died October 29, 1655, in Virginia.
Obedience Robins, 1655
   of Northampton County, Va.
   Born April 16, 1600. Died 1662, in Virginia.
Abraham Wood, 1657
   of Charles City (Prince George) County, Va.
   Born in England. Died in Virginia.
Nathaniel Bacon, I., 1657
   of "Queen's Creek," York County, Va.
   Born about 1620, in England. Died March 16, 1692, in Virginia.
Warham Horsmanden, 1657
   of Charles City County, Va.
   Born in England. Died after 1683, in England.
Anthony Elliot, 1657
   of Elizabeth City and Lancaster (Middlesex) Counties, Va.
   Born in England. Died about 1666, in Virginia.
John Carter, I., 1657-8
   of Nansemond County, and of "Corotoman," Lancaster County, Va.
   Born in England. Died June 10, 1669, in Virginia.
John Walker, 1657-8
   of Rappahannock County, Va.
   Born in England. Died about 1671, in Virginia.

GEORGE READE, 1657-8
    of York and Gloucester Counties, Va.
    Born in England. Died 1671, in Virginia.

FRANCIS WILLIS, 1658
    of York County, Va.
    Born in England. Died 1691, in England.

EDWARD CARTER, 1659
    of Nansemond County, Va.
    Born in England. Died 1682, in England.

WILLIAM WHITAKER, 1659
    of James City County, Va.
    Born in England. Died after 1662, in Virginia.

THOMAS SWANN, 1659
    of "Swann's Point," Surry County, Va.
    Born in Virginia. Died September 16, 1680, in Virginia.

AUGUSTINE WARNER, I., 1660
    of "Warner Hall," Gloucester County, Va.
    Born 1610, in England. Died December 24, 1674, in Virginia.

MAINWARING HAMMOND, 1660
    Born in England. Died after 1670, probably in Ireland.

THOMAS LUDWELL, 1661
    of James City County, Va.
    Born in England. Died 1678, in Virginia.

THOMAS BEALE, 1662
    of York County, Va.
    Born in England. Died after 1676, in Virginia.

HENRY CORBIN, 1663
    of Lancaster (Middlesex) County, Va.
    Born in England. Died January 8, 1676, in Virginia.

ROBERT SMITH, 1663
  of "Brandon," Lancaster (Middlesex) County, Va.
  Born in England. Died about 1687 in Virginia.
THOMAS STEGG, II., 1664
  Born in Virginia. Died in Virginia, 1670.
THEODORICK BLAND, 1665
  of "Westover," Charles City County, Va.
  Born January, 1629, in England. Died April 23, 1671, in Virginia.
MILES CARY, 1665
  of Warwick County, Va.
  Born about 1620, in England. Died June 10, 1667, in Virginia.
DANIEL PARKE, I., 1665
  of York County, Va.
  Born in England. Died March 6, 1679, in Virginia.
JAMES BRAY, 1670
  of James City County, Va.
PETER JENINGS, 1670
  Born in England. Died about 1671, in Virginia.
THOMAS BALLARD, 1670
  of James City County, Va.
  Born 1630, in England. Died 1689, in Virginia.
JOHN PATE, 1670
  of Gloucester County, Va.
  Born in England. Died in Virginia.
JOSEPH BRIDGER, 1670
  of "Whitemarsh," Isle of Wight County, Va.
  Born 1628. Died April 15, 1686, in Virginia.
SIR HENRY CHICHELEY, 1670
  of "Rosegill," Lancaster (Middlesex) County, Va.

Born 1632, in England. Died February 5, 1682, in Virginia.

NICHOLAS SPENCER, 1671
of Westmoreland County, Va.
Born in England. Died September 23, 1689, in Virginia.

PHILIP LUDWELL, I., 1674-5
of "Rich Neck" and "Green Spring," James City County, Va.
Born in England. Died after 1704, in England.

WILLIAM COLE, 1675
of "Baltrope," Warwick County, Va.
Born 1638. Died March 4, 1694, in Virginia.

ROWLAND PLACE, 1675
Born in England. Died after 1681, in England.

THOMAS BOWLER, 1675
of Rappahannock County, Va.
Born in England. Died 1679, in Virginia.

NATHANIEL BACON, II. ("The Rebel"), 1675
of "Curles" Henrico County, Va.
Born in England. Died 1676, in Virginia.

RICHARD LEE, II., 1676
of "Mt. Pleasant," Westmoreland County, Va.
Born 1647, in Virginia. Died March 12, 1714, in Virginia.

FRANCIS LEIGH, 1676
Born in England. Died after 1680, in Virginia.

ROBERT BEVERLEY, 1676
of Middlesex County, Va.
Born in Yorkshire, Eng. Died March 15, 1686, in Virginia.

JOHN CUSTIS, I.,   1677
of " Arlington," Northampton County, Va.
Born 1630, in Virginia. Died in Virginia, January 29, 1696.

RALPH WORMELEY,   1677
of " Rosegill," Middlesex County, Va.
Born 1650, in Virginia. Died December 5, 1700, in Virginia.

AUGUSTINE WARNER, II.,   1677
of " Warner Hall," Gloucester County, Va.
Born July 3 (?), 1642, in Virginia. Died June 19, 1681, in Virginia.

HENRY MEESE,   1680
Born in England. Died after December, 1681, in England.

MATTHEW KEMP,   1681
of Gloucester County, Va.
Born in Virginia. Died 1683, in Virginia.

JOHN PAGE,   1681
of York County, Va.
Born 1627, in England. Died January 23, 1691-2, in Virginia.

WILLIAM BYRD, I.,   1681
of " Belvidere," Henrico County, and " Westover," Charles City County, Va.
Born about 1653, in England. Died December 4, 1704, in Virginia.

JOHN LEAR,   1683
of Nansemond County, Va.
Born in England. Died 1695, in Virginia.

ISAAC ALLERTON, 1683
    of Westmoreland County, Va.
    Born 1630, in Massachusetts. Died 1702, in Virginia.
CHRISTOPHER WORMELEY, 1683
    of Middlesex County, Va.
    Born in England. Died 1701, in Virginia.
EDWARD HILL, II., 1688
    of "Shirley," Charles City County, Va.
    Born 1637, in Virginia. Died November 30, 1700, in Virginia.
JOHN ARMISTEAD, 1688
    of Gloucester County, Va.
    Born in England. Died after 1697, in Virginia.
JAMES BLAIR, 1689
    of James City County, Va.
    Born 1656, in Scotland. Died April 18, 1743, in Virginia.
SIR FRANCIS NICHOLSON, 1690
    Born in England. Died March 5, 1728, in England.
HENRY WHITING, 1690
    of Gloucester County, Va.
    Born in Virginia.
CHARLES SCARBOROUGH, 1691
    of Accomac County, Va.
    Born in Virginia. Died about 1703, in Virginia.
CHRISTOPHER ROBINSON, 1691
    of "Hewick," Middlesex County, Va.
    Born 1645, in England. Died April, 1693, in Virginia.
JOHN LIGHTFOOT, 1692
    of New Kent County, Va.
    Born in England. Died May 28, 1707, in Virginia.

HENRY HARTWELL, 1692
Born in England. Died 1699, in England.
DANIEL PARKE, II., 1692
of York County, Va.
Born 1669, in Virginia. Killed December 7, 1710, at Antigua, Leeward Islands.
RICHARD JOHNSON, 1696
of King and Queen County, Va.
Born in England. Died about 1698, in Virginia.
DUDLEY DIGGES, 1698
of "Bellfield," York County, Va.
Born about 1665, in Virginia. Died January 18, 1710-11, in Virginia.
BENJAMIN HARRISON, 1698
of "Wakefield," Surry County, Va.
Born September 20, 1645, in Virginia. Died January 30, 1712-13, in Virginia.
MATTHEW PAGE, 1699
of "Timber Neck," Gloucester County, Va.
Born 1659, in Virginia. Died January 9, 1703, in Virginia.
JOHN CUSTIS, II., 1699
of "Arlington," Northampton County, Va.
Born 1653, in Virginia. Died January 26, 1713, in Virginia.
EDMUND JENINGS, 1699
of "Ripon Hall," York County, Va.
Born 1659, in England. Died December 5, 1727, in Virginia.
ROBERT CARTER, 1699
of "Corotoman," Lancaster County, Va.

Born 1663, in Virginia. Died August 4, 1732, in Virginia.

LEWIS BURWELL, 1702
of "Carter's Creek," Gloucester County, and "King's Creek," York County, Va.
Born in Virginia. Died December 19, 1710, in Virginia.

WILLIAM BASSETT, 1702
of "Eltham," New Kent County, Va.
Born 1670, in Virginia. Died October 11, 1723, in Virginia.

HENRY DUKE, 1702
of James City County, Va.
Died 1713, in Virginia.

ROBERT QUARRY, 1702
Born in England.

PHILIP LUDWELL, II., 1702
of "Green Spring," James City County, Va.
Born February 4, 1672, in Virginia. Died January 11, 1726-7, in Virginia.

JOHN SMITH, 1704
of Gloucester County, Va.
Born in Virginia. Died about 1719-20, in Virginia.

JOHN LEWIS, I., 1704
of "Warner Hall," Gloucester County, Va.
Born November 30, 1669, in Virginia. Died November 14, 1725, in Virginia.

WILLIAM CHURCHILL, 1705
of "Wilton," and "Bushy Park," Middlesex County, Va.

Born 1650, in England. Died November, 1710, in Virginia.

WILLIAM BYRD, II.,   1708
of "Westover," Charles City County, Va.
Born March 28, 1674, in Virginia. Died August 26, 1744, in Virginia.

WILLIAM FITZHUGH,   1711
of "Eagle's Nest," Stafford County, Va.
Born in Virginia. Died about January, 1714, in Virginia.

ROBERT PORTEUS,   1713
of "Newbottle," Gloucester County, Va.
Born 1617, in Virginia. Died August 8, 1758, in England.

WILLIAM COCKE, M.D.,   1713
of Williamsburg, Va.
Born 1671, in England. Died October 20, 1720, in Virginia.

EDMUND BERKELEY,   1713
of "Barn Elms," Middlesex County, Va.
Born before 1674, in Virginia. Died 1718, in Virginia.

NATHANIEL HARRISON,   1713
of "Wakefield," Surry County, Va.
Born August 8, 1677, in Virginia. Died November 30, 1727, in Virginia.

MANN PAGE,   1714
of "Rosewell," Gloucester County, Va.
Born 1691, in Virginia. Died January 24, 1730, in Virginia.

PETER BEVERLEY,   1719
of Gloucester County, Va.

Born about 1668, in Virginia. Died 1728, in Virginia.

COLE DIGGES, 1719
of " Bellfield," York County, Va.
Born 1692, in Virginia. Died 1744, in Virginia.

JOHN ROBINSON, 1720
of " Piscataway," Essex County, Va.
Born 1683, in Virginia. Died September, 1749, in Virginia.

JOHN CARTER, 1724
of " Shirley," Charles City County, Va.
Born in Virginia. Died July 31, 1742, in Virginia.

JOHN GRYMES, 1725
of "Brandon," Middlesex County, Va.
Born 1692, in Virginia. Died November 2, 1748, in Virginia.

RICHARD FITZWILLIAM, 1725
Died, or removed to England, 1732.

JOHN CUSTIS, III., 1727
of " Arlington," Northampton County, Va.
Born 1678, in Virginia. Died November, 1749, in Virginia.

WILLIAM DANDRIDGE, 1727
of King William County.
Born in England. Died 1743, in Virginia.

WILLIAM RANDOLPH, 1728
of " Turkey Island," Henrico County, Va.
Born November, 1681, in Virginia. Died October 19, 1742, in Virginia.

HENRY HARRISON, 1730
of Surry County, Va.

Born 1692, in Virginia. Died September 24, 1732, in Virginia.

DAVID BRAY, 1731
of James City County, Va.
Born 1699, in Virginia. Died October 5, 1731, in Virginia.

JOHN TAYLOE, 1732
of "Mt. Airy," Richmond County, Va.
Born February 15, 1687, in Virginia. Died 1747, in Virginia.

GEORGE PHENNY, 1732

THOMAS LEE, 1732-3
of "Stratford," Westmoreland County, Va.
Born 1690, in Virginia. Died November 14, 1750, in Virginia.

PHILIP LIGHTFOOT, 1733
of "Sandy Point," Charles City County, Va.
Born 1689, in Virginia. Died May 30, 1748, in Virginia.

ROBERT DINWIDDIE, 1738
Born 1690, in Scotland. Died July 27, 1770, in England.

JOHN BLAIR, 1743
of Williamsburg, Va.
Born 1686, in Virginia. Died November 7, 1771, in Virginia.

WILLIAM FAIRFAX, 1743
of "Belvoir," Fairfax County, Va.
Born 1691, in England. Died September 3, 1757, in Virginia.

REV. WILLIAM DAWSON, 1743
    of Williamsburg, Va.
    Born 1704, in England. Died July 24, 1752, in Virginia.

WILLIAM NELSON, 1744
    of Yorktown, Va.
    Born 1711, in Virginia. Died November 19, 1772, in Virginia.

LEWIS BURWELL, 1744
    of " Carter's Creek," Gloucester County, Va.
    Born 1710, in Virginia. Died 1752, in Virginia.

JOHN LEWIS, II., 1748
    of " Warner Hall," Gloucester County, Va.
    Born 1694, in Virginia.

THOMAS NELSON, 1749
    of Yorktown, Va.
    Born 1716, in Virginia. Died 1782, in Virginia.

WILLIAM BEVERLEY, 1750
    of " Blandfield," Essex County, Va.
    Born about 1698, in Virginia. Died about March 1, 1756, in Virginia.

RICHARD CORBIN, 1750
    of " Laneville," King and Queen County, Va.
    Born in Virginia. Died about 1787, in Virginia.

PETER RANDOLPH, 1750
    of " Chatsworth," Henrico County, Va.
    Born 1713, in Virginia. Died July 8, 1767, in Virginia.

PHILIP GRYMES, 1751
    of " Brandon," Middlesex County, Va.
    Born in Virginia. Died 1762, in Virginia.

Rev. William Robinson, 1751
of King and Queen County, Va.
Born in Virginia, 1717. Died in Virginia, 1767.

Philip Ludwell, III., 1752
of " Green Spring," James City County, Va.
Born December 28, 1716, in Virginia. Died March 25, 1767, in Virginia.

William Byrd, III., 1754
of " Westover," Charles City County, Va.
Born in Virginia. Died January 1, 1777, in Virginia.

Rev. Thomas Dawson, 1756
Born in England. Died December, 1761, in Virginia.

John Tayloe, II., 1757
of " Mt. Airy," Richmond County, Va.
Born 1721, in Virginia. Died April 18, 1779, in Virginia.

Philip Ludwell Lee, 1757
of " Stratford," Westmoreland County, Va.
Born February 24, 1726-7, in Virginia. Died February 23, 1775.

Presley Thornton, 1760
of " Northumberland House," Northumberland County, Va.
Born in Virginia, 1721. Died in Virginia, December 8, 1769.

Robert Carter, II., 1764
of " Nominy Hall," Westmoreland County, Va.
Born in Virginia, 1728. Died in Baltimore, Md., 1804.

Rev. James Horrocks, 1764
Born in England. Died March 20, 1772, at Oporto, Portugal.

ROBERT CARTER BURWELL, 1764
of Isle of Wight County, Va.
Born in Virginia. Died in Virginia, 1777.

GEORGE WILLIAM FAIRFAX, 1768
of Fairfax County, Va.
Born 1724, in the Bahamas. Died April 3, 1787, in England.

JOHN PAGE, 1768
of " North End," Gloucester County, Va.
Born about 1720, in Virginia. Died October, 1774, in Virginia.

RALPH WORMELEY, III., 1771
of " Rosegill," Middlesex County, Va.
Born 1744, in Virginia. Died January 19, 1806, in Virginia.

JOHN PAGE, II., 1773
of " Rosewell," Gloucester County, Va.
Born April 17, 1744, in Virginia. Died October 11, 1808, in Virginia.

GAWIN CORBIN, 1775
Born in Virginia. Died in Virginia.

REV. JOHN CAMM, 1775
of Williamsburg, Va.
Born 1718, in England. Died 1779, in Virginia.

THE HOUSE OF BURGESSES

SPEAKERS

John Pory, 1619.
[From 1619 to 1642 there is no record of Speakers.]
Thomas Stegg, 1642-3.
Edward Hill, Sr., 1644-45, 1654, 1658-9.
Edmund Scarborough, November, 1645.
Ambrose Harmer, October, 1646.
Thomas Harwood, 1648-49.
Edward Major, April, 1652.
Thomas Dew, November, 1652.
William Whitby, 1653.
Francis Moryson, 1655-56.
John Smith, March, 1657-58.
Theoderick Bland, 1659-61.
Henry Soane, 1660-61.
Robert Wynne, 1661-74.
Augustine Warner, March, 1675-6; February, 1676-7.
Thomas Godwin, June, 1676.
William Travers, 1677.
Matthew Kemp, 1679.
Thomas Ballard, 1680-82.
Edward Hill, Jr., 1684.
Arthur Allen, 1686.
Thomas Milner, 1691-93.
Robert Carter, 1696, 1699.
William Randolph, 1698.
Peter Beverley, 1700-05, 1710-1714.

Benjamin Harrison, October, 1705.
Daniel McCarty, 1715-18.
John Halloway, 1720-34.
Sir John Randolph, 1736.
John Robinson, 1738-65.
Peyton Randolph, 1766-75.

MEMBERS
1619

Assembled July 30th

James City: Captain William Powell, Ensign William Spense.

Charles City: Samuel Sharpe, Samuel Jordan.

The City of Henricus: Thomas Dowse, John Polentine.

Kicoughtan: Captain William Tucker, William Capp.

Martin-Brandon (Captain John Martin's plantation): Thomas Davis, Robert Stacy.

Smythe's Hundred: Captain Thomas Graves, Walter Shelley.

Martin's Hundred: John Boys, John Jackson.

Argall's Gift: Thomas Pawlett, Mr. Gourgainy.

Flowerdieu Hundred: Ensign Rossingham, Mr. Jefferson.

Captain Lawne's Plantation: Captain Christopher Lawne, Ensign Washer.

Captain Ward's Plantation: Captain Ward, Lieutenant Gibbes.

Source: A manuscript copy of the Journal of this session is in the Public Record Office, London, and has several times been printed.

1623-4

Assembled March 5th

William Tucker,
Jabez Whitaker,
William Peeine,
Raleigh Croshaw,
Richard Kingsmell,
Edward Blany,
Luke Boyse,
John Pollington,
Nathaniel Causey,
Robert Adams,
Thomas Harris,
Richard Stephens,
Nathaniel Basse,
John Willcox,
Nicholas Martian,
Clement Dilke,
Isaac Chaplin,
John Chew,
John Utie,
John Southerne,
Richard Bigge,
Henry Watkins,
Gabriel Holland,
Thomas Morlatt.

Source: Hening's Statutes at Large of Virginia, I, 128-129. The counties are not given in this list.

1629

Assembled October 16th

The Plantation at the College: Lieutenant Thomas Osborne, Matthew Edlowe.
The Neck of Land: Sergeant Sharp.
Shirley Hundred Island: Cheney Boyse, John Browne.
Shirley Hundred Main: Thomas Palmer, John Harris.
Mr. Henry Throckmorton's Plantation: William Allen.
Jordan's Journey: William Popkton.
Chaplaine's Choice: Walter Price.
Westover: Christopher Woodward.
Flowerdieu Hundred: Anthony Pagett.
James City: George Menefie, Richard Kingsmell.
Pace's Paines: Lt. William Perry, John Smyth.
The Other Side of the Water: Captain John West, Captain [Robert] Fellgate.
Pasbehay: Thomas Bagwell.
The Neck of Land: Richard Brewster.
Archer's Hope: Theodore Moyse, Thomas Doe.
The Plantations between Archer's Hope and Martin's Hundred: John Utie, Richard Townsend.
Hogg Island: John Chew, Richard Tree.
Martin's Hundred: Thomas Kingston, Thomas Fawcett.
Mulberry Island: Thomas Harwood, Phettiplace Clause,
Warwick River: Christopher Stokes, Thomas Ceely, Thomas Flint, Zachary Cripps.
Warrosquoyacke: Captain Nathaniel Basse, Richard Bennett, Robert Savin, Thomas Jordan.
Nuttmegg Quarter: William Cole, William Bentley.
Elizabeth City: Lieutenant George Thompson, William

English, Adam Thoroughgood, Lionel Rowlston, John Browning, John Downman.
"For the Easterne shoare noe burgesses did appear."
Source: Hening I, 137-139.

1629-30

Assembled March 24th

The Plantations of the College and Neck of Land: Captain Thomas Osborne, Thomas Farmer.
Shirley Hundred Main: Thomas Palmer, John Harris.
Shirley Hundred Island: Cheney Boyse, Walter Aston.
Jordan's Journey and Chaplaine's Choice: Walter Price.
Flowerdieu Hundred: John Flood.
Westover: None appeared.
Weyanoke: John Trahorne.
Pace's Paines and Smythe's Mount: William Perry.
Pashbehay: Bridges Freeman.
James City Island: John Southerne, Robert Barrington.
The Other Side of the Water: Captain John West, Captain Robert Felgate.
Hog Island: Captain John Utie.
The Neck of Land in the Corporation of James City: Richard Brewster.
Archer's Hope and Glebe Land: Theodore Moyses, Henry Coney.
Harrap, and the plantations between Archer's Hope and Martin's Hundred: John Browning, Thomas Farley.
Martin's Hundred: Robert Scotchmore, Thomas Fossett.
Mulberry Island: Thomas Harwood, Anthony Barham.
Warwick River: Thomas Flint, John Brewer.

Denby: Thomas Ceely, Christopher Stokes, Thomas Key.

Nutmeg Quarter: Joseph Stratton.

Warrosqueake: John Upton, John Atkins, Robert Savin, Thomas Burges.

The Upper Part of Elizabeth City: Captain Thomas Willoughby, William Kempe, Thomas Hayrick.

The Lower Part of Elizabeth City: Captain Thomas Purifoy, Adam Thoroughgood, Lancelot Barnes.

Accomac: Captain Thomas Graves, Edmund Scarsborough, Obedience Robins, Henry Bagwell.

Source: Hening I, 147-149.

1631-2

Assembled February 21st

Arrowhattocks, Neck of Land, and Curles: Captain Thomas Osborne.

Both Shirley Hundreds, Mr. Farrar's and Chaplains: Captain Francis Epes, Walter Aston.

Westover, Flowerdieu Hundred, and Weyanoke: John Flood.

Captain Perry's downwards to Hogg Island: Captain William Perry, Richard Richards.

James City: John Southerne, Thomas Crampe [Crump].

Archer's Hope: Thomas Farley, Percival Wood.

Kethe's Creek to Mulberry Island and Saxon's Goal: Thomas Harwood, Captain Thomas Flint.

Warwick River: Thomas Seely, Thomas Ramshawe.

Water's Creek and the Upper Parish of Elizabeth City: Captain Thomas Willoughby.

The Lower Parish of Elizabeth City: George Downes.

Warrosqueake: Thomas Jordan.

Accomac: Edmund Scarborough, John Howe.
Kiskyacke and the Isle of Kent: Captain Nicholas Martian.
Source: Hening I, 153.

1632

Assembled September 4th

Arrowhattocks, Neck of Land, and Curles: Captain Thomas Osborne.
Shirley Hundred Main and Cawsey's Care: Walter Aston.
Shirley Hundred Island: Cheney Boyse.
Westover and Flowerdieu Hundred: John Flood.
Weyanoke: Richard Coxe.
Chickahominy: Bridges Freeman.
Smythe's Mount and Perry's Point: John Smythe.
James City Island: John Jackson.
Pasbehay: John Corker.
The Neck of Land: Sergeant Thomas Crump.
Glebe Land and Archer's Hope: Roger Webster, Henry Coney.
Over the Water against James City: Richard Richards.
Hogg Island: Richard Tree.
Mounts Bay: John Browning, John Wareham.
Martin's Hundred: Robert Scotchmore, Percival Wood.
Mulberry Island: Thomas Harwood, Thomas Bennett.
Stanley Hundred: Thomas Barnett, Thomas Flint.
Denbigh, and to Waters Creek: Pettiplace Clause.
Warrosqueake: Thomas Jordan, William Hutchison.
From Waters Creek to Marie's Mount: Joseph Stratton, John Powell.

The Upper Parish of Elizabeth City: Captain Thomas Willoughby, (absent), Henry Seawell, John Sipsey.

The Lower Parish of Elizabeth City: Adam Thoroughgood, William English, George Downes.

Kiskyacke: Captain Nicholas Martian.

Yorke: Lyonel Rowlston.

Accomac: Captain Thomas Graves, John Howe, Henry Bagwell, Charles Harmer.

Source: Hening I, 178-179.

1632-3

Assembled February 1st

Arrowhattocks, Henrico Neck of Land, and Curles: Captain Thomas Osborne.

Shirley Hundred Main and Cawsey's Care: Walter Aston.

Shirley Hundred Island: Rice Hooe.

Westover and Flowerdieu Hundred: Captain Thomas Pawlett.

Weyanoke: William Emerson.

James City, Chickahominy, and Pasbehay: John Corker.

Neck of Land: Thomas Crump.

Archer's Hope and Glebe Land: Henry Coney.

Smythe's Mount, the Other Side of the Water and Hogg Island: Thomas Grindon.

Harrop and to Martin's Hundred: Richard Brewster, John Wareham.

Martin's Hundred: David Mansfield, Robert Scotchmore.

Mulberry Island: Thomas Harwood, William Spencer.

Stanley Hundred: Zachary Cripps, Roger Dilke.

Denbigh: Captain Thomas Flint, Thomas Hawkins.

Warrosqueake: John Upton, Robert Savin.
Nutmeg Quarter: Francis Hough.
The Upper Parts of Elizabeth City: Thomas Sheppard, John Sipsey.
The Lower Parts of Elizabeth City: William English, John Arundel.
Accomac: Captain Edmund Scarborough, John Howe, Roger Saunders, John Wilkinson.
Kiskyacke: Captain Nicholas Martian.
Yorke: Lyonel Rowlston.
Source: Hening I, 202-203.

1633

Assembled August 21st

The acts of this session are in Hening I, 209-222, but there is no list of members.

1634

All that is known of this session is derived from the brief notice in Hening I, 223.

1635

Assembled May 7th

" An Assembly to be called to receive complaints against Sir John Harvey, on the petition of many inhabitants, to meet 7th of May," Hening I, 223. That this Assembly met at the appointed time is shown by a letter of Samuel Mathews *(Va. Mag. Hist. and Biog. I, 422)* and of Governor Harvey (ib. 427.)

There is no list of members or any detailed account of the proceedings of this Assembly.

1639

Assembled January 6th

(As will be seen by reference to *Hening I, 224*, there is no printed list of the members of the House of Burgesses in 1639. The following list is from a copy made by the late Conway Robinson from the original [now destroyed] in the office of the General Court. This original seems to have been partially obliterated, and addition of names which seemed probable has been made in brackets. The persons named were members of other sessions about the same time).

Henrico: Captain Thomas Harris, Christopher Branch, Edward Tonshall [Tunstall].

Charles City: Captain Francis Eppes, Captain Thomas Pawlett, Edward Hill, Joseph Johnson.

James City:

Chickahominy Parish or the Upper Chippokes and Smiths Fork:

Lower Chippokes, Hogg Island, Lawn Creek:

Martin's Hundred to Kethe's Creek: Thomas [Kingston, or Fawcett].

Farloes' Neck to Waroues' Ponds: Mr. Richard.

Johnson's Neck, Archer's Hope, and The Neck of Land: David [Mansfield, or Mansell].

Warwick River: Thomas [Flint], Thomas [Harwood], Thomas [Ceely], Zachary Crip.

Charles River: William ———, Hugh Gwyn, Peregrine Bland.

Upper Norfolk: Randall Crew, John Gookin, Tristam Norsworthy.

Lower Norfolk: Captain John Sibsey, John Hill.

Isle of Wight: Captain John Upton, Anthony Jones, John Moone, James Tuke.

Elizabeth City: Thomas Oldis, Mr. Strafferton.

Accomac: Obedience Robins, John Neale.

1641

Assembled January 12*th*

James City: Captain Robert Hutchinson, Mr. Francis Fowler, Mr. John White, Mr. Thomas Hill, Mr. Richard Richards, Mr. Ferdinand Franklin, Mr. Jeremie Clement, Mr. Thomas Follis, Mr. William Butler.

Henrico: Mr. John Baugh, Mr. Francis Fulford.

Charles City: Mr. Walter Aston, Mr. Joseph Jackson, Mr. Walter Chiles.

Charles River: Captain Richard Townsend, Mr. George Ludlowe, Mr. George Worleigh.

Warwick River: Mr. Thomas Barnett, Mr. William Whittbey.

Isle of Wight: Captain John Upton, Mr. Joseph Salmon, Mr. George Harddie.

Upper Norfolk: Captain Daniel Coogan [Gookin], Mr. John Carter.

Lower Norfolk: Captain John Shipsie [Sibsie], Mr. John Hill.

Elizabeth City: Mr. John Branch, Mr. Flo. Payne.

Accomack: Mr. John Wilkins, Mr. John Neale.

Source: A manuscript, evidently of contemporary date, which contains the list of members and some of the acts of a session of Assembly begun January 12, 1641, has just been presented to the Virginia Historical Society. It was picked up in Virginia during the Civil War.

This session is not mentioned in Hening.

1642

Assembled April 1st

Richard Townsend,
John Upton,
Obedience Robins,
Benjamin Harrison,
Thomas Dewe,
John Hill,
Ferdinand Franklin,
William Butler,
George Worleigh,
Francis Fowler,
John Weale,
Edward Hill,
Thomas Harwood,
Nathaniel Gough,
Joseph Johnson,
Matthew Chiles,
William Dacker,
Thomas Fallowes,
George Hardy,
Thomas Bernard,
Edward Windham.

Source: Hening I, 236. No counties are given in this list, but they may generally be learned from that of 1641.

1642-3

Assembled March 2nd

Henrico: Captain Matthew Gough, Arthur Bayly, Daniel Luellin.

Charles City: Walter Aston, Thomas Stegg, Speaker, Walter Chiles.

James City: Captain Robert Hutchinson, Rowland Sadler, Henry Filmer, Captain John Fludd, Stephen Webb, William Davis.

Warwick River: Captain Thomas Flint, Toby Smith.

Elizabeth City: John Branch, John Hoddin.

The Isle of Wight: Anthony Jones, Richard Death.

Upper Norfolk: John Carter, Randall Crew.

Lower Norfolk: Cornelius Lloyd, Edward Windham.

York: John Chew, Captain John Chesman, William Tayler.

Northampton: Philip Tayler, Edmond Scarbrough.

Source: Hening I, 239.

1644

Assembled October 1st

James City: Captain Robert Hutchinson, Stephen Webb, Edward Travis, Thomas Loveing, George Jordan, John Shepherd, Thomas Warren.

York: John Chew, Rowland Burnham, Captain X'pher Caultropp [Calthorpe].

Isle of Wight: Peter Hull, George Hardy, Richard Death.

Lower Norfolk: Cornelius Lloyd, John Sidny.

Elizabeth City: Lieutenant William Worbrigh [Wooldridge], John Hodin.

Warwick: Captain Thomas Bernard, John Walker, Hen. Heyrick.

Northampton: Obedience Robins, Edward Douglas.

Upper Norfolk: Randall Crew, Moore Fauntleroy.

Charles City: Edward Hill, Speaker, Francis Poythers [Poythress], John Bishop, John Westropp.
Henrico: Dan. Llewellin, Richard Cocke, Abra. Wood, William Hatcher.
Source: Hening I, 283.

1644-5

Assembled February 17th

James City: Ambrose Harmer, Captain Robert Hutchinson, William Barrett, John Corker, Peter Ridley, George Stephens, John Rogers.
Henrico: John Baugh, Abraham Wood.
Charles City: Captain Edward Hill, Speaker, Rice Hooe, Lieutenant Francis Poythres, Edward Prince.
Warwick River: Captain Thomas Harwood, Captain Thomas Bernard, Hen. Heyricke.
Isle of Wight: Arthur Smith, George Hardy.
Upper Norfolk: Philip Bennett, Moore Fauntleroy.
Elizabeth City: Captain Leonard Yeo, Captain X'pher Caulthropp, Arthur Price.
Northampton: Edmon. Scarbrough, Stephen Charlton.
Lower Norfolk: Edward Lloyd, Thomas Meares, X'pher Burroughs.
Source: Hening I, 289.

1645

Assembled November 20th

James City: John Flood, Walter Chiles, Thomas Swan, Robert Weatherall, Ambrose Harmer, Thomas Warne, Peter Ridley, George Stephens.

York: Captain X'pher Coltrop, Rowland Burnham, Arthur Price.

Isle of Wight: John Upton, George Hardin [Hardy], John Seward.

Lower Norfolk: Cornelius Lloyd, X'pher Burrowes.

Elizabeth City: Captain Leonard Yeo, John Chandler.

Warwick: Thomas Bernard, John Walker, Randall Crew.

Northampton: E'd. Scarbrough, Speaker, Thomas Johnson.

Upper Norfolk: Philip Bennett, Edward Major, Richard Wells.

Charles City: Captain Fra. Eps, Captain Edward Hill, Edward Prince, Rice Hooe, William Barker, Charles Sparrow, Anthony Wyatt.

Henrico: Abra. Wood. William Hatcher.

Northumberland [first time this country seems to have been represented in the Assembly]: John Matrum.

Source: Hening I, 298-299.

1645-6

Assembled March

Second session of Assembly which first met on Nov. 25, 1645. The acts of this session are printed in Hening I, 309-323, and though there is no list of members, the membership must have been, with possibly a few exceptions, the same as in the previous session.

1646

Assembled October 5th

James City: Ambrose Harmer, Speaker, Walter Chiles,

Captain Robert Shepheard, George Jordayne, Thomas Lovinge, William Barrett.
Henrico: Captain Abra. Wood, William Cocke.
Charles City: Rice Hoe, Dan Lluellen.
Isle of Wight: George Fawdowne, Ja. Bagnall.
Elizabeth City: John Robbins, Hen. Ball.
Yorke: Hugh Gwin, William Luddington.
Warwick: Thomas Taylor, Randall Crew, John Walker.
Lower Norfolk: Edw. Lloyd, Thomas Meares, Robert Eyres.
Northampton: Edward Douglas, Thomas Johnson.
Nansemond: Edward Major, Sam. Stoughton.
Source: Hening I, 322-323.

1647

Assembled November 3rd

James City: Captain Robert Hutchinson, Captain Bridges Freeman, Captain Robert Shepheard, George Jorden, William Davis, Peter Ridley.
Charles City: Captain Edward Hill, Captain Francis Poythers.
Elizabeth City: Anth. Elliot, John Chandler, Hen. Poole.
York: Richard Lee, Captain William Tayler, Fra. Morgan.
Upper Norfolk: Moore Fauntleroy, Sam. Stoughton, Richard Wells.
Warwick: Captain Thomas Flint, Randle Crew.
Isle of Wight: Captain John Upton, John George.
Lower Norfolk: Lieutenant John Sidney, Hen. Woodhouse, Cor. Lloyd, Thomas Meeres.

Northampton: E'd. Scarbrough, Stephen Charleton.
Northumberland: William Presley.
Henrico: Captain Thomas Harris.
Source: Hening I, 339-340.

1648

Assembled October 12th

The acts of this session are printed in Hening I, 352-357. There is no list of members, but this was an adjourned session of the Assembly which met in November, 1647. See Hening I, 341 and 352, *note*. The membership in general, must therefore have been the same. But there was a change in at least one county, for the records of Lower Norfolk show that the members from that county at the session of October, 1648, were:

Lower Norfolk: Robert Eyre or [Eyres], Thomas. Lambert.

1649

Assembled October 10th

James City: Walter Chiles, Thomas Swan, William Barret, George Read, William Whittaker, John Dunston.
Henrico: William Hatcher.
Charles City: Captain Edward Hill, Charles Sparrow.
Warwick: Captain Thomas Harwood, Speaker; John Walker.
Isle of Wight: George Hardy, Robert Pitt.
Nansemond: Jo. Carter, Toby Smith.
Elizabeth City: Lieutenant William Worlich [Wooldridge], Jo. Robbins.
Lower Norfolk: Bartho. Hoskins, Thomas Lambert, John Chandler.

Yorke: Captain Ralph Wormeley, Rowland Burnham.
Northumberland: Captain Francis Poythers, Jo. Trussell.

Sources: Hening I, 358-359, and for John Chandler, the records of Lower Norfolk County.

1651

Assembled in March

We only know of this Assembly from Hening I, 363-368 and from the county records. There is no complete list of members.

Northumberland: John Trussell, Thomas Baldridge, Mr. [William] Presley, "Mr. Lee" [probably Richard, though there were other Lees living in Northumberland at this time], Mr. Speke, Thomas Wilford.

Lancaster: Moore Fauntleroy, Raleigh Travers.

Lower Norfolk: Cornelius Lloyd, Thomas Lambert, John Martin, Bartholomew Hoskins.

Sources: The records of the counties named.

1652

Assembled April 26th

Henrico: William Hatcher.

Charles City: Colonel Edward Hill, Captain John Bishopp.

James City: Robert Wetherall, Lieutenant Colonel John Fludd, Hen. Soane, Da. Mansill, George Stephens, William Whittakere.

Isle of Wight: Robert Pitt, George Hardie, John George, John Moone.

Nansemond: Captain Thomas Due, Ed. Major, Speaker.
Lower Norfolk: Cor. Lloyd, Thomas Lambert, Henry Woodhouse, Charles [Chris?] Burrowes.
Elizabeth City: Peter Ransom, John Sheppard.
Warwick River: Lieutenant Colonel Sam. Mathews, William Whittbye.
York: Captain Fra. Morgan, Hen. Lee, Captain Austin Warner.
Northampton: Obedience Robins, Edm. Scarbrough, Thomas Johnson, William Jones, Antho, Hoskins.
Northumberland: Jno. Mottram, Geo. Fletcher.
Gloucester: (First time this County appears). Hugh Gwinne, Fra. Willis.
Source: Hening I, 369-371.

1652

Assembled November 25th

Henrico: Captain William Harris.
Charles City: Captain Hen. Perry, Captain Dan. Llewellin, Major Abraham Woode, Captain Woodlife, Captain Charles Sparrow.
James City: Robert Wetherall, William Whittaker, Abraham Wattson, Hen. Soane.
Surry: William Thomas, William Edwards, George Stephens.
Isle of Wight: Charles Reynolds.
Warwick: Lientenant Colonel Samuel Mathews, Wm. Whittley.
Nansemond: Colonel Thomas Dew, Speaker, Peter Montague.
Lower Norfolk: Lieutenant Colonel Cor. Lloyd, Major Thomas Lambert, Charles Burrowes.

Elizabeth City: Peter Ransome, Theo. Hone.

York: Captain Stephen Gill, William Gouge, Major X'pher Calthrope.

Gloucester: Colonel Hugh Gwinne, Fra. Willis.

Northampton: Lieutenant Colonel Robbins, Stephen Charlton.

Lancaster: Captain Hen. Fleet, William Underwood.

Source: Hening I, 373-374.

1653

Assembled July 5th

James City: Colonel Walter Chiles, William Whittaker, Hen. Soane, Abra. Wattson.

Surry: Captain William Butler, William Edwards.

Warwick: Colonel Sam. Mathews, William Whittby, Speaker.

Charles City: Captain John Bishopp, Anthony Wyatt.

Nansemond: Col. Thomas Dew, Lieutenant Colonel Edw'd Major, Peter Montague.

Lower Norfolk: Colonel Francis Yardly, Colonel Cornelius Lloyd.

Gloucester: Abraham Iversonn, Richard Pate.

Isle of Wight: Lieutenant Colonel Robert Pitt, Major George Fowden, Daniel Boucher.

Northampton: Captain Thomas Johnson, William Mellin, Stephen Horsey.

Lancaster: Captain Moore Fauntleroy, Captain Thomas Hackett.

York: Major X'pher Calthropp, Robert Booth, William Hockaday, Captain Fra. Morgan.

Northumberland: Lieutenant Colonel George Fletcher, Walter Broadhurst.

Henrico: Captain William Harris.
Elizabeth City: John Sheppard, Thomas Thornbury.
Source: Hening I, 379.

1654

Assembled November 20th

Charles City: Colonel Edward Hill, Speaker, Captain Henry Perry, Major Abraham Wood, Stephen Hamlin.
Elizabeth City: Major William Worlich, John Sheppard.
Gloucester: Thomas Breman, Wingfield Webb.
Henrico: Richard Cock.
James City: Thomas Dipnall, Abraham Watson, William Whitaker, Henry Soane.
Isle of Wight: Lieutenant Colonel Robert Pitt, Captain John Moone, Fra. Hobbs, Captain John Bond.
Lower Norfolk: Barthol. Hoskins, Lemuell Mason.
Lancaster: John Carter, James Bagnall.
Northampton: Peter Walker, Wm. Waters, Tho. Johnson.
Nansemond: Colonel Tho. Dew, Sam. Stoughton, Tho. Godwin.
Northumberland: John Trussell.
Surry: Wm. Batt, James Mason.
Warwick: Lieutenant Colonel Sam. Matthewes, William Whitbye.
New Kent: Capt. Robt. Abrell [the first time this county is represented].
York: Captain Wm. Gooch, Robert Booth, John Hayward.

Westmoreland: Major John Holland, Major Alex. Baynham.

Source: Hening I, 386-387.

Assembly of 1655-1656

This Assembly first met in March 1654-5, and, by adjournments, on March 10, 1655-56, and December 1st, 1656 (Hening I, 407, 414). There is no complete list of members.

Lancaster: Lt. Col. Moore Fauntleroy, Sir Henry Chicheley, Knt.

Northampton: Col. [Edmund] Scarborough.

Lower Norfolk: Col. John Sidney, Lemuel Mason, Bartholomew Hoskins, Thos. Lambert, Capt. Richard Foster.

James City: Lt. Col. [William]Whittaker, Theophilus Hone, Col. John Flood, Robert Holt, Robert Ellyson.

Isle of Wight: Major John Bond, Nicholas Smith, Robert Beazley.

Henrico: Thomas Lyggon, Major William Harris.

Charles City: Anthony Wyatt, Col. Abraham Wood, Captain Daniel Lluellin.

York: Lt. Col. George Reade, John Page, Joseph Croshaw, Capt. Ralph Langley, Capt. Francis Willis, Nathaniel Bacon, Armiger Wade.

Warwick: Thomas Davis.

Northumberland: John Trussell.

Gloucester: Capt. Thos. Ramsey.

Nansemond: Capt. Edward Streeter, John Wilcox, Captain Blake.

Elizabeth City: Peter Ashton.

"Mr. Holmewood," George Lobb, William Thomas, "Mr. Wright," and Lt. Colonel John Walker (who was soon afterwards a member of the Council), can not, with certainty, be assigned to counties.

Sources: Hening I, 414, 421, 422. "Proceedings" of this Assembly in "Edmund Randolph MS," Congressional Library, printed in Va. Mag. Hist. and Biog. VIII, 388-389. In a number of instances Christian names and counties are not given; but these can be readily and certainly supplied from lists of other years, and from other contemporary records.
Records of York County, 1657.

1657-8

Assembled March 13th

Henrico: Major Wm. Harris.

James City: Hen. Soane, Major Richard Webster, Thomas Loveinge, William Corker.

Surry: Lieut. Colonel Thos. Swann, William Edwards, Major Wm. Butler, Captain Wm. Cawfield.

New Kent: William Blacky.

Gloucester: Lieut. Colonel Anth. Elliott, Captain Thomas Ramsey.

Rappahannock: Thomas Lucas.

Lancaster: Colonel John Carter, Peter Montague.

Isle of Wight: Major John Bond, Thomas Tabenor, John Brewer, Joseph Bridger.

Charles City: War'm Horsmenden, Captain Robert Wynne.

Upper Norfolk: Lieut. Colonel Edw'd Carter, Thomas Francis, Giles Webb.

Lower Norfolk: Colonel John Sidney, Major Lemuell Mason.

Elizabeth City: Major William [Wooldridge], John Powell.
Warwick: John Smith, Speaker, Thomas Davis.
York: Jeremy Ham, James Goodwin, Robert Borne, William Hay.
Northumberland: Peter Knight, John Haney.
Northampton: William Kendall, William Mellings, Captain William Michell, Randall Revell, John Willcox.
Source: Hening I, 429-432. York Co. Records 1658.

1658-9

Assembled March 1st

Henrico: William Hatcher.
Charles City: The Speaker; War'm Horsmenden.
James City: Walter Chiles, Captain William Whittacre, Captain Thomas Foulke, Captain Matthew Edloe.
Surry: Captain Geo. Jordan, Thomas Warren, Captain Wm. Cawfield.
Isle of Wight: Colonel Robert Pitt, Major John Bond, Captain Wm. English, James Pyland.
Upper Norfolk: Lieut. Colonel Edw'd Carter, Captain Thomas Goodwyn, Giles Webb.
Lower Norfolk: Captain John Sidney, Major Lemuell Mason.
Warwick: John Harlowe.
Elizabeth City: William Batte, Florentine Paine.
York: Nathaniel Bacon, Major Joseph Crowshaw, Thomas Bushrod, William Hay.
New Kent: William Blacke.
Lancaster: Colonel John Carter, Hen. Corbin.
Rappahannock: Colonel Moore Fauntleroy, John Weye.

Gloucester: Captain Francis Willis, Captain Augustine Warner.
Northumberland: George Collclough.
Northampton: John Stringer, William Jones.
Source: Hening I, 506-507.

1659-60

Assembled March 13*th*

Henrico: Theodorick Bland, Speaker, Captain William Farrer.
Charles City: Theodorick Bland, Captain Robert Wynne, Charles Sparrow.
James City: Henry Soane, Captain Robert Ellison, Richard Ford, William Morley.
Surry: Major William Cawfield, William Browne.
Isle of Wight: Colonel Robert Pitt, Major Nich. Hill, Major John Bond, Nicholas Smith.
Upper Norfolk: Giles Webb, William Denson, George Catchmaie.
Lower Norfolk: Captain John Sidney, Lemuell Mason.
Northampton: Colonel Edm'd Scarbrough, Major Wm. Waters, Lieut. Colonel John Stringer.
Warwick: Colonel Miles Cary, Major Edw. Griffith.
Elizabeth City: Lieut. Colonel Wm. Worleich, Captain John Powell.
York: Christ'r Calthropp, Major Joseph Crowshaw, Nathaniel Bacon, Robert Baldry, Thos. Bushrod "returned Burgess."
New Kent: Colonel Manwaring Hammond, Lieut. Colonel Robert Abrahall.
Rappahannock: Colonel Moore Fantleroy, John Weyre.

Lancaster: Colonel John Carter, Henry Corbin, John Curtis.
Northumberland: Captain Peter Ashton.
Westmoreland: Captain Thomas Foulke [Fowke].
Gloucester: Captain Francis Willis, Captain Peter Jenings, Peter Knight, David Cant.
Source: Hening I, 527-530. York Records.

1660

Assembled October 11th

There is no list of the members of this, the first Assembly held after the Restoration; though the orders and resolutions are printed. Hening II, 9-16.

Assembly of 1661-1676

The Assembly which convened for the first time on March 23d, 1660-61, lasted by various prorogations and adjournments for fifteen years, the last session beginning March 7, 1675-6. Though there was no general election during this long period the membership of the House of Burgesses must have been during the period considerably changed by deaths and seats made vacant by the acceptance of office.

There are only two complete lists, 1663 and 1666; but the county records supply the names of various persons who were certainly members during other years.

Session of March 23, 1660-61

Northumberland: Peter Presley.
Lancaster: Raleigh Travers.
Sources: The records of the respective counties.

Session of March 23, 1661-62

Northumberland: William Presley.
Lancaster: Raleigh Travers.
Sources: The records of the respective counties.

Session of December 23, 1662

Northumberland: William Presley.
Lancaster: Raleigh Travers.
Sources: The records of the respective counties.

Session of September 10, 1663

Henrico: Captain Wm. Farrar.
Charles City: Captain Robert Wynne, Speaker, Stephen Hamelyn, Captain Francis Gray.
James City County: Captain Robt. Ellyson, Walter Chiles, Captain Edward Ramsey.
Surry: Thomas Warren, Captain Wm. Cockerain.
Isle of Wight: Major Nicholas Hill, Captain Joseph Bridger, Dr. Robt. Williamson.
Nansemond: George Wallings.
Lower Norfolk: Major Lemuel Mason.
Elizabeth City: Captain John Powel, Colonel Leonard Yeo.
Warwick: Major Edward Griffith.
York: Lieut. Colonel Wm. Barber.
New Kent: Col. Wm. Claiborne.
Gloucester: Captain Peter Jennings, Captain Thos. Walker.
Lancaster: Rawleigh Travers.
Rappahannock: Thomas Lucas, Captain John Weye.
Northumberland: Wm. Presley.
Westmoreland: Colonel Gerard Fowke.

Northampton: Lieut. Colonel Wm. Kendall, Major Wm. Andrews.
Accomac: Devoreux Browne, Hugh Yeo.
Source: Hening II, 196-197.

Session of September 20, 1664

Northumberland: William Presley.
Lancaster: Raleigh Travers.
Sources: The respective county records.

Session of October 10, 1665

Northumberland: William Presley.
Lancaster: Raleigh Travers.
Lower Norfolk: Adam Thoroughgood, William Carver.
Sources: The respective county records.

Session of June 5, 1666

Northumberland: William Presley.
Lancaster: Raleigh Travers.
Sources: The respective county records.

Session of October 23, 1666

Henrico: Captain William Farrar.
Charles City: Captain Robert Wynne, Speaker, Captain Thomas Southcoat.
York: Lieut. Colonel Wm. Barber, Captain Danl. Parke.
New Kent: Colonel William Clayborn, Captain William Berkley.
James City County: Captain Edward Ramsey, Thomas Ballard.

James City: Theo. Hone.
Surry: Captain Laur. Baker, Thomas Warren.
Isle of Wight: Adjutant General Joseph Bridger, Major Nich. Hill, Robert Williamson.
Nansemond: Colonel John Blake, Captain John Leare.
Lower Norfolk: Captain Adam Thorowgood, Captain Wm. Carver.
Elizabeth City: Colonel Leond. Yeo, Captain John Powell.
Gloucester: Adjutant General Peter Jenyngs, Major Thomas Walker.
Lancaster: Rawleigh Traverse.
Rappahannock: Captain John Weye, Thomas Lucas.
Stafford: Colonel Henry Mees. [First time this county appears in proceedings of Assembly.]
Westmoreland: Colonel Nich. Spencer, Colonel John Washington.
Northumberland: William Presley.
Northampton: Lieut. Colonel Wm. Kendall, Captain John Swavage [Savage].
Accomac: Colonel Edmund Scarburgh, Hugh Yeo.
Source: Hening II, 249-250.

Session of September 23, 1667

Lancaster: " Mr. Wyllis."
Source: The county records.

Session of September 17, 1668

Northumberland: Isaac Allerton.
Lancaster: William Ball.
Sources: The respective county records.

Session of October 20, 1669

Northumberland: Isaac Allerton.
Lancaster: Raleigh Travers.
Sources: The respective county records.

Session of October 3, 1670

Lancaster: William Ball, Raleigh Travers.
Source: The county records.

Session of September 20, 1671

Lancaster: William Ball.
Source: The county records.

Session of September 24, 1672

Northumberland: Isaac Allerton, William Presley.
Surry: Lawrence Baker.
Lancaster: William Ball.
Sources: The respective county records.

Session of October 20, 1673

Northumberland: William Presley, Isaac Allerton.
Lancaster: William Ball.
Westmoreland: "Captain Lee."
Surry: Laurence Baker, William Browne.
Sources: The records of the respective counties.

Session of September 21, 1674

Northumberland: Isaac Allerton, William Presley
Surry: George Jordan, Laurence Baker.
Middlesex: Walter Whitaker, Ralph Wormeley.

Lancaster: William Ball.
Sources: The records of the respective counties.

Session of March 7, 1675-6

Surry: George Jordan, Laurence Baker.
Middlesex: Walter Whitaker, John Burnham.
Westmoreland: John Appleton, John Washington.
Sources: The records of the respective counties.
At the close of this session the Assembly was dissolved.

1676

Assembled June 5th

Lower Norfolk: Arthur Moseley, Richard Church.
Surry: Robert Canfield, Francis Mason.
Stafford: Thomas Mathew, George Mason.
Henrico: Nathaniel Bacon, Jr.
Northumberland: William Presley.
Middlesex: Robert Beverley.
Sources: The records of the respective counties, T. M's Account of Bacon's Rebellion. Northumberland County records, identifying T. M. as Thomas Mathew.

Addenda: The levy of Middlesex County for 1677 contains payments to Richard Perrott, Sr., and Abraham Weekes, for their services as "burgesses in October, 1676." No trace of such a session is to be found elsewhere; but it is possible that either Berkeley or Bacon may have summoned an Assembly for October, which never convened.

1676-77

Assembled February 20th

Westmoreland: "Major Lee" [Richard Lee], John Washington, Isaac Allerton.

Surry: William Browne, Benjamin Harrison.
Stafford: William Fitzhugh.
Sources: The records of the respective counties, and Va. Mag. Hist. and Biog. II, 21.

1677

Assembled October 10th

Henrico: William Byrd, Thomas Cocke.
Stafford: William Fitzhugh.
Northumberland: Isaac Allerton, William Presley, Peter Presley.
Middlesex: Richard Perrott, Sr., Abraham Weekes.
Surry: William Browne, Samuel Swann.
Lancaster: David Fox, Edward Dale, William Ball.
Sources: The records of the respective counties, and letters of William Fitzhugh.

1679

Assembled April 25th

Henrico: William Byrd, Abel Gower.
Surry: Thomas Swann, William Browne.
Stafford: William Fitzhugh.
Sources: The respective County records, and letters of Wm. Fitzhugh.

1680

Assembled June 8th

Surry: Samuel Swann, Benjamin Harrison.
Northumberland: William Presley, St. Leger Codd.
Henrico: William Byrd, John Farrar.
Lancaster: David Fox.

Stafford: William Fitzhugh.
Sources: The respective County records, and letters of Wm. Fitzhugh.

1682
Assembled November 20th

Henrico: William Byrd, John Farrar.
Surry: Samuel Swann, Benjamin Harrison.
Northumberland: St. Leger Codd, William Presley.
Lancaster: " Captain Ball."
Stafford: William Fitzhugh.
Sources: The respective County records, and Fitzhugh letters.

1682
(Another session.)

Northumberland: Thomas Brereton, William Presley.
Surry: William Browne, Arthur Allen.
Stafford: William Fitzhugh.
Lower Norfolk: Lemuel Mason.
Lancaster: Edward Dale, " Captain Ball."
Sources: This session is not mentioned in Hening, nor in the Jameson nor Ludwell lists, and yet the records of the counties named above show payments to the persons mentioned for their services as Burgesses in two Assemblies.

1684
Assembled April 16th

Henrico: William Randolph, John Farrar.
Northumberland: Peter Presley, Peter Knight.
Stafford: William Fitzhugh.
Sources: The records of the respective counties, and Fitzhugh letters.

Assembly of 1685-86

This Assembly first met on October 1st, 1685, and on the same day was prorogued to the 2d of November following. It met on the day appointed and sat some time; but though several bills were passed, none received the Governor's assent. See Hening III, 29, *note*. The Ludwell list says an Assembly was called in 1685, but that there was no session. The Jameson list contains no mention of this session. The Assembly met again, by prorogation, on October 20, 1686. See also Hening III, 40, 41, in regard to the session of 1685.

Session begun November 2, 1685

In the "McDonald Papers," Virginia State Library, is a copy of the journal of the Council, sitting as Upper House of the General Assembly, copied from the English Public Record Office. The names of a number of Burgesses, probably nearly all present, appear in this journal, and are printed. The counties they represented, were, in most cases, easily obtained from other contemporary records:

Accomac: Col. William Kendall, Speaker.
Charles City: Major John Stith.
Elizabeth City or York: Henry Jenkins.
Elizabeth City: William Wilson.
Gloucester: Col. John Armistead.
Henrico: Captain William Randolph and Richard Kennon.
Isle of Wight: Lt. Col. Arthur Smith and Henry Applewhaite.
James City: Col. Thomas Ballard.
Lancaster: Captain William Ball and David Fox.

Lower Norfolk: Col. Lemuel Mason and Capt. Wm. Robinson.

Middlesex: Robert Dudley, Robert Beverley (vacated seat, on election as clerk of the House of Burgesses), Matthew Kemp (elected in place of Beverley), Christopher Robinson.

Nansemond: John Brasseur and Thomas Lear.

New Kent: Col. John West and Richard Littlepage.

Northampton: Captain John Custis.

Northumberland: Christopher Neale and Captain Peter Knight.

Rappahannock: Col. William Lloyd and Arthur Spicer.

Surry: Major Samuel Swan and Major Arthur Allen.

Warwick: Richard Whittaker and Humphrey Harwood.

Westmoreland: Capt. Lawrence Washington and Wm. Hardinge [Hardidge].

Stafford: Samuel Hayward.

York: Thos. Cheesman and Thos. Barber.

Captain John Smith, William Anderson, John Anderson, and Captain Henry Batts [Batte] cannot be, with certainty, assigned to counties. A Captain John West, whose name appears as a member, may have been the same as Colonel John West, of New Kent, or he may have been the John West, who, about the same time, was a justice of Stafford county. The name "Capt. John Casslis," which twice appears, is believed to be an error of the copyist for "Custis." "Capt. John Lear," also appears as a member. This may be a mistake for Thomas Lear, or John Lear may have been elected during the session to fill a vacancy from Nansemond County. Thomas Lear was certainly a member.

The records of Surry, Lancaster, Northumberland and Henrico also show that the persons given in the list above were members of both sessions, 1685, and 1686. Va. Mag. Hist. and Biog. II, 131 for Hayward.

Session begun October 20, 1686

No list, except as shown above; but the membership was probably the same as in the preceding session.

1688

Assembled April 19th

Henrico: William Randolph, Peter Feild.
Nansemond: Thomas Milner, Thomas Lear.
Warwick: Miles Cary, Richard Whittaker.
James City County: Philip Ludwell, James Bray.
James City: William Sherwood.
York: Francis Page, Thomas Barber.
Surry: Arthur Allen, Samuel Swan.
Rappahannock: Arthur Spicer, Henry Aubrey.
Westmoreland: Thomas Yowell, William Hardage.
Accomack: Charles Scarburgh, William Anderson.
Northampton: Thomas Harmanson, William Kendall.
Middlesex: Christopher Robinson, Robert Dudley.
Elizabeth City: William Wilson, Thomas Allonby.
Northumberland: Richard Kenner, Hancock Lee.
Lancaster: William Ball, John Pinkard.
Stafford: George Mason, George Brent.
New Kent: John West, Joseph Foster.
Lower Norfolk: Anthony Lawson, William Crawford.
Isle of Wight: Arthur Smith, Henry Applewhite.
Charles City: Peter Perry.

Source: There is no mention of this session in Hening or in the Jameson list; in the Ludwell list there is, under 1688, "one called April 19, no session." "No session" here means doubtless the same as in reference to 1685, that is, that none of the bills offered became laws. The list of members given above is derived from the English "Calendar of State Papers, Colonial Series, 1685-1688." We are indebted to Mr. Edw'd Wilson James, of Norfolk, Va., for the copy used. The members from Henrico are derived from the county records.

The Jameson list of sessions, frequently referred to, is that by Prof. J. F. Jameson, in the collections of the American Historical Association. The Ludwell list is one among the Ludwell Papers, Virginia Historical Society.

Assembly of 1691-2

This Assembly first met on April 16, 1691, and, by prorogation, on April 1st, 1692.

Session of April 16, 1691

Lancaster: Robert Carter.
Henrico: William Randolph, Francis Epes [Eppes].
Middlesex: Christopher Wormeley, William Churchill.
Surry: Francis Mason, Benjamin Harrison.
Northumberland: Peter Presley, Sr., Richard Kenner.
Sources: The records of the respective counties.

Session of April 1, 1692

Northumberland: Peter Presley, George Cooper.
Middlesex: Christopher Robinson, William Churchill.
Surry: Benjamin Harrison, Francis Mason.
Henrico: Wm. Randolph, Francis Epes.
Lancaster: Wm. Ball, Robert Carter.
Sources: Records of the respective counties.

1692-93

Assembled March 2d

Henrico: John Pleasants, Captain Peter Field. [John Pleasants declined to take the oath, and Capt. William Randolph was elected in his stead.]

Charles City: Captain John Taylor, Captain John Styth.

James City County: Michael Sherman, Captain Henry Duke.

James City: Captain Miles Cary.

Surry: Major Samuel Swann, Captain Francis Clements. [The levy of Surry, September 28, 1693, provides for payment of these burgesses 40 days each, and Thos. Swan and John Thompson 33 days each.]

Isle of Wight: Major Henry Baker, Anthony Holiday.

Nansemond: Lieut. Colonel Thomas Milner, Speaker, Thomas Lear.

Norfolk: Colonel Lemuel Mason, Major Francis Sawyer.

Princess Anne: John Richardson, Jacob Johnson (Sr.)

Elizabeth City: Captain Willis Wilson, Captain William Armistead.

York: Captain Thomas Ballard, Daniel Parke.

New Kent: Captain John Lyddall, Captain William Bassett.

Gloucester: Captain James Ransom, John Baylor.

Middlesex: Captain Matthew Kemp, John Cant.

Essex: Captain John Battaile, Captain Edward Thomas.

Richmond: Captain Arthur Spicer, William Colston.

Stafford: Captain Martin Scarlett, Captain Thomas Ousley.

Accomac: Major Richard Baylie, Samuel Sandford.

Lancaster: Captain David Fox, John Stretchley.
Westmoreland: Captain Thomas Yowell, Captain William Harddige.
Warwick: Captain William Cary, Major Humphrey Harwood.
Northumberland: Richard Rogers, Richard Flint. [These seats were contested, and the sheriff of Northumberland was required to amend his return in favor of Mr. John Downing and Capt. Wm. Jones.]
King and Queen: Captain Wm. Leigh, Captain John Lane. [Captain Lane's seat was vacated by order of the House.]
Northampton: Captain John Custis, Captain Wm. Kendall.
Source: MS. journal, Va. State Library.

1693
Assembled October 10th

Essex: John Catlett, Thomas Edmondson.
Henrico: William Randolph, Francis Epes.
Lancaster: John Downing, William Jones.
Northumberland: William Lee, Cuthbert Span.
Norfolk: Lemuel Mason, ———— Sayres.
Middlesex: Matthew Kemp, John Cant.
Sources: Records of the respective counties.

1695
Assembled April 18th

Henrico: William Randolph, William Soane.
Northumberland: Richard Haynie, Rodham Kenner.
Surry: Samuel Swan, John Thompson.
Lancaster: Joseph Ball, George Heale, John Stretchley.

Essex: William Moseley, John Catlett.
Sources: Records of the respective counties.

1696

Assembled April 23d

Henrico: William Randolph, William Soane.
Northumberland: Richard Haynie.
Surry: Thomas Swan, John Thompson.
Norfolk: William Craford [Crawford], Thomas Hodges.
Essex: John Catlett, William Moseley.
Sources: Records of the respective counties. Hening has a note, III, 137, to prove that this session was never held; but the County records and the journal referred to in Jameson's list prove that it was.

Assembly of 1696-97

This Assembly met September 24, 1696, and by prorogations, on April 29, and October 21st, 1697, See under "Sources," for names of some members at the last session.

Session of September 24, 1696

"A Roll of the Burgesses at an Assembly beginning the 24th day of September, 1696:"
Henrico: Wm. Byrd,* Wm. Randolph, James Cocke.
New Kent: Wm. Bassett, Gideon Macon.
Princess Anne: Benjamin Borough, John Thorowgood.
King and Queen: Wm. Leigh, Joshua Story, sheriff.
Isle of Wight: James Benn, dead; John Giles.
Gloucester: James Ransone, Mordecai Cooke.

* Out of the country.

Northumberland: Richard Haynie, Rodham Kenner.
Surry: Benjamin Harrison, John Thompson.
Westmoreland: Alexander Speare, Isaac Allerton.
James City County: Henry Duke, Miles Sherman.
James City: Philip Ludwell, Jr., Wm. Sherwood, dead.
Lancaster: Robert Carter, George Heale.
Nansemond: John Brassieur, Thomas Jordan, sheriff.
Norfolk: Thomas Hodges, Thomas Mason.
Elizabeth City: Anthony Armistead, Willis Wilson.
Warwick: Dudley Digges, Robt. Hubbard, Rich'd Whitaker, sheriff.
Accomack: John Washburn, Rich'd Bayley.
Richmond: Alex'r Newman.
Charles City: Chas. Goodrich, John Taylor.
Middlesex: Matthew Kemp, Robert Dudley.
Stafford: George Mason, John Withers.
Essex: John Battaile, Thos. Edmondson.
York: Henry Jenkins, Thomas Ballard.
Northampton: John Custis, Wm. Waters, sheriff.

Sources: A list derived from one in the State Council Chamber, printed in the Va. Mag. Hist. and Biog. III, 425. The records of Norfolk, Surrey, Northumberland and Henrico contain payments to the Burgesses here named for service at this session. Except that the Henrico record says Wm. Byrd, Jr. Where the words " death," or " sheriff " follow names, the cause of a vacancy during the session is indicated.

The County records and the Cal. Va. State Papers, Vol. I, show that Kenner, Haynie, Edmundson, Ransone, Brasseur, Ludwell, Jr., Hubbard, Randolph, Heale, Harrison and Thompson were members at the session of October, 1697; but that Thos. Cocke was Burgess for Henrico in place of

James Cocke, and Benoni Burroughs and John Thoroughgood for Norfolk, in place of Hodges and Mason. The Essex records show that Thos. Edmundson, and John Battaile were also members at both sessions in 1697.

1698

Assembled September 28th

Henrico: William Randolph, Speaker, Thomas Cocke.
Lancaster: Joseph Ball, Robert Carter.
Surry: Benjamin Harrison, Thomas Swan.
Northumberland: Hancock Lee, Richard Haynie.
Essex: James Boughan.
Sources: The records of the respective counties, and Hening III, 166, *note*.

1699

Assembled April 27th

Henrico: Wm. Randolph (served three days), James Cocke, Thomas Cocke (in place of Randolph).
Essex: John Taliaferro, James Baughan.
Northumberland: George Cooper, Rodham Kenner.
Richmond: Thomas Lloyd, William Colston.
Surry: Thomas Holt, Nathaniel Harrison.
Lancaster: Alexander Swan, Robert Carter.
Sources: The records of the respective counties.

Assembly of 1700-1702

This Assembly first met on December 5, 1700, and, by successive prorogations, on August 6, 1701; May 13, 1702; June 18, 1702, and August 14, 1702. It was dissolved on August 28, 1702.

[Though not mentioned in Hening or in Jameson's list it seems that there was an Assembly in session in May, 1700. See Calendar Va. State Papers, Vol. I, under date May 26, 1700, Wm. Bassett, Burgess for New Kent, and William Byrd, Burgess for King and Queen, refused to take the oaths, believing that King William was dead, and new writs were issued to fill their places.

There would also seem to have been a session in October, 1700, not mentioned by Hening or Jameson. In the Norfolk County levy, laid January 16, 1700, are payments to Thomas Butt, services as Burgess, " 27 days in October last," and Matthew Godfrey, " October last 28 days and December last 27 days." The Northumberland levy, dated January 16, 1700-1701, provides payment for two sets of Burgesses, Col. George Cooper and Rodham Kenner, and Rodham Kenner and Thomas Hobson.

The Surry levy for 1700 also provides for two sets of Burgesses: Thomas Holt and Nathaniel Harrison, 5 days; and Nathaniel Harrison and Samuel Thompson, 24 days in December. Whatever the facts may be in regard to this session, the persons named were undoubtedly Burgesses.]

Session of December 5, 1700

Henrico: Thomas Cocke, William Randolph.
Surry: Nathaniel Harrison, Samuel Thompson.
Norfolk: Matthew Godfrey.
Essex: Thomas Edmondson, John Catlett.
Northumberland: Rodham Kenner, Thomas Hobson.
Richmond: George Taylor, William Tayloe.
King and Queen: William Leigh.
Warwick: Miles Cary.
Charles City: Richard Bland.

Princess Anne: Jacob Johnson, Jr.

Sources: The records of Henrico, Surrey, Norfolk, Essex, Northumberland and Richmond Counties. Journal of the Council, sitting as Upper House of Assembly, in Va. State Library.

Session of August 6, 1701

Surry: Nathaniel Harrison, Samuel Thompson.
Northumberland: Rodham Kenner, Thomas Hobson.
Richmond: George Taylor, William Tayloe.
Westmoreland: Alexander Spence, James Westcombe.
Henrico: William Farrar, Thomas Cocke.
Lancaster: Joseph Ball, William Fox.
Stafford: George Mason, William Fitzhugh.
Sources: The respective county records.

Sessions of May 13 and June 18, 1702

Accomac: Tho. Welburn, Tully Robinson.
Charles City: Rich'd Bland, Jno. Wynn.
Elizabeth City: Wm. Wilson, Wm. Armistead.
Essex: Jno. Catlett, Tho. Edmondson.
Gloucester: Petr. Beverley, Speaker, Mord. Cook.
Henrico: Tho. Cock, Wm. Farrar.
James City: James Bray, Geo. Marable, Rob't Beverley.
Isle of Wight: Henry Applethwaite, Tho. Giles.
King and Queen: Wm. Leigh, James Taylor.
King William: Jno. West, Natt. West.
Lancaster: Jos. Ball, Wm. Fox.
Middlesex: Gawin Corbin, Edwin Thacker.
Nansemond: Tho. Milner, Danl. Sullivan.
Norfolk: Rich'd Church, Matt. Godfrey.
New Kent: Wm. Bassett, Jos. Foster.

Northumberland: Rodham Kenner, Tho. Hobson.
Northampton: Wm. Waters, Jno. Powell.
Princess Anne: Adam Thorogood, Edw'd Moseley.
Richmond: Wm. Tayloe, Geo. Taylor.
Surry: Natt. Harrison, Sam'l Thompson.
Stafford: Geo. Mason, Wm. Fitzhugh.
Warwick: Miles Cary, Wm. Cary.
Westmoreland: Alex. Spence, James Westcomb.
York: Tho. Barbar, Tho. Ballard.

Source: A list, dated July 8, 1702, in a report to the Board of Trade, made by Edmund Jenings, Secretary of State of Virginia, as printed in the Virginia Magazine of History and Biography, I, 364-373. It is evident that the membership during the four sessions of this Assembly was unchanged.

The records of Northumberland, Essex, Stafford, Henrico, Lancaster, Richmond and Surry show that these members in the session of August, 1702, were the same as at the previous sessions.

Assembly of 1702-3-1705

This Assembly first met on March 19, 1702-3, and by various prorogations, on April 20, 1704 and April 18, 1705, See Hening III, 224 note, and Jameson. There are no complete lists of the members during this Assembly.

Session of March 19, 1702-3

Essex: Richard Covington, James Boughan.
Lancaster: William Ball, John Turberville.
Northumberland: John Harris, Richard Haynie.
Stafford: Rice Hooe, Richard Fosaker.
Surry: Nathaniel Harrison, Wm. Edwards.

Westmoreland: Henry Ashton, Charles Ashton.
Richmond: William Robinson, David Gwyn.
Nansemond: Thomas Swan.
King and Queen: William Leigh.
Middlesex: Edwin Thacker.
Sources: Records of Lancaster, Northumberland, Stafford, Surry, Westmoreland and Richmond. Journal of Council, as Upper House in Va. State Library.

Session of April 20, 1704

Henrico: William Randolph, Francis Epes.
Essex: Richard Covington, James Boughan.
Surry: Nathaniel Harrison, William Edwards.
Westmoreland: Charles Ashton, Henry Ashton.
Northumberland: John Harris, Richard Haynie.
Charles City: Edward Hill, Benjamin Harrison.
Lancaster: John Turberville, William Ball.
Middlesex: Gawin Corbin, William Churchill (in place of Thacker, deceased).
Nansemond:——(in place of Swan, deceased).
King and Queen: ——— (in place of Leigh, deceased), William Bird.
Richmond: William Robinson.
Warwick: Miles Cary.
Prince George: Robert Bolling.
Essex: Richard Covington.
Sources: Records of Henrico, Surry, Northumberland, Westmoreland and Lancaster. Journal of Council as Upper House, Va. State Library.

Session of April 18, 1705

Essex: Richard Covington, James Boughan.

Charles City: Edward Hill, Benjamin Harrison.
Henrico: William Randolph.
Surry: Nathaniel Harrison, William Edwards.
Westermoreland: Charles Ashton, Henry Ashton.
Northumberland: Richard Haynie, John Harris.
Lancaster: William Ball, William Lister.
—— Co: " Mr. Jenkins."
Sources: Records of Henrico, Surry, Westmoreland, Northumberland, and Lancaster. Calendar Va. S. P., I. Extract from the Journal of the House printed in Va. Mag. Hist. and Biog. VIII, 133, 134.

Assembly of 1705-1706

This Assembly met twice, the first session beginning October 23, 1705, and the second, April 24, 1706.

Session of October 23, 1705

Northumberland: Peter Hack, Christopher Neale.
Source: Records of Northumberland county.

Session of April 24, 1706

Northumberland: Peter Hack, Christopher Neale.
Richmond: William Tayloe, William Robinson.
Westmoreland: George Eskridge, Daniel McCarty.
Surry: Nathaniel Harrison, William Edwards.
Lancaster: William Lister, William Ball.
King and Queen: Robert Beverley.
Gloucester: Peter Beverley.
Essex: Francis Gouldman, Francis Meriwether.
Henrico: William Randolph.
Warwick: Miles Cary.

Prince George: Richard Bland.

Sources: Records of Northumberland, Richmond, Westmoreland, Surry and Lancaster. Journal of Council sitting as Upper House, Va. State Library.

Assembly of 1710-1712

This Assembly first met on Oct. 25, 1710, and, by prorogations, on Nov. 7, 1711, and Jan. 24, 1712.

Session of October 25, 1710

Richmond: John Tarpley, William Robinson.
Surry: William Gray, John Simmons.
Henrico: William Randolph, John Bolling.
Essex: James Boughan, John Hawkins.
Middlesex: Christopher Robinson.
Princess Anne: Maximilian Boush.
Gloucester: Nathaniel Burwell, Peter Beverley Speaker, Ambrose Dudley.
Westmoreland: Willoughby Allerton.
Elizabeth City: Nicholas Curle, William Armistead.
Warwick: William Cary.
Norfolk: James Wilson.
King William: John Waller.
New Kent: Nicholas Meriwether.
Sources: Records of Richmond and Surry. Cal. Va. S. P. I, under date 1710.

Session of November 7, 1711

Essex: John Hawkins.
Lancaster: William Ball.
Northumberland: Christopher Neale, Peter Presley.

Norfolk: George Newton.
Princess Anne: Maximilian Boush.
Surry: John Simmons, William Gray.
Richmond: John Tarpley, William Robinson.
King and Queen: John Holloway.
Middlesex: John Robinson.
Sources: Records of Lancaster, Northumberland, Norfolk, Princess Anne, Surry and Richmond. Journal of Council as Upper House, Va. State Library.

Session of January 24, 1712

No names; but doubtless same as the other sessions.

Assembly of 1712-1714

This Assembly first met on October 22, 1712, and, by prorogations, on November 5, 1713, and November 16, 1714.

Session of October 22, 1712

Northumberland: Peter Presley, Christopher Neale, Richard Neale.
Princess Anne: Maximilian Boush.
Richmond: William Thornton, William Robinson.
Surry: William Gray, Jr., John Simmons.
Lancaster: Edwin Conway, William Ball.
Essex: Francis Meriwether, Francis Gouldman.
Sources: Records of the respective counties.

Session of November 5, 1713

Northumberland: Christopher Neale, Richard Neale.
Surry: William Gray, John Simmons.
Lancaster: Edwin Conway, William Ball.

Princess Anne: Maximilian Boush.
Westmoreland: Willoughby Allerton, George Eskridge.
Sources: Records of respective counties.

Session of November 16, 1714

Accomac: Tully Robinson, Richard Drumond.
Charles City: Littlebury Epes, Samuel Harwood.
Elizabeth City: Wm. Armistead, Robt. Armistead.
Essex: Fra. Gouldman, Jno. Hawkins.
Gloucester: Peter Beverley, Mordecai Cooke.
Henrico: Jno. Bolling, Fra. Epes, Jr.
James City: Geo. Marable, Henry Soane, Jr., Edwd. Jacquelin, for ye city
Isle of Wight: Wm. Bridger, Joseph Godwin.
King and Queen: Jno. Holloway, Wm. Bird.
King William: Jno. Waller, Orlando Jones.
Lancaster: Wm. Ball, Edwin Conway.
Middlesex: Jno. Robinson, Chr. Robinson.
Nansemond: Tho. Godwin, Wm. Wright.
Norfolk: Geo. Newton, Wm. Crawford.
New Kent: Nicho. Meriwether, Jno. Stanup.
Northumberland: Chr. Neale, Richd. Neale.
Northampton: Wm. Waters. Cha. Floyd.
Princess Anne: Max. Boush, Tho. Walke.
Prince George: Edwd. Goodrich, Jno. Hamlyn.
Richmond: Wm. Robinson, Wm. Thornton.
Surry: Wm. Gray, Jno. Simmons.
Stafford: Henry Fitzhugh, Jno. Waugh.
Warwick: Miles Wills, Wm. Harwood.
Westmoreland: Willoughby Allerton, Geo. Eskridge.
York: Wm. Buckner, Wm. Barbar.
Source: A list in the British Public Record Office, Vir-

ginia—Board of Trade—Vol: 14; printed in the Virginia Magazine of History and Biography II, 1-15.

Assembly of 1715

This Assembly had but one session beginning August 3, 1715.
Northumberland: Peter Presley, Christopher Neale.
Lancaster: James Ball, Edwin Conway, William Ball.
Princess Anne: Maximilian Boush.
Richmond: William Woodbridge, Thomas Griffin.
Surry: Henry Harrison, Samuel Thompson, William Gray, John Simmons.
Norfolk: William Langley, William Craford.
Westmoreland: Henry Ashton, Daniel McCarty.
Sources: Records of the respective counties.

Assembly of 1718

There were two sessions of this Assembly, both held in 1718. One began on April 23, and the other on November 11. Though the list of only one session has been preserved there is every reason to believe that the membership was the same for both.

Session of April 23, 1718

Henrico: William Randolph, John Bolling.
Charles City: John Stith, Francis Hardiman.
Prince George: Edward Goodrich, Robert Hall.
Surry: Henry Harrison, Samuel Thompson.
Isle of Wight: William Bridger, Arthur Smith.

Nansemond: John Lear, James Reddick.
Norfolk: William Crafford, Willis Wilson.
Princess Anne: Maximilian Boush. Horatio Woodhouse.
Elizabeth City: Henry Jenkins, Thomas Wyth.
Warwick: William Cole, Cole Digges.
York: William Barber, James Burwell.
James City: William Brodnax, George Marable.
Jamestown: Arch. Blair.
College: Major John Custis.
New Kent: Nich. Meriwether, James Stanup [Stanhope].
King William: Orlando Jones, Thomas Johnson.
King and Queen: John Baylor, George Braxton.
Gloucester: Henry Willis, Thomas Buckner.
Middlesex: Gawin Corbin, John Grymes.
Essex: John Hawkins, Wm. Daingerfield.
Stafford: George Mason, George Fitzhugh.
Westmoreland: Daniel McCarty, Speaker, George Eskridge.
Northumberland: Peter Presley, Christopher Neale.
Richmond: Wm. Woodbridge, Thomas Griffin.
Lancaster: Edwin Conway, James Ball.
Accomac: Tully Robinson, Solomon Ewell.
Northampton: William Waters, Charles Floyd.
'Source: A list derived from the Virginia Colonial records and printed in the Virginia Historical Register IV, 18.

Assembly of 1720-22

There were two sessions of this Assembly, meeting on November 2, 1720, and May 9, 1722.

Sessions of 1720 and 1722

Accomack: John Teackle (deceased), Solomon Ewell.
Charles City: John Stith, Samuel Harwood, Jr.
College: Thomas Jones.
Elizabeth City: James Rickets, Mr. Anthony Armistead.
Essex: John Hawkins, Richard Covington.
Gloucester: Henry Willis, Nathaniel Burwell (deceased).
Henrico: Wm. Randolph, Thos. Randolph.
Isle of Wight: William Bridger, Arthur Smith.
James City: Archibald Blair, John Clayton.
Jamestown: William Brodnax.
King William: John Waller, Thos. Johnson.
King and Queen: George Braxton, Robert Beverley (deceased).
Lancaster: Wm. Ball, James Ball.
Middlesex: John Grymes, Gawin Corbin.
New Kent: Nicholas Meriwether, John Stanhope (deceased).
Nansemond: John Lear, James Reddick.
Norfolk: Willis Wilson, Wm. Crawford.
Northumberland: Peter Presley, Peter Hack.
Northampton: William Waters (deceased), George Harmanson.
Prince George: Edward Goodrich (deceased), Robert Mumford [Munford], John Hamlin.
Princess Anne: Maximilian Boush, Anthony Walk.
Richmond: Wm. Woodbridge, Chas. Barber.
Stafford: Geo. Mason, Wm. Robinson.
Surrey: Henry Harrison, John Simmons.
Warwick: William Cole, James Roscow (dec'd).

Westmoreland: George Eskridge, Thomas Lee, unduly elected, Daniel McCarty.

York: John Holloway, Speaker, Lawrence Smith.

1722

New Burgesses chosen for the new counties of—

Hanover: Nicholas Meriwether, John Syme.

King George: Nicholas Smith, Wm. Thornton.

Mr. Meriwether being declared a burgess for Hanover county and Mr. Stanope being dead, a new writ was issued, and for

New Kent: John Thornton, Thomas Massey were duly returned Burgesses.

Chosen in the room of the deceased—

Gloucester: Giles Cook.

Accomack: Tully Robinson.

King and Queen: Richard Johnson.

Northampton: Thomas Harmanson.

Warwick: Nath. Hoggard.

Source: A list, apparently contemporary, in the collection of the Virginia Historical Society. This was among the papers of Godfrey Pole, a committee clerk of this Assembly, presented to the Society many years ago.

Assembly of 1723-26

The first session of this Assembly was called for December 5, 1722; but was prorogued and did not meet until May 9, 1723. The second and last session met May 12, 1726.

Session of May 9, 1723

Accomac: Tully Robinson, Edm'd Scarburgh.

Charles City: Sam'l Harwood, John Stith.

Essex, Rob't Jones, Wm. Dangerfield.

Elizabeth City: James Rickets, Thomas Wythe.
Gloucester: Giles Cooke, Henry Willis.
Henrico: Wm. Randolph, John Bolling.
Hanover: Nich. Merriwether, Richard Harris.
Jamestown: Wm. Brodnax.
James City: Archibald Blair, John Clayton.
Isle of Wight: Henry Applewhaite, Joseph Godwyn.
King and Queen: Richard Johnson, George Braxton.
King William: William Aylet, John Childs.
King George: Nicholas Smith, William Thornton.
Lancaster: Edwin Conway, William Ball.
Middlesex: Matthew Kemp, Edwin Thacker.
Northumberland: Peter Presley, George Ball.
Nansemond: Thomas Goodwin, Henry Baker.
New Kent: John Thornton, Thomas Massey [Massie].
Norfolk: William Crafford, George Newton.
Prince George: Robert Bolling, John Poythress.
Princess Anne: Henry Sprat, Maximilian Boush.
Richmond: Charles Barber, Thomas Griffin.
Spotsylvania: Larkin Chew, Francis Thornton.
Stafford: George Mason, William Robinson.
Westmoreland: George Eskridge, Daniel McCarty.
Williamsburgh: Jno. Holloway, Speaker.
Warwick: William Cole, William Roscoe.
Northampton: Geo. Harmanson, Thos. Harmanson.
Surry: William Gray, Henry Harrison.
York: Lawrence Smith, Edward Tabb.
Source: Virginia Historical Register IV. 66.

Session of May 12, 1726

Accomac: Henry Scarburgh, Edmund Scarburgh.
Charles City: Sam'l. Harwood, Jr., John Stith.

Nansemond: Thomas Godwin, Henry Baker.
New Kent: John Thornton, Thomas Massie.
Elizabeth City: Robert Armistead, Thomas Wythe.
Essex: Robt. Jones, Wm. Dangerfield.
Gloucester: Giles Cook, Henry Willis.
Hanover: Nich. Meriwether, Richard Harris.
Henrico: Wm. Randolph, John Bolling.
James City: Archibald Blair, John Clayton.
Jamestown: Wm. Brodnax.
Isle of Wight: Henry Applewhaite, Joseph Godwin.
King and Queen: Richard Johnson, George Braxton.
King George: Nicholas Smith, William Thornton.
King William: William Aylett, Philip Whitehead.
Lancaster: Edwin Conway, Wm. Ball.
Middlesex: Matthew Kemp, Edwin Thacker.
Norfolk: William Crafford, George Newton.
Northampton: George Harmanson, Thomas Marshall.
Northumberland: Peter Presly, George Ball.
Princess Anne: Henry Spratt, Maximilian Boush.
Prince George: Robert Bolling, John Poythress.
Richmond: Charles Barber, Thomas Griffin.
Spotsylvania: Larkin Chew, Francis Thornton.
Stafford: George Mason, William Robinson.
Surry: Wm. Gray, Henry Harrison.
Warwick: Wm. Cole, Wm. Roscow.
Westmoreland: George Eskridge, Thomas Lee.
Williamsburg: Jno. Holloway, Speaker.
York: Lawrence Smith, Edward Tabb.
Source: Virginia Historical Register IV, 73.

Assembly of 1727-8-1734

This Assembly met first on February 1, 1727-8, and by prorogations, on May 21, 1730, May 18, 1732, and August

22, 1734. There are no complete lists of any session of this Assembly.

Session of February 1, 1727-8

Richmond: Charles Grymes, John Tayloe.
Goochland: Richard Randolph, John Bolling.
Lancaster: Edwin Conway, Charles Burgess.
Hanover: Nicholas Meriwether.
Surry: Henry Harrison.
James City: Archibald Blair, John Clayton.
King and Queen: George Braxton.
Gloucester: Henry Willis, Francis Willis.
Essex: William Dangerfield.
Middlesex: Matthew Kemp.
Westmoreland: Thomas Lee, George Eskridge.
Northumberland: Peter Presley.
Caroline: Henry Armistead.
———: ——— Fitzhugh.

Sources: Records of Richmond, Goochland and Lancaster, Journal of Council sitting as Upper House; Va. State Library.

Session of May 21, 1730

Surry: Henry Harrison.
Prince George: Robert Bolling.
Middlesex: Matthew Kemp.
James City: John Clayton.
Lancaster: Edwin Conway.
Richmond: John Tayloe.
Stafford: William Robinson
Westmoreland: George Eskridge.

Source: Journal of Council sitting as Upper House, Va. State Library.

Session of May 18, 1732

Lancaster: Edwin Conway, Charles Burgess.
Goockland: John Fleming, Dudley Digges.
Westmoreland: Thomas Lee, George Eskridge.
Sources: The records of the respective counties.

Session of August 22, 1734

Lancaster: Edwin Conway, James Ball.
Essex: Thomas Waring, Salvator Muscoe.
Sources: The county records.

Assembly of 1736-1740

This Assembly first met on August 5, 1736, and by prorogations, on November 1, 1738, May 22, 1740, and August 21, 1740.

Session of August 5, 1736

Accomac: Henry Scarburgh, Sacker Parker.
Amelia: Edward Booker, Richard Jones.
Brunswick: Henry Embry, John Wall.
Charles City: W. Acrill, B. Harrison.
Caroline: Robert Fleming, Jonathan Gibson.
Elizabeth City: W. Westwood, Merit Sweny.
Essex: Tho. Waring, Salvator Muscoe.
Gloucester: Fran. Willis, Lawrence Smith.
Goochland: Edw. Scott, James Holman.
Hanover: None elected.
Henrico: Richard Randolph.
James City County: W. Marable, J. Eaton.
Jamestown: Lewis Burwell.
Isle of Wight: Joseph Grey, John Simmons.

King George: Charles Carter, Tho. Turner.
King William: Cornel. Lyde, Leon. Claiborne.
King and Queen: J. Robinson, Gawin Corbin.
Lancaster: Edwin Conway, James Ball.
Middlesex: Tho. Price, Edmund Berkeley.
Nansemond: Daniel Pugh, Lemuel Riddick.
New Kent: William Macon.
Norfolk: William Craford, Samuel Boush.
Northampton: Matth. Harmanson, P. Bowdoin.
Northumberland: Peter Presley, George Ball.
Orange: Robert Green, William Beverley.
Princess Anne: Anth. Walke, Jacob Elligood.
Prince George: Fran. Eppes, Rob. Munford.
Prince William: Tho. Osborn, Val. Peyton.
Richmond: J. Woodbridge, William Fantleroy.
Spotsylvania: William Johnson, Rice Curtis.
Stafford: Henry Fitzhugh, John Peyton.
Surry: Thomas Edmunds.
Warwick: William Roscow, Thomas Haynes.
Westmoreland: William Aylett, Dan. McCarty.
Williamsburg: John Blair.
York: Edw. Digges, John Buckner.
College of William and Mary: Sir John Randolph, Knt., Speaker.

Source: The Virginia Historical Register IV, 135.

The following changes during the session are noted in the Virginia Gazette (Va. Historical Society):

Hanover: William Meriwether, Robert Harris.

Prince William: Peter Hedgman in place of Thomas Osborne, expelled.

Caroline: Jonathan Gibson declared unduly elected was reëlected.

Session of November 1, 1738

Accomac: Henry Scarburgh, Edmund Scarborough (in place of Sacker Parker, deceased.)
Amelia: Edward Booker, Richard Jones.
Brunswick: Henry Embry, John Wall.
Charles City: Benjamin Harrison, Richard Kennon.
Caroline: John Martin (in place of Robert Fleming, deceased), Jonathan Gibson.
Elizabeth City: W. Westwood, Merit Sweny.
Essex: Thomas Waring, Salvator Muscoe.
Gloucester: Francis Willis, Lawrence Smith.
Hanover: William Meriwether, Robert Harris.
Henrico: Richard Randolph.
Goochland: James Holman, Isham Randolph (in place of Edward Scott, deceased.)
James City: W. Marable, J. Eaton.
Jamestown: Lewis Burwell.
Isle of Wight: Joseph Gray.
King George: Charles Carter, Thomas Turner.
King William: Leonard Clarborne, John Aylett (in place of Cornelius Lyde, deceased.)
King and Queen: John Robinson, Gawin Corbin.
Lancaster: Edwin Conway, James Ball.
Middlesex: Thomas Price, Edmund Berkeley.
Nansemond: Daniel Pugh, Lemuel Riddick.
New Kent: William Macon.
Norfolk: William Craford, Samuel Boush.
Northampton: Matthew Harmanson, P. Bowdoin.
Northumberland: Peter Presley, George Ball.
Orange: Robert Green, William Beverley.
Princess Anne: Anthony Walke, Jacob Elligood.
Prince George: Francis Eppes, Robert Munford.

Prince William: Valentine Peyton, Peter Hedgman.
Richmond: J. Woodbridge, William Fauntleroy.
Stafford: Henry Fitzhugh, John Peyton.
Spotsylvania: William Johnson, Rice Curtis.
Surry: Thomas Edmunds, John Ruffin.
Warwick: William Roscow, Thomas Haynes.
Westmoreland: William Aylett, Daniel McCarty.
Williamsburg: John Blair.
York: Edward Digges, John Buckner.
Norfolk Borough: John Hutchings.
College of William and Mary: Attorney General Edward Barradall (in place of Sir John Randolph, deceased).
Source: The list of the previous session corrected by the changes noted in the Virginia Gazette.

Session of May 22, 1740

Accomac: Edmund Scarborough, Edward Allen, in place of Henry Scarburgh, deceased).
Amelia: Richard Jones, Edward Booker.
Brunswick: Henry Embry, John Wall.
Caroline: John Martin, Jonathan Gibson.
Charles City: Benjamin Harrison, Richard Kennon.
Elizabeth City: William Westwood, Merit Sweny.
Essex: Thomas Waring, Salvator Muscow (Wm. Beverley was also member for Essex at this session.)
Gloucester: Beverley Whiting (in place of Lawrence Smith, deceased), Francis Willis. During the session Whiting's seat was successfully contested and a new election ordered.
Goochland: Isham Randolph, James Holman.
Hanover: William Meriwether, Robert Harris.

Henrico: Richard Randolph.
James City: William Marable,—(in place of John Eaton, deceased.)
Isle of Wight: John Simmons, Joseph Gray.
King George: Thomas Turner, Charles Carter.
King and Queen: Gawin Corbin, John Robinson.
King William: Leonard Claiborne, John Aylett.
Lancaster: Edwin Conway, James Ball.
Middlesex: Thos. Price, Edmund Berkeley.
Nansemond: David Pugh, Lemuel Riddick.
New Kent: William Macon.
Norfolk: Samuel Boush, William Craford.
Northumberland: George Ball, Peter Presley.
Northampton: Matthew Harmanson, P. Bowdoin.
Orange: William Beverley, (in place of Robert Green, who had accepted the place of sheriff.)
Prince George: Robert Munford, Francis Eppes.
Princess Anne: Jacob Elligood, Anthony Walke.
Prince William: Valentine Peyton, Peter Hedgman.
Richmond: J. Woodbridge, Wm. Fauntleroy.
Spotsylvania: William Johnson, Henry Willis.
Stafford: Henry Fitzhugh, John Peyton.
Surry: John Ruffin, Thos. Edmunds.
Warwick: Thomas Haynes, William Roscow.
Westmoreland: Daniel McCarty, William Aylett.
York: John Buckner, Dudley Digges.
College of William and Mary: The Attorney General.
Jamestown: Lewis Burwell.
Norfolk Borough: John Hutchings.
Williamsburg: John Blair.

It appears from the Journal of this session that a Mr. Cary was a member. As both seats for Warwick and Elizabeth City were held by others, this may be Henry Cary of Henrico (the part now Chesterfield.)

Source: Journal of the House of Burgesses, Congressional Library.

Session of August 1, 1740

There is no list of this session, but no doubt the membership was the same as in the session before.

Assembly of 1742-1747

This Assembly first met on May 6, 1742, and, by prorogations, on Sept. 4, 1744, Feb. 20, 1746, July 11, 1746, and March 30, 1747, and was dissolved on April 8. The Journal of the first session of the House of Burgesses states that the Assembly was called to meet on May 6, 1741, but was prorogued before convening. The Journal of the Council, sitting as Upper House, states the same fact. Both Journals, however, say that the first session began on May 6, 1742.

Though there is no other record of a session in 1741, the records of Essex show that in the levy for that county laid Nov. 20, 1741, William Beverley and James Garnett were paid for their services as Burgesses. And the records of Northumberland show that on Nov. 17, 1741, Peter Presley and Samuel Blackwell were elected members for that county. And in the same year William Fairfax and Thomas Harrison were elected for Prince William, and Andrew Monroe for Westmoreland.

While there are no lists of the members of the Assembly, there are printed Journals of the sessions of 1742, in the Congressional Library, and of 1744 and 1745 in the Va. State Library, and also, in the latter, manuscript journals of the Council sitting as Upper House. These enable us to supply the names of most of the members.

There was a Mr. Lee a member in 1742, and perhaps other years, and a Mr. Cunningham, in 1745, 1746, and 1747, who cannot be identified or their counties fixed. A William Randolph was a member in 1745, 1746, and 1747, after the death of William Randolph of "Tuckahoe," who represented Goochland. This seems to be certainly William Randolph of "Wilton;" but he did not apparently represent Henrico or Goochland. Possibly it was Goochland.

Session of May 6, 1742

Accomack: Henry Scarburgh, George Douglas. (Douglas was unseated on contest, and William Andrews seated in his place. Not long afterwards Andrews was expelled and a new election ordered), George Douglas (reëlected.)

Amelia: Samuel Cobbs, Joseph Scott (unseated on contest), Edward Booker.

Brunswick: John Wall.

Caroline: Lunsford Lomax, John Baylor.

Charles City: Benjamin Harrison, Richard Kennon.

Elizabeth City: Wm. Westwood, Merit Sweny.

Essex: William Beverley, James Garnett.

Fairfax: Lawrence Washington.

Frederick: Samuel Earle.

Gloucester: Lewis Burwell, Beverley, Whiting.

Goochland: William Randolph, Benjamin Cocke.

Hanover: Robert Harris, John Chiswell.

Henrico: Richard Randolph, John Bolling.

Isle of Wight: John Simmons, Joseph Gray.

James City: Col. Lewis Burwell, Carter Burwell.

King George: Charles Carter, Henry Turner.
King and Queen: George Braxton, John Robinson, Speaker.
King William: Thomas West, James Power.
Lancaster: Edwin Conway, Robt Mitchell.
Louisa: Abraham Venable, Charles Barret.
Middlesex: Ralph Wormeley, Gawin Corbin.
Nansemond: Lemuel Riddick, ―― Baker.
New Kent: William Bassett, Wm. Gray.
Norfolk: William Crawford, Samuel Boush.
Northampton: Littleton Eyre, Matthew Harmanson.
Northumberland: Peter Presley, Samuel Blackwell.
Orange: Henry Downs (expelled during the session for misconduct prior to his candidacy), Robert Slaughter (unseated on contest, and new election ordered for both seats.)
Prince George: Richard Bland, Francis Eppes.
Princess Anne: Anthony Walke, Jacob Elligood.
Prince William: William Fairfax, Thomas Harrison.
Richmond: John Woodbridge, William Fauntleroy.
Spotsylvania: William Waller, Francis Thornton.
Stafford: Henry Fitzhugh, Peter Hedgman.
Surry: John Cargill, John Ruffin.
Warwick: William Harwood.
Westmoreland: Daniel McCarty, Andrew Monroe.
York: William Nelson, Edward Digges.
The College: Edward Barradall, Attorney General.
Norfolk Borough: John Hutchings.
Williamsburg: John Harmer.
Jamestown: Philip Ludwell.

Session of September 4, 1744
Accomac: George Douglas, Henry Scarburgh (died

shortly before October 11th); ———, in place of Henry
Scarburgh (deceased).

Amelia: Samuel Cobbs, Edward Booker.

Brunswick: John Wall.

Caroline: Lunsford Lomax, John Baylor.

Charles City: Benj. Harrison, Richard Kennon.

Elizabeth City: William Westwood, Merit Sweny.

Essex: James Garnet, William Beverley.

Fairfax: Lawrence Washington.

Frederick: Samuel Earle. ("Mr. Campbell" was a member at this session, and as a bill relating to Frederick was referred to him, it is probable that he represented that county. Probably he was Andrew Campbell, one of the first justices of Frederick.)

Gloucester: Beverley Whiting, Samuel Buckner (in place of Lewis Burwell, promoted to the Council).

Goochland: Benjamin Cocke, William Randolph.

Hanover: John Chiswell, William Meriwether (in place of Robert Harris, who had accepted the place of surveyor of a county [Louisa]).

Henrico: Richard Randolph, John Bolling.

James City: Carter Burwell, Lewis Burwell (died during session), Benj. Waller (in place of Lewis Burwell, deceased—a new writ was asked for on September 7, 1744).

Isle of Wight: John Simmons, Joseph Gray.

King George: Charles Carter, Henry Turner.

King and Queen: John Robinson, Speaker, George Braxton.

King William: Bernard Moore (in place of Thomas West, deceased), James Power.

Lancaster: Edwin Conway, Robert Mitchell.

Louisa: Charles Barret, Abraham Venable (unseated). Robert Lewis (in place of Abraham Venable).

Middlesex: Gawin Corbin, Ralph Wormeley.
Nansemond: Lemuel Rddick,i —— Baker.
New Kent: —— —— (In place of William Bassett, deceased), Wm. Gray.
Norfolk: Samuel Boush, William Crawford.
Northumberland: Peter Presley, Samuel Blackwell.
Northampton: Littleton Eyre, Matthew Harmanson.
Prince George: Richard Bland, Francis Eppes.
Princess Anne: Anthony Walke, Jacob Elligood.
Prince William: Thomas Harrison, John Colville (in place of William Fairfax, promoted to the Council).
Richmond: John Woodbridge, William Fauntleroy.
Spotsylvania: William Waller, Francis Thornton.
Stafford: Peter Hedgman, James Waugh (in place of Henry Fitzhugh, deceased).
Surry: Rich'd Cocke (in place of John Cargill, deceased), John Ruffin.
Warwick: William Harwood.
Westmoreland: George Lee (in place of Daniel McCarty, deceased); Andrew Monroe.
York: William Nelson, Edward Digges.
College of William and Mary: Beverley Randolph (in place of Edward Barradall, deceased).
Jamestown: Philip Ludwell.
Norfolk Borough: John Hutchings.
Williamsburg: John Harmer.

Session of February 20, 1745

Accomac: George Douglas.
Albemarle: Joshua Fry.
Amelia: Samuel Cobbs, Edward Booker.
Brunswick: John Wall.

Caroline: Lunsford Lomax, John Baylor.
Charles City: Richard Kennon, —— —— (in place of Benjamin Harrison, deceased.)
Elizabeth City: William Westwood, Merit Sweny.
Essex: William Beverley, James Garnett.
Fairfax: Lawrence Washington.
Frederick: Samuel Earle, [Andrew?] Campbell.
Gloucester: Beverley Whiting, Francis Willis (in place of Samuel Buckner, who accepted a place of profit.)
Goochland: Benjamin Cocke, George Carrington (in place of William Randolph, deceased).
Hanover: William Meriwether, John Chiswell.
Henrico: Richard Randolph, John Bolling.
James City: Carter Burwell, Benjamin Waller.
Isle of Wight: John Simmons, Joseph Gray.
King George: Charles Carter, Henry Turner.
King and Queen: George Braxton, John Robinson, Speaker.
King William: Bernard Moore, James Power.
Lancaster: Edwin Conway, Robert Mitchell.
Louisa: Charles Barret, Robert Lewis.
Middlesex: Ralph Wormeley.
Nansemond: Lemuel Riddick, —— Baker.
New Kent: William Gray.
Norfolk: William Crawford, Samuel Boush.
Northumberland: Peter Presley, Samuel Blackwell.
Northampton: Littleton Eyre, Matthew Harmanson.
Prince George: Richard Bland, Francis Eppes.
Princess Anne: Anthony Walke, Jacob Elligood.
Prince William: John Colville, Major [Richard?] Blackburn.
Richmond: John Woodbridge, William Fauntleroy.

Spotsylvania: William Waller, Francis Thornton.
Stafford: Peter Hedgman, John Waugh.
Surry: John Ruffin, Richard Cocke.
Warwick: William Harwood.
Westmoreland: George Lee, Andrew Monroe.
York: Edward Digges, Sec'y Thos Nelson (in place of William Nelson, promoted to the Council).
College of William and Mary: Beverley Randolph.
Jamestown: Philip Ludwell.
Norfolk Borough: John Hutchings.
Williamsburg: John Harmer.

Session of July 11, 1746

Accomac: George Douglas.
Albemarle: Joshua Fry.
Amelia: Samuel Cobbs, Edward Booker.
Brunswick: John Wall.
Caroline: Lunsford Lomax, John Baylor.
Charles City: Richard Kennon.
Elizabeth City: William Westwood, Merit Sweny.
Essex: William Beverley, James Garnet.
Fairfax: Lawrence Washington.
Frederick: Samuel Earle, [Andrew?] Campbell.
Gloucester: Beverley Whiting, Francis Willis.
Goochland: Benjamin Cocke.
Hanover: William Meriwether, John Chiswell.
Henrico: Richard Randolph, John Bolling.
James City: Benjamin Waller, Carter Burwell.
Isle of Wight: Joseph Gray, John Simmons.
King George: Charles Carter, Henry Turner.
King and Queen: George Braxton, John Robinson, Speaker.

King William: Bernard Moore, James Power.
Lancaster: Edwin Conway, Richard Mitchell.
Louisa: Charles Barret, Robert Lewis.
Middlesex: Ralph Wormeley.
Nansemond: Lemuel Riddick, —— Baker.
New Kent: William Gray.
Norfolk: William Crawford, Samuel Boush.
Northumberland: Peter Presley, Samuel Blackwell.
Northampton: Littleton Eyre, Matthew Harmanson.
Prince George: Richard Bland, Francis Eppes.
Princess Anne: Anthony Walke, Jacob Elligood.
Prince William: John Colville, Major [Richard?] Blackburn.
Richmond: John Woodbridge, William Fauntleroy.
Spotsylvania: William Waller, Francis Thornton.
Stafford: Peter Hedgman, John Waugh.
Surry: Richard Cocke, John Ruffin.
Warwick: William Harwood.
Westmoreland: John Bushrod, George Lee.
York: Secretary Thomas Nelson, Edward Digges.
William and Mary College: Beverley Randolph.
Jamestown: Philip Ludwell.
Norfolk Borough: John Hutchings.
Williamsburg: John Harmer.

Session of March 30, 1747

Accomac: George Douglas.
Albemarle: Joshua Fry.
Amelia: Samuel Cobbs, Edward Booker.
Brunswick: John Wall.
Caroline: Lunsford Lomax, John Baylor.
Charles City: Richard Kennon.

Elizabeth City: William Westwood, Merit Sweny.
Essex: William Beverley, James Garnet.
Fairfax: Lawrence Washington.
Frederick: Samuel Earle, [Andrew?] Campbell.
Gloucester: Beverley Whiting, Francis Willis.
Goochland: George Carrington, Benjamin Cocke.
Hanover: William Meriwether, John Chiswell.
Henrico: Richard Randolph, John Bolling.
James City: Benj. Waller, Carter Burwell.
Isle of Wight: Joseph Gray, John Simmons.
King George: Charles Carter, Henry Turner.
King and Queen: George Braxton, John Robinson, Speaker.
King William: Bernard Moore, James Power.
Lancaster: Edwin Conway, Robert Mitchell.
Louisa: Charles Barret.
Middlesex: Ralph Wormeley.
Nansemond: Lemuel Riddick, —— Baker.
New Kent: William Gray.
Norfolk: William Crawford, Samuel Boush.
Northumberland: Peter Presley, Samuel Blackwell.
Northampton: Littleton Eyre, Matthew Harmanson.
Orange: George Taylor.
Prince George: Richard Bland, Francis Eppes.
Princess Anne: Anthony Walke, Jacob Elligood.
Prince William: John Colville, Major [Richard?] Blackburne.
Richmond: John Woodbridge, William Fauntleroy.
Spotsylvania: William Waller, Francis Thornton.
Stafford: Peter Hedgman, John Waugh.
Surry: Richard Cocke, John Ruffin.
Warwick: William Harwood.

Westmoreland: John Bushrod, George Lee.
York: Secretary Thomas Nelson, Edward Digges.
College of William and Mary: Beverley Randolph.
Jamestown: Philip Ludwell.
Norfolk Borough: John Hutchings.
Williamsburg: John Harmer.

Assembly of 1748-1749

This Assembly was summoned to meet on June 30, 1748; but before the date of meeting it was prorogued by proclamation to May 27 of that year, when it first actually met. Jameson's list (compiled in this instance from an imperfect journal of the House of Burgesses) states that there was one session extending from October 27, 1748, to May 11, 1749; but the journal of the Council sitting as Upper House, shows that the Assembly was prorogued on November 11, 1748, and met again on April 10, 1749, making two sessions. It is probable that though this Assembly did not meet again, it was kept in existence for a year or more after by successive prorogations.

—— Kemp, who was a member at the session beginning October 27, 1748, cannot be identified.

Session of Oct. 27, 1748.

Accomac: Thomas Parramore, Edward Allen.
Albemarle: Joshua Fry, Charles Lynch.
Amelia: Thomas Tabb, Wood Jones.
Augusta: John Wilson, John Madison.
Brunswick: Sterling Clack, Drury Stith.
Caroline: John Baylor, Lunsford Lomax.
Charles City: Richard Kennon, Edward Brodnax (**died before the Assembly met**).

Elizabeth City: William Westwood, John Tabb.
Essex: Wm. Beverley, Wm. Dangerfield.
Fairfax: Lawrence Washington, Richard Osborne.
Frederick: Geo. Fairfax, Gabriel Jones.
Gloucester: Beverley Whiting, Francis Willis.
Goochland: Geo. Carrington, Archibald Cary.
Hanover: William Meriwether, John Chiswell.
Henrico: John Bolling, Rd. Randolph.
James City: Carter Burwell, Benj. Waller.
Isle of Wight: John Simmons, Joseph Gray.
King George: Chas. Carter, Henry Turner.
King and Queen: John Robinson, George Braxton.
King William: Bernard Moore, Francis West.
Lancaster: Joseph Chinn, Peter Conway.
Louisa: Abraham Venable, Charles Barrett.
Lunenburg: Clement Reade, Henry Embry.
Middlesex: Ralph Wormeley, Philip Grymes.
Nansemond: Lemuel Riddick, Wm. Hunter.
New Kent: William Hockaday, Wm. Massie.
Norfolk: Willis Wilson, Wm. Portlock.
Northampton: Littleton Eyre, Matthew Harmanson.
Northumberland: Presley Thornton, Spencer Ball.
Orange: George Taylor, John Spotswood.
Princess Anne: Anthony Walke, Jacob Elligood.
Prince George: Rd. Bland, Francis Eppes.
Prince William: Thomas Harrison, Joseph Blackwell.
Richmond: Wm. Fauntleroy, John Woodbridge.
Spotsylvania: Wm. Waller, Rice Curtis.
Stafford: Wm. Fitzhugh, Peter Hedgman.
Surry: Robt. Jones, Augustine Claiborne.
Warwick: Wm. Harwood, John Langhorne.
Westmoreland: John Bushrod, Geo. Lee.

York: Thos. Nelson (Secretary), Edward Digges.
Jamestown: Phil. Ludwell.
Williamsburg: The Attorney General.
Norfolk Town: Robt. Todd.
The College: Beverley Randolph.
Sources: Burk's History of Virginia III, 133. Journal of the House of Burgesses, Congressional Library. Journal of the Council, sitting as Upper House, Va. State Library.

Session of April 10, 1749

Accomack: Thomas Parramore, Edward Allen.
Albemarle: Joshua Fry, Charles Lynch.
Amelia: Thomas Tabb, Samuel Cobbs.
Augusta: John Wilson, John Madison.
Brunswick: Sterling Clack, Drury Stith.
Caroline: John Baylor, Lunsford Lomax.
Charles City: Richard Kennon, Benjamin Harrison (in place of Edwd Brodnax, deceased.)
Elizabeth City: William Westwood, John Tabb.
Essex: William Beverley, William Dangerfield.
Fairfax: Lawrence Washington, Richard Osborne.
Frederick: George Fairfax, Gabriel Jones.
Gloucester: Beverley Whiting, Francis Willis.
Goochland: George Carrington, Archibald Cary.
Hanover: William Meriwether, John Chiswell.
Henrico: John Bolling, Peter Randolph.
James City: Carter Burwell, Benjamin Waller.
Isle of Wight: John Simmons, Joseph Gray.
King George: Charles Carter, Harry Turner.
King and Queen: John Robinson, Sp.; George Braxton.
King William: Bernard Moore, Francis West.
Lancaster: Joseph Chinn, Peter Conway.

Louisa: Abraham Venable, Charles Barret.
Lunenburg: Clement Reade, Henry Embry.
Middlesex: Ralph Wormeley, Richard Corbin.
Nansemond: Lemuel Riddick, William Hunter.
New Kent: William Hockaday, William Massie.
Norfolk: Willis Wilson, William Portlock.
Northampton: Littleton Eyre, Matthew Harmanson.
Northumberland: Presley Thornton, Spencer Ball.
Orange: George Taylor, John Spotswood.
Princess Anne: Anthony Walke, Jacob Elligood.
Prince George: Richard Bland, Francis Eppes.
Prince William: Thomas Harrison, Joseph Blackwell.
Richmond: William Fauntleroy, John Woodbridge.
Spotsylvania: William Waller, Rice Curtis.
Stafford: William Fitzhugh, Peter Hedgman.
Surry: Robert Jones, Augustine Claiborne.
Warwick: William Harwood, John Langhorne.
Westmoreland: John Bushrode, George Lee.
York: Edward Digges, John Norton. (Thomas Nelson was Burgess for York during part of the session.)
Jamestown: Philip Ludwell.
Williamsburg: Attorney General.
Norfolk Borough: Robert Todd.
The College: Beverley Randolph.

Chesterfield, Culpeper, Cumberland, and Southampton, are Counties erected by an Act of the last Assembly, and have not yet elected their representatives.

Sources: Virginia Almanacs of 1750 and 1751. Journal of the Council sitting as Upper House.

Assembly of 1752-1755

This Assembly first convened February 5, 1752, and met, by various prorogations, on November 1, 1753; February 14, 1754; August 22, 1754; October 17, 1754; May 1, 1755; August 5, 1755; October 27, 1755, and was dissolved November 8, 1755.

The lists of members here given are derived from the journals of the respective sessions, now in the Virginia State Library and Congressional Library; a list published in the Virginia Gazette, of November 27, 1752, and copied in the Va. Magazine of History and Biography, III, 191; Virginia Almanacs of 1754, 1755, and 1756 in the Congressional Library, and a Virginia Almanac of 1756 in the collection of the Virginia Historical Society.

Session of February 5, 1752

Accomack: Edmund Allen, George Douglas.
Albemarle: Joshua Fry, Allen Howard.
Amelia: Thomas Tabb, Wood Jones.
Augusta: John Madison, John Wilson.
Brunswick: Drury Stith, John Willis.
Caroline: Edmund Pendleton, Lunsford Lomax.
Charles City: Benjamin Harrison, Richard Kennon.
Chesterfield, Richard Eppes, John Bolling.
Culpeper: John Spotswood, William Green.
Cumberland: George Carrington, Samuel Scott.
Elizabeth City: William Westwood, John Tabb.
Essex: Francis Smith, Thomas Waring.
Fairfax: Hugh West, Gerrard Alexander.
Frederick: George William Fairfax, Gabriel Jones.
Gloucester: Beverley Whiting, John Page.
Goochland: John Payne, John Smith.

Hanover: John Chiswell, John Syme.*
Henrico: William Randolph, Bowler Cocke.
James City: Carter Burwell, Benjamin Waller.
Isle of Wight: Robert Burwell, Thomas Gale.
King George: Charles Carter, Thomas Turner.
King and Queen: John Robinson, Speaker, Philip Johnson.
King William: John Martin, Bernard Moore.
Lancaster: Edwin Conway, Joseph Chinn.
Louisa: Abraham Venable, Thomas Walker.
Lunenburg: William Byrd, Clement Reade.
Middlesex: Ralph Wormeley, Christopher Robinson.
Nansemond: Lemuel Riddick, Anthony Holladay.
New Kent: Richard Adams, James Power.
Norfolk: Robert Tucker, Samuel Boush, Jun.
Northampton: Littleton Eyre, John Kendall.
Northumberland: Presley Thornton, Spencer Ball.
Orange: George Taylor, Benjamin Cave.
Prince George: Richard Bland, Stephen Dewey.
Princess Anne: Edward Hacke Moseley, Anthony Walke, Jun.
Prince William: Thomas Harrison, Joseph Blackwell.
Richmond: John Woodbridge, Landon Carter.
Southampton: Etheldred Taylor, Thomas Jarrell.
Spotsylvania: William Waller, Rice Curtis.
Stafford: William Fitzhugh, Peter Hedgman.
Surry: Robert Jones, Augustine Claiborne.
Warwick: William Harwood, William Digges.
Westmoreland: John Bushrod, Robert Vaulx.
York: John Norton, Dudley Digges.

* On contest, Chiswell and Syme were unseated, and a new election ordered, when John Chiswell and Henry Robinson were chosen.

Jamestown: Edward Champion Travis.
Norfolk Borough: John Hutchings.
Williamsburg: Armistead Burwell.
William and Mary College: Attorney General.
Sources: Virginia Gazette, February 27, 1752. Journal of the House, Virginia State Library.

Session of November 1, 1753

Accomack: Ralph Justice (in place of Edmund Allen, who had accepted the place of sheriff).
Albemarle: Joshua Fry, Allen Howard.
Amelia: Thomas Tabb, Wood Jones.
Augusta: John Madison, John Wilson.
Brunswick: Drury Stith, John Willis.
Charles City: Benjamin Harrison, Richard Kennon.
Culpeper: John Spotswood, William Green.
Caroline: Edmund Pendleton, Lunsford Lomax.
Chesterfield: Richard Eppes, John Bolling.
Cumberland: George Carrington, Samuel Scott.
Dinwiddie: John Jones, Isham Eppes.
Elizabeth Ctiy: William Westwood, John Tabb.
Essex: Francis Smith, Thomas Waring.
Fairfax: Hugh West, Gerard Alexander.
Frederick: George W. Fairfax, Gabriel Jones.
Gloucester: Beverley Whiting, John Page.
Goochland: John Payne, John Smith.
Halifax: John Bates, William Harris. George Currie was returned for this county, but was unseated and a new election ordered.
Hanover: John Chiswell, Henry Robinson.
Henrico: William Randolph, Bowler Cocke.
James City: Carter Burwell, Benjamin Waller.

Isle of Wight: Robert Burwell, Thomas Gale.
King and Queen: John Robinson, Speaker, Philip Johnson.
King William: John Martin, Bernard Moore.
King George: Charles Carter, Thomas Turner.
Lancaster: Edwin Conway, Joseph Chinn.
Louisa: Abraham Venable, Thomas Walker.
Lunenburg: William Byrd, Clement Reade.
Middlesex: Ralph Wormeley, Christopher Robinson.
Nansemond: Lemuel Riddick, Anthony Holladay.
New Kent: Richard Adams, James Power.
Norfolk: Robert Tucker, Samuel Boush, Jr.
Northampton: Littleton Eyre, John Kendall.
Northumberland: Presley Thornton, Spencer Ball.
Orange: George Taylor, Benjamin Cave.
Princess Anne: Anthony Walke, Jr., E. H. Moseley.
Prince George: Richard Bland, Stephen Dewey.
Prince William: Thomas Harrison, Joseph Blackwell.
Richmond: John Woodbridge, Landon Carter.
Spotsylvania: John Thornton (in place of William Waller, who had accepted the place of coroner), Rice Curtis.
Stafford: William Fitzhugh, Peter Hedgman.
Surry: Robert Jones, Augustine Claiborne.
Southampton: Robert Jones (in place of Thomas Jarrell, deceased), Etheldred Taylor.
Warwick: William Harwood, William Digges.
Westmoreland: John Bushrod, Robert Vaulx.
York: John Norton, Dudley Digges.
Jamestown: Edward Travis.
Williamsburg: Armistead Burwell.
Norfolk Borough: John Hutchings.
The College: The Attorney General.

Session of February 14, 1754

Accomack: George Douglas, Ralph Justice.
Albemarle: Allen Howard, Joshua Fry.
Amelia: Thomas Tabb, Wood Jones.
Augusta: John Wilson, John Madison.
Brunswick: Drury Stith, John Willis.
Cumberland: George Carrington, Samuel Scott.
Charles City: Benjamin Harrison, Richard Kennon.
Culpeper: John Spotswood, William Green.
Caroline: Edmund Pendleton, Lunsford Lomax.
Chesterfield: Richard Eppes, John Bolling.
Dinwiddie: John Jones, Isham Eppes.
Elizabeth City: William Westwood, John Tabb.
Essex: Francis Smith, William Dangerfield (in place of Thomas Waring, deceased).
Fairfax: Gerard Alexander, Hugh West.
Frederick: George William Fairfax, Gabriel Jones.
Gloucester: Beverley Whiting, John Page.
Goochland: John Payne, John Smith.
Halifax: John Bates, William [Samuel?] Harris.
Hanover: John Chiswell, Henry Robinson.
Henrico: William Randolph, Bowler Cocke.
James City: Carter Burwell, Benjamin Waller.
Isle of Wight: Robert Burwell, Thomas Gale.
King and Queen: John Robinson, Speaker, Philip Johnson.
King William: John Martin, Bernard Moore.
King George: Charles Carter, Thomas Turner.
Lancaster: Edwin Conway, James Ball (in place of Joseph Chinn, who had accepted the place of coroner).
Louisa: Abraham Venable, Robert Anderson (in place

of Thomas Walker, who had accepted the position of assistant surveyor).

Lunenburg: William Byrd.
Middlesex: Ralph Wormeley, Christopher Robinson.
Nansemond: Lemuel Riddick, Anthony Holladay.
New Kent: Richard Adams, James Power.
Norfolk: Robert Tucker, John Willoughby (in place of Samuel Boush, who had accepted a clerkship).
Northampton: Littleton Eyre, John Kendall.
Northumberland: Presley Thornton, Spencer Ball.
Orange: George Taylor, Benjamin Cave.
Princess Anne: Anthony Walke, Jr., Edward Hacke Moseley.
Prince Edward: John Nash, Charles Anderson.
Prince George: Richard Bland, Stephen Dewey.
Prince William: Thomas Harrison, Joseph Blackwell.
Richmond: John Woodbridge, Landon Carter.
Spotsylvania: Rice Curtis, John Thornton.
Stafford: William Fitzhugh, Peter Hedgman.
Surry: Robert Jones, John Ruffin (in place of Augustine Claiborne, who had accepted a Clerkship).
Sussex: Gray Briggs, John Edmunds.
Southampton: Etheldred Taylor, Joseph Gray.
Warwick: William Harwood, William Digges.
Westmoreland: John Bushrod, Robert Vaulx.
York: John Norton, Dudley Digges.
Jamestown: Edward Champion Travis.
Williamsburg: Armistead Burwell.
Norfolk Borough: John Hutchings.
The College: Peyton Randolph.

Session of August 22, 1754

Accomac: George Douglas, Ralph Justice.
Albemarle: Allen Howard, Peter Jefferson (in place of Joshua Fry, deceased).
Amelia: Thomas Tabb, Wood Jones.
Augusta: John Madison, James Patton (in place of John Wilson, who had accepted a surveyor's place).
Brunswick: Drury Stith, John Willis.
Bedford: William Callaway, John Phelps.
Cumberland: George Carrington, Samuel Scott.
Charles City: Benjamin Harrison, Richard Kennon.
Culpeper: John Spotswood, William Green.
Chesterfield: Richard Eppes, John Bolling.
Dinwiddie: John Jones, Isham Eppes.
Elizabeth City: William Westwood, John Tabb.
Essex: Francis Smith, William Dangerfield.
Fairfax: Gerard Alexander, —— —— (in place of Hugh West, deceased).
Frederick: George William Fairfax, —— Perkins.
Gloucester: Beverley Whiting, John Page.
Goochland: John Payne, John Smith.
Halifax: John Bates, William [Samuel?] Harris.
Hampshire: Gabriel Jones, —— Parker.
Hanover: John Chiswell, Henry Robinson.
Henrico: William Randolph, Bowler Cocke.
James City: Carter Burwell, Benjamin Waller.
Isle of Wight: Robert Burwell, Thomas Gale.
King and Queen: John Robinson, Philip Johnson.
King William: John Martin, Bernard Moore.
Lancaster: Edwin Conway, James Ball.
Louisa: Abraham Venable, Robert Anderson.

Lunenburg: William Byrd, William Embry (in place of Clement Reade who had accepted a surveyor's place).

Middlesex: Ralph Wormeley, Christopher Robinson.

Nansemond: Lemuel Riddick, Anthony Holladay.

New Kent: Richard Adams, James Power.

Norfolk: Robert Tucker, John Willoughby.

Northampton: Littleton Eyre, John Kendall.

Northumberland: Presley Thornton, Spencer Ball.

Orange: George Taylor, Benjamin Cave.

Princess Anne: Anthony Walke, Jr., Edward Hack Moseley.

Prince Edward: John Nash, Charles Anderson.

Prince George: Richard Bland, Stephen Dewey.

Prince William: Thos. Harrison, Joseph Blackwell.

Richmond: John Woodbridge, Landon Carter.

Spotsylvania: Rice Curtis, John Thornton.

Surry: Robert Jones, John Ruffin.

Sussex: Gray Briggs, John Ruffin (in place of John Edmunds who had accepted a surveyor's place).

Stafford: William Fitzhugh, Peter Hedgman.

Southampton: Etheldred Taylor, Joseph Gray.

Warwick: William Harwood, William Digges.

Westmoreland: John Bushrod, Augustine Washington (in place of Robert Vaulx, deceased).

York: John Norton, Dudley Digges.

Jamestown: Edward Champion Travis.

Williamsburg: George Wythe (in place of Armistead Burwell, deceased).

Norfolk Borough: John Hutchings.

The College: Attorney General Peyton Randolph.

Session of October 17, 1754

Accomack: George Douglas, Ralph Justice.
Albemarle: Allen Howard, Peter Jefferson.
Augusta: John Wilson, James Patton.
Amelia: Thomas Tabb, Wood Jones.
Bedford: William Callaway, John Phelps.
Brunswick: Drury Stith, John Willis.
Cumberland: George Carrington, Samuel Scott.
Charles City: Benjamin Harrison, Richard Kennon.
Culpeper: John Spotswood, William Green.
Caroline: Edmund Pendleton, Lunsford Lomax.
Chesterfield: Richard Eppes, John Bolling.
Dinwiddie: John Jones, Isham Eppes.
Elizabeth City: William Westwood, John Tabb.
Essex: Francis Smith, William Dangerfield.
Fairfax: Gerard Alexander, Hugh West.
Frederick: George William Fairfax, Gabriel Jones.
Gloucester: Beverley Whiting, John Page.
Goochland: John Payne, John Smith.
Halifax: John Bates, William Harris.
Hanover: John Chiswell, Henry Robinson.
Henrico: William Randolph, Bowler Cocke.
James City: Carter Burwell, Benjamin Waller.
Isle of Wight: Robert Burwell, Thomas Gale.
King and Queen: John Robinson, Speaker, Philip Johnson.
King William: John Martin, Bernard Moore.
King George: Charles Carter, Thomas Turner.
Lancaster: Edwin Conway, James Ball.
Louisa: Abraham Venable, Robert Anderson.
Lunenburg: William Embry, Matthew Marrable (in place of William Byrd, appointed to the Council).

Middlesex: Ralph Wormeley, Christopher Robinson.
Nansemond: Lemuel Riddick, Anthony Holladay.
New Kent: Richard Adams, James Power.
Norfolk: Robert Tucker, John Willoughby.
Northampton: Littleton Eyre, John Kendall.
Northumberland: Presley Thornton, Spencer Ball.
Orange: George Taylor, Benjamin Cave.
Princess Anne: Anthony Walke, Jr., Edw'd Hack Moseley.
Prince Edward: John Nash, Charles Anderson.
Prince George: Richard Bland, Stephen Dewey.
Prince William: Thomas Harrison, Joseph Blackwell.
Richmond: John Woodbridge, Landon Carter.
Spotsylvania: Rice Curtis, John Thornton.
Stafford: William Fitzhugh, Peter Hedgman.
Surry: Robert Jones, John Ruffin.
Sussex: Gray Briggs, John Edmunds.
Southampton: Etheldred Taylor, Joseph Gray.
Warwick: William Harwood, William Digges.
Westmoreland: John Bushrod, Augustine Washington.
York: John Norton, Dudley Digges.
Jamestown: Edward Champion Travis.
Williamsburg: George Wythe.
Norfolk Borough: John Hutchings.
College of William and Mary: Peyton Randolph.

Session of May 1, 1755

Accomack: George Douglas, Ralph Justice.
Albemarle: Allen Howard, Peter Jefferson.
Amelia: Thomas Tabb, Wood Jones.
Augusta: John Wilson, James Patton.
Bedford: William Callaway, John Phelps.

Brunswick: Drury Stith, John Willis, Edward Goodrich. (On July 1st the House requested the Governor to issue a writ for a new election in Brunswick to fill the place of John Willis, who had accepted the office of coroner).

Cumberland: George Carrington, John Fleming (in place of Samuel Scott, deceased).

Charles City: Benjamin Harrison, Richard Kennon.

Culpeper: John Spotswood, William Green.

Caroline: Edmund Pendleton, Lunsford Lomax.

Chesterfield: Richard Eppes, John Bolling.

Dinwiddie: John Jones, Isham Eppes.

Elizabeth City: William Westwood, John Tabb.

Essex: Francis Smith, William Dangerfield.

Fairfax: Gerard Alexander, Hugh West.

Frederick: George William Fairfax, —— Perkins.

Gloucester: John Page, Thomas Whiting (in place of Beverley Whiting, deceased).

Goochland: John Payne, John Smith.

Halifax: John Bates, William Harris.

Hanover: John Chiswell, Henry Robinson.

Henrico: William Randolph, Bowler Cocke.

James City: Carter Burwell, Benjamin Waller.

Isle of Wight: Robert Burwell, Thomas Gale.

King and Queen: John Robinson, Speaker, Philip Johnson.

King William: John Martin, Bernard Moore.

King George: Charles Carter, Thomas Turner.

Lancaster: Edwin Conway, James Ball.

Louisa: Abraham Venable, Robert Anderson.

Lunenburg: William Embry, Matthew Marrable.

Middlesex: Ralph Wormeley, Christopher Robinson.

Nansemond: Lemuel Riddick, Anthony Holladay.

New Kent: Richard Adams, James Power.
Norfolk: Robert Tucker, John Willoughby.
Northampton: Littleton Eyre, John Kendall.
Northumberland: Presley Thornton, Spencer Ball.
Orange: George Taylor, Benjamin Cave.
Princess Anne: Anthony Walke, Jr., Edw'd Hack Moseley.
Prince Edward: John Nash, Charles Anderson.
Prince George: Richard Bland, Stephen Dewey.
Prince William: Thomas Harrison, Joseph Blackwell.
Richmond: John Woodbridge, Landon Carter.
Spotsylvania: Rice Curtis, John Thornton.
Stafford: William Fitzhugh, Peter Hedgman.
Surry: Robert Jones, John Ruffin.
Sussex: Gray Briggs, John Edmunds.
Southampton: Etheldred Taylor, Joseph Gray.
Warwick: William Harwood, William Digges.
Westmoreland: John Bushrod, Augustine Washington.
York: John Norton, Dudley Digges.
Jamestown: Edward Champion Travis.
College of William and Mary: The Attorney (Peyton Randolph).
Williamsburg: George Wythe.
Norfolk Borough: John Hutchings.

Session of August 5th 1755

Membership as in preceding session, except that a writ was requested for an election in Augusta to fill the vacancy caused by the death of James Patton, who was killed by the Indians on his return home from the last session of Assembly.

Session of October 27, 1755

Accomac: George Douglas, Ralph Justice.
Albemarle: Allen Howard, Peter Jefferson.
Amelia: Thomas Tabb, Wood Jones.
Augusta: John Wilson.
Brunswick: Drury Stith, Edward Goodrich.
Bedford: William Callaway, John Phelps.
Caroline: Edmund Pendleton, Lunsford Lomax.
Charles City: Benjamin Harrison, Richard Kennon.
Chesterfield: Richard Eppes, John Bolling.
Culpeper: John Spotswood, William Green.
Cumberland: George Carrington, John Fleming.
Dinwiddie: John Jones, Isham Eppes.
Elizabeth City: William Westwood, John Tabb.
Essex: Francis Smith, William Dangerfield.
Fairfax: Gerard Alexander, John West.
Frederick: Geo. Wm. Fairfax, —— Perkins.
Gloucester: John Page, Thomas Whiting.
Goochland: John Payne, John Smith.
Hanover: John Chiswell, Henry Robinson.
Hampshire: Gabriel Jones, —— Parker.
Halifax: Samuel Harris, John Bates.
Henrico: William Randolph, Bowler Cocke.
James City: Carter Burwell, Benjamin Waller.
Isle of Wight: Robert Burwell, Thomas Gale.
King George: Charles Carter, Thomas Turner.
King and Queen: John Robinson, Speaker, Philip Johnson.
King William: John Martin, Bernard Moore.
Lancaster: Edwin Conway, —— —— (in place of James Ball, who had accepted the office of sheriff).
Louisa: Abraham Venable, Robert Anderson.

Lunenburg: William Embry, Matthew Marrable.
Middlesex: Ralph Wormeley, Christopher Robinson.
Nansemond: Lemuel Riddick, Anthony Holladay.
New Kent: Richard Adams, James Power.
Norfolk: —— —— (in place of Rob't Tucker, who had accepted the office of sheriff), John Willoughby.
Northampton: Littleton Eyre, John Kendall.
Northumberland: Presley Thornton, Spencer Ball.
Orange: George Taylor, Benjamin Cave.
Prince Edward: John Nash, Charles Anderson.
Prince George: Richard Bland, Stephen Dewey.
Princess Anne: Anthony Walke, Jr., —— —— (in place of E. H. Moseley, who had accepted the office of Surveyor and Searcher of Elizabeth and Nansemond Rivers).
Prince William: Thomas Harrison, Joseph Blackwell.
Richmond: John Woodbridge, Landon Carter.
Southampton: Joseph Gray, —— —— (in place of Etheldred Taylor, deceased.)
Spotsylvania: Rice Curtis, John Thornton.
Stafford: William Fitzhugh, Peter Hedgman.
Surry: Robert Jones, John Ruffin.
Sussex: Gray Briggs, John Edmunds.
Warwick: William Harwood, William Digges.
Westmoreland: John Bushrod, Augustine Washington.
York: John Norton, Dudley Digges.
Jamestown: Edward Champion Travis.
Norfolk Borough: John Hutchings.
Williamsburg: George Wythe.
The College: The Attorney (Peyton Randolph).

[This Assembly was dissolved on November 8, 1755, and it is not probable that any Burgesses were elected to fill the vacancies in this session.]

Assembly of 1756-1758

This Assembly began March 25, 1756, and met by various prorogations, on September 20, 1756; April 30, 1757, and March 30, 1758. At the close of the last session the Assembly was prorogued to June succeeding; but it was evidently dissolved by proclamation during the recess, for the next meeting of Assembly, September 14, 1758, is described as a first session. The lists here given are derived from the journals of the respective sessions in the Va. State Library, and Virginia Almanacs of 1757 and 1758, in the collection of the Virginia Historical Society.

Session of March 25, 1756

Accomac: Edmund Allen, Ralph Justice.
Albemarle: John Nicholas, William Cabell.
Amelia: Thomas Tabb, Richard Booker.
Augusta: John Wilson, Gabriel Jones.
Bedford: William Callaway, —— Stith.
Brunswick: Edward Goodrich, William Thornton.
Caroline: Edmund Pendleton, John Baylor.
Charles City: Benjamin Harrison, William Lightfoot.
Chesterfield: Archibald Cary, John Bolling.
Culpeper: Thomas Slaughter, Henry Field.
Cumberland: George Carrington, John Fleming.
Dinwiddie: John Jones, Robert Bolling.
Elizabeth City: William Westwood, John Tabb.
Essex: William Dangerfield, Francis Smith.
Fairfax: John West, George Wm. Fairfax.
Frederick: Hugh West, Thomas Swearingen.
Gloucester: John Page, Thomas Whiting.
Goochland: John Payne, John Smith.
Hanover: John Syme, Henry Robinson.

Hampshire: Thomas Bryan Martin, Thomas Walker.
Halifax: Samuel Harris, John Bates.
Henrico: William Randolph, Bowler Cocke.
James City: Benjamin Waller, Joseph Morton.
Isle of Wight: Joseph Bridger, Robert Burwell.
King George: Charles Carter, Charles Carter, Jr.
King and Queen: John Robinson, Speaker, Philip Johnson.
King William: John Martin (died during session), Bernard Moore, Francis West (elected in place of Martin, deceased).
Lancaster: William Ball, Richard Selden.
Louisa: Robert Anderson, Charles Barret.
Lunenburg: Thomas Nash, William Embry.
Middlesex: Christopher Robinson, Ralph Wormeley.
Nansemond: Lemuel Riddick, Willis Riddick.
New Kent: James Power, Richard Adams.
Norfolk: George Veale, Joshua Corprew.
Northampton: Littleton Eyre, John Kendall.
Northumberland: Spencer Ball, Presley Thornton.
Orange: George Taylor, Benjamin Cave.
Prince Edward: John Nash, Charles Anderson.
Prince George: Richard Bland, Alexander Bolling.
Princess Anne: Thomas Walke, William Keeling.
Prince William: Henry Lee (unseated on contest, and new election ordered), John Bell.
Richmond: Landon Carter, John Woodbridge.
Southampton: Joseph Gray, William Taylor.
Spotsylvania: William Waller, John Spotswood.
Stafford: Peter Hedgman, William Fitzhugh.
Surry: Benjamin Harrison, Jr., William Clinch.
Sussex: John Edmunds, Gray Briggs.

Warwick: William Digges, William Harwood.
Westmoreland: Augustine Washington, Philip Ludwell Lee.
York: Dudley Digges, Robert Carter Nicholas.
Jamestown: Edward Champion Travis.
Norfolk Borough: John Hutchings.
Williamsburg: John Chiswell.
The College: Mr. Attorney.

Session of September 20th, 1756

There is no journal of the session preserved, though the acts passed are printed in Hening. The membership was the same as that of the preceding session.

Session of April 30, 1757

Accomac: Edmund Allen, Ralph Justice.
Albemarle: John Nicholas, William Cabell.
Amelia: Thomas Tabb, Richard Booker.
Augusta: John Wilson, Gabriel Jones.
Bedford: William Callaway, —— Stith.
Brunswick: Edward Goodrich, William Thornton.
Caroline: Edmund Pendleton, John Baylor.
Charles City: Benjamin Harrison, William Lightfoot.
Chesterfield: Archibald Cary, John Bolling.
Culpeper: Thomas Slaughter, Henry Field.
Cumberland: George Carrington, John Fleming, Jun.
Dinwiddie: John Jones, Robert Bolling.
Elizabeth City: William Westwood, John Tabb.
Essex: William Dangerfield, Francis Smith.
Fairfax: John West, George Wm. Fairfax.
Frederick: Hugh West, Thomas Swearingen.

Gloucester: John Page, Thomas Whiting.
Goochland: John Payne, John Smith.
Hanover: John Syme, N. West Dandridge.
Hampshire: Thomas Bryan Martin, Thomas Walker.
Halifax Samuel Harris, John Bates.
Henrico: William Randolph, Bowler Cocke.
James City: Benjamin Waller, Joseph Morton.
Isle of Wight: Robert Burwell, Joseph Bridger.
King George: Charles Carter, Charles Carter, Jun.
King and Queen: John Robinson, Speaker, Philip Johnson.
King William: Bernard Moore, Francis West.
Lancaster: William Ball, Richard Selden.
Louisa: Robert Anderson, Charles Barret.
Lunenburg: William Embry, Thomas Nash.
Middlesex: Ralph Wormeley, Christopher Robinson.
Nansemond: Lemuel Riddick, Willis Riddick.
New Kent: James Power, Richard Adams.
Norfolk: George Veale, Joshua Corprew.
Northampton: Littleton Eyre, John Kendall.
Northumberland: Presley Thornton, Spencer Ball.
Orange: George Taylor, Benjamin Cave.
Prince Edward: John Nash, Charles Anderson.
Prince George: Richard Bland, Alexander Bolling.
Princess Anne: Thomas Walke, William Keeling.
Prince William: John Bell, Henry Peyton:
Richmond: Landon Carter, John Woodbridge.
Southampton: Joseph Gray, William Taylor.
Spotsylvania: Zachary Lewis, John Spotswood.
Stafford: Peter Hedgeman, William Fitzhugh.
Surry: Benjamin Cocke (in place of William Clinch, expelled April 26th), Benjamin Harrison, Jun.

Sussex: Gray Briggs, John Edmunds.
Warwick: William Harwood, William Digges.
Westmoreland: Augustine Washington, Richard Lee (in place of P. L. Lee, appointed to the Council.)
York: Dudley Digges, Robert C. Nicholas.
Williamsburg: John Chiswell.
College of William and Mary: Mr. Attorney General.
Norfolk Borough: John Hutchings, Jun.
Jamestown: Edward Champion Travis.

Session of March 30, 1758

Accomac: Edmund Allen, Ralph Justice.
Albemarle: John Nicholas, William Cabell.
Amelia: Thomas Tabb, Richard Booker.
Augusta: John Wilson, Gabriel Jones.
Brunswick: Edward Goodrich, William Thornton.
Bedford: William Callaway, —— Stith.
Caroline: Edmund Pendleton, John Baylor.
Charles City: Benjamin Harrison, William Lightfoot.
Chesterfield: Archibald Cary, —— —— (in place of John Bolling, deceased).
Culpeper: Thomas Slaughter, Henry Field.
Cumberland: George Carrington, John Fleming, Jun.
Dinwiddie: —— —— (in place of John Jones, who had accepted the place of tobacco inspector), Robert Bolling.
Elizabeth City: William Westwood, John Tabb.
Essex: William Dangerfield, Francis Smith.
Fairfax: John West, Geo. William Fairfax.
Frederick: Hugh West, Thomas Swearingen.
Gloucester: John Page, Thomas Whiting.
Goochland: John Payne, John Smith.
Hanover: John Syme, Nathaniel West Dandridge.

Hampshire: Thomas Bryan Martin, Thomas Walker.
Halifax: Samuel Harris, John Bates.
Henrico: William Randolph, Bowler Cocke.
James City: Benjamin Waller, Joseph Morton.
Isle of Wight: Robert Burwell, Joseph Bridger.
King George: Charles Carter, Charles Carter, Jun.
King and Queen: John Robinson, Speaker, Philip Johnson.
King William: Bernard Moore, Francis West.
Lancaster: William Ball, Richard Selden.
Louisa: Robert Anderson, Charles Barret.
Lunenburg: William Embry, Thomas Nash.
Middlesex: Ralph Wormeley, Christopher Robinson.
Nansemond: Lemuel Riddick, Willis Riddick.
New Kent: James Power, Richard Adams.
Norfolk: George Veale, Joshua Corprew.
Northumberland: Presley Thornton, Spencer Ball.
Northampton: Littleton Eyre, John Kendall.
Orange: George Taylor, Benjamin Cave.
Prince Edward: John Nash, Charles Anderson.
Prince George: Richard Bland, Alexander Bolling.
Princess Anne: Thomas Walke, William Keeling.
Prince William: John Bell, Henry Peyton.
Richmond: Landon Carter, John Woodbridge.
Southampton: Joseph Gray, William Taylor.
Spotsylvania: William Waller, John Spotswood.
Stafford: Peter Hedgeman, William Fitzhugh.
Surry: Benjamin Cocke, Benjamin Harrison, Jun.
Sussex: Gray Briggs, John Edmunds.
Warwick: William Harwood, William Digges.
Westmoreland: Augustine Washington, Richard Lee.
York: Dudley Digges, Robert C. Nicholas.

College of William and Mary: Mr. Attorney General.
Jamestown: Edward Champion Travis.
Norfolk Borough: John Hutchings, Jun.
Williamsburg: John Chiswell.

Assembly of 1758-1761

This Assembly first met on September 14, 1758, and, by prorogations, on November 7, 1758; February 22 and November 1, 1759, and on March 4, May 19, and October 6, 1760. The last named session continued until October 20th and the Assembly was then prorogued. It met again for one day on the 11th, and was then prorogued to March 5, 1761. It met on the day appointed and remained in session until April 10th, when it was dissolved.

Sessions of September 14, and November 9, 1758

Accomac: Edmund Allen, Thomas Parramore.
Albemarle: Allen Howard, William Cabell, Jun.
Amelia: Edmund Booker, Richard Booker.
Augusta: John Wilson, Israel Christian.
Brunswick: William Thornton, Edward Goodrich.
Bedford: Samuel Hairstone, Zachariah Burnley.
Caroline: Edmund Pendleton, John Baylor.
Charles City: Benjamin Harrison, William Kennon, Jun.
Chesterfield: Archibald Cary, Richard Eppes.
Culpeper: Thomas Slaughter, William Green.
Cumberland: George Carrington, John Fleming.
Dinwiddie: Leonard Claiborne, Jun., Robert Ruffin.
Elizabeth City: William Wager, John Tabb.
Essex: John Upshaw, Francis Waring.
Fairfax: George Johnston, George Mason.

Frederick: George Washington, Thomas Bryan Martin.
Gloucester: John Page, Thomas Whiting.
Goochland: Reuben Skelton, John Payne.
Halifax: Robert Wade, Nathaniel Terry.
Hampshire: Gabriel Jones, Thomas Walker.
Hanover: N. West Dandridge, John Syme.
Henrico: William Randolph, Bowler Cocke.
James City: Benjamin Waller, Lewis Burwell.
Isle of Wight: James Bridger, Joseph Bridger.
King George: Charles Carter, Charles Carter, Jr.
King and Queen: John Robinson, Speaker, George Braxton.
King William: Peter Robinson, Harry Gaines.
Lancaster: Charles Carter, William Ball.
Loudoun: Francis Lightfoot Lee, James Hamilton.
Louisa: Thomas Johnson, Thomas Walker.
Lunenburg: Clement Reade, Matthew Marrable.
Middlesex: Ralph Wormeley, Thomas Price.
Nansemond: Lemuel Riddick, Willis Riddick.
New Kent: Richard Adams, Lewis Webb.
Norfolk: George Veal, John Tatem.
Northumberland: Presley Thornton, Spencer Ball.
Northampton: Littleton Eyre, John Kendall.
Orange: Benjamin Cave, William Taliaferro.
Prince Edward: Peter Legrand, Charles Anderson.
Prince George: Richard Bland, Alexander Bolling.
Princess Anne: Anthony Walke, Jun., Thomas Walke.
Prince William: Henry Lee, Henry Peyton.
Richmond: John Woodbridge, Landon Carter.
Southampton: Benjamin Symmons, William Taylor.
Spotsylvania: William Waller, Zachariah Lewis.
Stafford: Thomas Ludwell Lee, Thompson Mason.

Surry: Hartwell Cocke, William Allen.
Sussex: John Edmunds, David Mason.
Warwick: William Digges, William Harwood.
Westmoreland: Richard Lee, Richard Henry Lee.
York: Dudley Digges, Robert C. Nicholas.
College of William and Mary: George Wythe.
Jamestown: Edward Champion Travis.
Norfolk Borough: William Atchison.
Williamsburg: Mr. Attorney.
Sources: Virginia Almanac of 1759. Journal (incomplete) of the House of Burgesses, Congressional Library.

Session of February 22, 1759

Accomac: Edmund Allen, Thomas Parramore.
Albemarle: Allen Howard, William Cabell, Jr.
Amelia: Edmund Booker, Richard Booker.
Augusta: John Wilson, Israel Christian.
Brunswick: William Thornton, Edward Goodrich.
Bedford: Samuel Hairston, Zachariah Burnley.
Caroline: Edmund Pendleton, John Baylor.
Charles City: Benjamin Harrison, William Kennon, Jr.
Chesterfield: Archibald Cary, Richard Eppes.
Culpeper: Thomas Slaughter, William Green.
Cumberland: George Carrington, John Fleming.
Dinwiddie: Leonard Claiborne, Jr., Robert Ruffin.
Elizabeth City: William Wager, John Tabb.
Essex: John Upshaw, Francis Waring.
Fairfax: George Johnston, George Mason.
Frederick: George Washington, Thos. Bryan Martin.
Gloucester: John Page, Thomas Whiting.
Goochland: John Payne, Reuben Skelton.
Halifax: Robert Wade, Nathaniel Terry.

Hampshire: Gabriel Jones, Thomas Walker.
Hanover: Nathaniel West Dandridge, John Syme.
Henrico: William Randolph, Bowler Cocke.
James City: Benjamin Waller, Lewis Burwell.
Isle of Wight: James Bridger, Joseph Bridger.
King George: Charles Carter, Charles Carter, Jr.
King and Queen: John Robinson, Speaker, George Braxton.
King William: Peter Robinson, Harry Gaines.
Lancaster: Charles Carter, George Heale.
Loudoun: Francis Lightfoot Lee, James Hamilton.
Louisa: Thomas Johnson, Thomas Walker.
Lunenburg: Clement Reade, Matthew Marrable.- (On contest during this session the last named Burgess was unseated, and a new election ordered.)
Middlesex: Ralph Wormeley, Thomas Price.
Nansemond: Lemuel Riddick, Willis Riddick.
New Kent: Richard Adams, Lewis Webb.
Norfolk: George Veal, John Tatem.
Northumberland: Presley Thornton, Spencer Ball.
Northampton: Littleton Eyre, John Kendall.
Orange: Benjamin Cave, William Taliaferro.
Prince Edward: Peter Legrand, Charles Anderson.
Prince George: Richard Bland, Alexander Bolling.
Princess Anne: Anthony Walke, Jr., Thomas Walke.
Prince William: Henry Lee, Henry Peyton.
Richmond: John Woodbridge, Landon Carter.
Southampton: Benjamin Symmons, William Taylor.
Spotsylvania: William Waller, Zachariah Lewis.
Stafford: Thos. Ludwell Lee, Thompson Mason.
Surry: Hartwell Cocke, William Allen.
Sussex: John Edmunds, David Mason.

Warwick: William Digges, William Harwood.
Westmoreland: Richard Lee, R. H. Lee.
York: Dudley Digges, Robert C. Nicholas.
College of William and Mary: George Wythe.
Jamestown: Edward Champion Travis.
Norfolk Borough: William Atchison.
Williamsburg: Mr. Attorney.
Sources: List of former session. Journal of the House, Congressional Library.

Session of November 1, 1759

Accomac: Edmund Allen, Thomas Parramore.
Albemarle: Allen Howard, William Cabell, Jr.
Amelia: Edmund Booker, Richard Booker.
Brunswick: William Thornton, John Clack (in place of Edward Goodrich, who had accepted the office of sheriff).
Bedford: Samuel Hairston, Zachariah Burnley.
Caroline: Edmund Pendleton, John Baylor.
Charles City: Benjamin Harrison, William Kennon, Jr.
Chesterfield: Archibald Cary, Richard Eppes.
Culpeper: Thomas Slaughter, William Green.
Cumberland: George Carrington, John Fleming.
Dinwiddie: Leonard Claiborne, Jr., Robert Ruffin.
Elizabeth City: William Wager, John Tabb.
Essex: John Upshaw, Francis Waring.
Fairfax: George Johnston, George Mason.
Frederick: George Washington, Thomas Bryan Martin.
Gloucester: John Page, Thomas Whiting.
Goochland: John Payne, John Smith (in place of Reuben Skelton, deceased).
Halifax: Robert Wade, Nathaniel Terry.
Hampshire: Gabriel Jones, Thomas Walker.

Hanover: Nathaniel West Dandridge, John Syme.
Henrico: William Randolph, Bowler Cocke.
James City: Benjamin Waller, Lewis Burwell.
Isle of Wight: James Bridger, Joseph Bridger.
King George: Charles Carter, Charles Carter, Jr.
King and Queen: John Robinson, Speaker, George Braxton.
King William: Peter Robinson, Harry Gaines.
Lancaster: Charles Carter, George Heale.
Loudoun: Francis Lightfoot Lee, James Hamilton.
Louisa: Thomas Johnson, Thomas Walker.
Lunenburg: Clement Reade, Matthew Marrable (re-elected).
Middlesex: Ralph Wormeley, Thomas Price.
Nansemond: Lemuel Riddick, Willis Riddick.
New Kent: Richard Adams, Lewis Webb.
Norfolk: John Tatem, William Bradley (in place of George Veal, who had accepted the place of sheriff).
Northumberland: Presley Thornton, Spencer Ball.
Northampton: Littleton Eyre, John Kendall.
Orange: Benjamin Cave, William Taliaferro.
Prince Edward: Peter Legrand, Charles Anderson.
Prince George: Richard Bland, Alexander Bolling.
Princess Anne: Anthony Walke, Jr., Thomas Walke.
Prince William: Henry Lee, Henry Peyton.
Richmond: John Woodbridge, Landon Carter.
Southampton: Benjamin Symmons, William Taylor.
Spotsylvania: William Waller, Zachariah Lewis.
Stafford: Thos. Ludwell Lee, Thompson Mason.
Surry: Hartwell Cocke, William Allen.
Sussex: John Edmunds, David Mason.
Warwick: William Digges, William Harwood.

Westmoreland: Richard Lee, R. H. Lee.
York: Dudley Digges, Richard C. Nicholas.
College of William and Mary: George Wythe.
Jamestown: John Ambler (in place of E. C. Travis, who had accepted the office of coroner).
Norfolk Borough: William Atchison.
Williamsburg: Mr. Attorney.
Sources: Journal of the House, Congressional Library. Lists of succeeding and preceding sessions.

Sessions of 1760 and 1761

Accomac: Edmund Allen, Thomas Parramore.
Albemarle: Allen Howard, William Cabell, Jun.
Amelia: Edmund Booker, [John?] Winn.
Augusta: John Wilson, Israel Christian.
Brunswick: William Thornton, John Clack.
Bedford: Samuel Hairstone, Zachariah Burnley.
Caroline: Edmund Pendleton, John Baylor.
Charles City: Benjamin Harrison, William Kennon, Jun.
Chesterfield: Archibald Cary, Richard Eppes.
Culpeper: William Green, Henry Pendleton.
Cumberland: George Carrington, John Fleming.
Dinwiddie: Leonard Claiborne, Jr., Robert Ruffin.
Elizabeth City: William Wager, John Tabb.
Essex: John Upshaw, Francis Waring.
Fairfax: George Johnston, George Mason.
Fauquier: Thomas Harrison, John Bell.
Frederick: George Washington, Thomas Bryan Martin.
Gloucester: John Page, Thomas Whiting.
Goochland: John Payne, John Smith.
Halifax: Robert Wade, Nathaniel Terry.

Hampshire: Gabriel Jones, Thomas Walker.
Hanover: N. West Dandridge, John Syme.
Henrico: William Randolph, Bowler Cocke.
James City: Benjamin Waller, Lewis Burwell.
Isle of Wight: James Bridger, Joseph Bridger.
King George: Charles Carter, Charles Carter, Jun.
King and Queen: John Robinson, Speaker, George Braxton.
King William: Peter Robinson, Harry Gaines.
Lancaster: Charles Carter, George Heale.
Loudoun: Francis Lightfoot Lee, James Hamilton.
Louisa: Thomas Johnson, Charles Smith.
Lunenburg: Clement Reade, Matthew Marrable.
Middlesex: Ralph Wormeley, Thomas Price.
Nansemond: Lemuel Riddick, Willis Riddick.
New Kent: Richard Adams, Lewis Webb.
Norfolk: John Tatem, William Bradley.
Northumberland: Presley Thornton, Spencer Ball.
Northampton: Littleton Eyre, John Kendall.
Orange: Benjamin Cave, James Taylor.
Prince Edward: Peter Legrand, Charles Anderson.
Prince George: Richard Bland, Alexander Bolling.
Princess Anne: Anthony Walke, Jun. Thomas Walke.
Prince William: Henry Lee, Henry Peyton.
Richmond: John Woodbridge, Landon Carter.
Southampton: Benjamin Symmons, William Taylor.
Spotsylvania: Zachariah Lewis, Fielding Lewis.
Stafford: Thomas Ludwell Lee, Thompson Mason.
Surry: Hartwell Cocke, William Allen.
Sussex: John Edmunds, David Mason.
Warwick: William Digges, William Harwood.
Westmoreland: Richard Lee, Richard Henry Lee.

York: Dudley Digges, Robert C. Nicholas.
College of William and Mary: George Wythe.
Jamestown: John Ambler.
Norfolk Borough: William Atchison.
Williamsburg: Mr. Attorney.
Sources: Journals and Va. Almanacs.

Assembly 1761-1765

This Assembly first convened on Nov. 3, 1761, and met by successive prorogations on Jan. 14, 1762; March 30, 1762; November 2, 1762; May 19, 1763; January 12, 1764; Oct. 30, 1764, and May 1, 1765. On June 1, 1765, not long after the adoption of the famous resolutions offered by Patrick Henry, it was dissolved.

The lists of members here given are compiled from the Journals of the several sessions, now in the Virginia State Library, and from a Virginia Almanac of 1762, in the Congressional Library, and one of 1765, cited by Mr. W. W. Henry in his Life of Patrick Henry, II, appendix II. There are several errors in Mr. Henry's list of members of the session of May-June, 1765, which have been corrected in the list here printed.

Session of November 3, 1761

Accomac: Thomas Parramore, Southey Simpson.
Albemarle: Thomas Walker, John Fry.
Amelia: David Greenhill, Thomas Tabb.
Augusta: Israel Christian, John Wilson.
Amherst: William Cabell, Cornelius Thomas.
Brunswick: Isaac Rowe Walton, William Thornton.
Bedford: William Callaway, John Talbot.
Buckingham: Robert Bolling, Joseph Cabell.

Caroline: Edmund Pendleton, John Baylor.
Charles City: Benjamin Harrison, William Kennon.
Chesterfield: Archibald Cary, Richard Eppes.
Culpepper: James Barber [Barbour], John Field.
Cumberland: George Carrington, John Fleming.
Dinwiddie: Robert Bolling, Leonard Claiborne, Jun.
Elizabeth City: George Wythe, William Wager.
Essex: John Upshaw, John Lee.
Fairfax: George Johnston, John West.
Fanquier: Thomas Marshall, Thomas Harrison.
Frederick: George Washington, George Mercer.
Gloucester: John Page, Thomas Whiting.
Goochland: John Payne, Josias Payne.
Halifax: Nathaniel Terry, Robert Wade.
Hampshire: James Keith ,Thomas Rutherford.
Hanover: John Syme, Nathaniel West Dandridge.
Henrico: Bowler Cocke, William Randolph (died since election.)
James City: Lewis Burwell, Philip Johnson.
Isle of Wight: James Bridger, Joseph Bridger.
King George: Charles Carter, Charles Carter, Jun.
King and Queen: John Robinson, Speaker, George Braxton (died since election).
King William: Bernard Moore, Carter Braxton.
Lancaster: Charles Carter, Richard Mitchell.
Loudoun: F. L. Lee, James Hamilton.
Louisa: William Johnson, Thomas Johnson.
Lunenburg: Clement Reade, Henry Blagrave.
Middlesex: John Smith, Ralph Wormeley.
Nansemond: Lemuel Riddick, Willis Riddick.
New Kent: Gill Armistead, Richard Adams.
Norfolk: Names of members cannot be ascertained.

Northumberland: Presley Thornton (promoted to Council since election). Spencer Ball.
Northampton: John Harmanson, Thomas Dalby.
Orange: James Taylor, James Walker.
Prince Edward: Peter Legrand, Abner Nash.
Prince George: Richard Bland, Richard Bland, Jun.
Princess Anne: Anthony Walke, E. H. Moseley.
Prince William: Henry Lee, John Baylis.
Richmond: Landon Carter, John Woodbridge.
Southampton: Joseph Gray, Benjamin Symmons.
Spotsylvania: Fielding Lewis, Benjamin Grymes.
Stafford: William Fitzhugh, Thomas L. Lee.
Surry: Hartwell Cocke, Henry Browne.
Sussex: David Mason, John Edmunds.
Warwick: William Digges, William Harwood.
Westmoreland: R. H. Lee, Richard Lee.
York: Dudley Digges, Thomas Nelson, Jun.
College of William and Mary: Mann Page.
Jamestown: Edward Champion Travis.
Norfolk Borough: Joseph Hutchings.
Williamsburg: Mr. Attorney.

Session of January 14, 1762

Accomac: Thomas Parramore, Southey Simpson.
Albemarle: Thomas Walker, John Fry.
Amelia: David Greenhill, Thomas Tabb.
Augusta: Israel Christian, John Wilson.
Amherst: William Cabell, Cornelius Thomas.
Brunswick: Isaac Rowe Walton, William Thornton.
Bedford: William Callaway, John Talbot.
Buckingham: Robert Bolling, Joseph Cabell.
Caroline: Edmund Pendleton, John Baylor.

Charles City: Benjamin Harrison, William Kennon.
Chesterfield: Archibald Cary, Richard Eppes.
Culpeper: James Barber, John Field.
Cumberland: George Carrington, John Fleming.
Dinwiddie: Robert Bolling, Leonard Claiborne, Jun.
Elizabeth City: George Wythe, William Wager.
Essex: John Upshaw, John Lee.
Fairfax: George Johnston, John West.
Fauquier: Thomas Marshall, Thomas Harrison.
Frederick: George Washington, George Mercer.
Gloucester: John Page, Thomas Whiting.
Goochland: John Payne, Josias Payne.
Halifax: Nathaniel Terry, Robert Wade.
Hampshire: James Keith, Thomas Rutherford.
Hanover: John Syme, Nathaniel West Dandridge.
Henrico: Philip Mayo (in place of William Randolph, deceased), Bowler Cocke.
James City: Lewis Burwell, Philip Johnson.
Isle of Wight: James Bridger, Joseph Bridger.
King George: Charles Carter, Charles Carter, Jun.
King and Queen: John Pendleton (in place of George Braxton, deceased), John Robinson, Speaker.
Lancaster: Charles Carter, Richard Mitchell.
King William: Bernard Moore, Carter Braxton.
Loudoun: F. L. Lee, James Hamilton.
Louisa: William Johnson, Thomas Johnson.
Lunenburg: Clement Reade, Henry Blagrave.
Middlesex: John Smith, Ralph Wormeley.
Nansemond: Leonard Riddick, Willis Riddick.
New Kent: Gill Armistead, Richard Adams.
Norfolk: Names of members cannot be ascertained.
Northumberland: Richard Hull (in place of Presley Thornton promoted to Council), Spencer Ball.

Northampton: John Harmanson, Thomas Dalby.
Orange: James Taylor, James Walker.
Prince Edward: Peter Legrand, Abner Nash.
Prince George: Richard Bland, Richard Bland, Jun.
Princess Anne: Anthony Walke, E. H. Moseley.
Prince William: Henry Lee, John Baylis.
Richmond: Landon Carter, John Woodbridge.
Southampton: Joseph Gray, Benjamin Symons.
Spotsylvania: Fielding Lewis, Benjamin Grymes.
Stafford: William Fitzhugh, Thomas L. Lee.
Surry: Hartwell Cocke, Henry Browne.
Sussex: David Mason, John Edmunds.
Warwick: William Digges, William Harwood.
Westmoreland: R. H. Lee, Richard Lee.
York: Dudley Digges, Thomas Nelson, Jun.
College of William and Mary: Mann Page.
Jamestown: Edward Champion Travis.
Norfolk Borough: Joseph Hutchings.
Williamsburg: Mr. Attorney.

Session of March 30, 1762

Accomac: Thomas Parramore, Southey Simpson.
Albemarle: Thomas Walker, John Fry.
Amelia: David Greenhill, Thomas Tabb.
Augusta: Israel Christian, John Wilson.
Amherst: William Cabell, Cornelius Thomas.
Brunswick: Isaac Rowe Walton, William Thornton.
Bedford: William Callaway, John Talbot.
Buckingham: Robert Bolling, Joseph Cabell.
Caroline: Edmund Pendleton, John Baylor.
Charles City: Benjamin Harrison, William Kennon.
Chesterfield: Archibald Cary, Richard Eppes.

Culpeper: James Barber [Barbour], John Field.
Cumberland: George Carrington, John Fleming.
Dinwiddie: Robert Bolling, Leonard Claiborne, Jun.
Elizabeth City: George Wythe, William Wager.
Essex: John Upshaw, John Lee.
Fairfax: George Johnston, John West.
Fauquier: Thomas Marshall, Thomas Harrison.
Frederick: George Washington, George Mercer.
Gloucester: John Page, Thomas Whiting.
Goochland: John Payne, Josias Payne.
Halifax: Nathaniel Terry, Robert Wade.
Hampshire: James Keith, Thomas Rutherford.
Hanover: John Syme, Nathaniel West Dandridge.
Henrico: Philip Mayo, Bowler Cocke.
James City: Lewis Burwell, Philip Johnson.
Isle of Wight: James Bridger, Joseph Bridger.
King George: Charles Carter, Charles Carter, Jun.
King and Queen: John Pendleton, John Robinson, Speaker.
King William: Bernard Moore, Carter Braxton.
Lancaster: Charles Carter, Richard Mitchell.
Loudoun: F. L. Lee, James Hamilton.
Louisa: William Johnson, Thomas Johnson.
Lunenburg: Clement Reade, Henry Blagrave.
Middlesex: John Smith, Ralph Wormeley.
Nansemond: Lemuel Riddick, Willis Riddick.
New Kent: Gill Armistead, Richard Adams.
Norfolk: William Bradley.
Northumberland: Richard Hull, Spencer Ball.
Northampton: John Harmanson, Thomas Dalby.
Orange: James Taylor, James Walker.
Prince Edward: Peter Legrand, Abner Nash.

Prince George: Richard Bland, Richard Bland, Jun.
Princess Anne: Anthony Walke, E. H. Moseley.
Prince William: Henry Lee, John Baylis.
Richmond: Landon Carter, John Woodbridge.
Southampton: Joseph Gray, Benjamin Symmons.
Spotsylvania: Fielding Lewis, Benjamin Grymes.
Stafford: William Fitzhugh, Thomas L. Lee.
Surry: Hartwell Cocke, Henry Browne.
Sussex: David Mason, John Edmunds.
Warwick: William Digges, William Harwood.
Westmoreland: R. H. Lee, Richard Lee.
York: Dudley Digges, Thomas Nelson, Jun.
College of William and Mary: Mann Page.
Jamestown: Edward Champion Travis.
Norfolk Borough: Joseph Hutchings.
Williamsburg: Mr. Attorney.

Session of November 2, 1762

Accomac: Southey Simpson, Thomas Parramore.
Albemarle: Thomas Walker, John Fry.
Amelia: David Greenhill, Thomas Tabb.
Augusta: John Wilson, Israel Christian.
Amherst: William Cabell, Cornelius Thomas.
Brunswick: William Thornton, Isaac Rowe Walton.
Bedford: William Callaway, John Talbot.
Buckingham: Robert Bolling, Jun., Joseph Cabell.
Caroline: John Baylor, Edmund Pendleton.
Charles City: Benjamin Harrison, William Kennon.
Chesterfield: Archibald Cary, Richard Eppes.
Culpeper: John Field, James Barber [Barbour].
Cumberland: George Carrington, John Fleming.
Dinwiddie: Robert Bolling, Leonard Claiborne, Jun.

Elizabeth City: William Wager, George Wythe.
Essex: John Lee, John Upshaw.
Fairfax: George Johnston, John West.
Fauquier: Thomas Harrison, Thomas Marshall.
Frederick: George Washington, George Mercer.
Gloucester: Tl.omas Whiting, John Page.
Goochland: J. Payne, Josias Payne.
Halifax: Nathaniel Terry, Robert Wade.
Hampshire: James Mercer (in place of James Keith, who had accepted a clerkship), Thomas Rutherford.
Hanover: N. W. Dandridge, John Syme.
Henrico: Bowler Cocke, Philip Mayo.
James City: Lewis Burwell, Philip Johnson.
Isle of Wight: J. Bridger, Joseph Bridger.
King George: Charles Carter, Charles Carter, Jun.
King and Queen: John Pendleton, John Robinson, Speaker.
Lancaster: Charles Carter, Richard Mitchell.
King William: Bernard Moore, Carter Braxton.
Loudoun: F. L. Lee, James Hamilton.
Louisa: William Johnson, Thomas Johnson.
Lunenburg: Henry Blagrave, Clement Reade.
Middlesex: John Smith, Ralph Wormeley.
Nansemond: Willis Riddick, Lemuel Riddick.
New Kent: Burwell Bassett (in place of Gill Armistead, deceased), Richard Adams.
Norfolk: William Bradley, Thomas Veal.
Northumberland: Richard Hull, Spencer Ball.
Northampton: John Harmanson, Thomas Dalby.
Orange: James Taylor, James Walker.
Prince Edward: Peter Legrand, Abner Nash.
Prince George: Richard Bland, Richard Bland, Jr.

Princess Anne: E. H. Moseley, Anthony Walke.
Prince William: John Baylis, Henry Lee.
Richmond: John Woodbridge, Landon Carter.
Southampton: Joseph Gray, Benjamin Symmons.
Spotsylvania: Fielding Lewis, Benjamin Grymes.
Stafford: William Fitzhugh, Thomas L. Lee.
Surry: Hartwell Cocke, Thomas Bailey (in place of Henry Browne, deceased.)
Sussex: David Mason, John Edmunds.
Warwick: William Harwood, William Digges.
Westmoreland: R. H. Lee, Richard Lee.
York: Dudley Digges, Thomas Nelson, Jun.
College of William and Mary: Mann Page.
Jamestown: E. C. Travis.
Norfolk Borough: Joseph Hutchings.
Williamsburg: Mr. Attorney.

Session of May 19, 1763

Accomac: Thomas Parramore, Southey Simpson.
Albemarle: Thomas Walker, John Fry.
Amelia: David Greenhill, Thomas Tabb.
Augusta: John Wilson, Israel Christian.
Amherst: William Cabell, Cornelius Thomas.
Brunswick: William Thornton, Isaac Rowe Walton.
Bedford: William Callaway, John Talbot.
Buckingham: Robert Bolling, Jr., Joseph Cabell.
Caroline: John Baylor, Edmund Pendleton.
Charles City: Benjamin Harrison, William Kennon.
Chesterfield: Archibald Cary, Richard Eppes.
Culpeper: John Field, James Barbour.
Cumberland: George Carrington, John Fleming.
Dinwiddie: Robert Bolling, Leonard Claiborne, Jr.

Elizabeth City: George Wythe, William Wager.
Essex: John Lee, John Upshaw.
Fairfax: George Johnston, John West.
Fauquier: Thomas Harrison, Thomas Marshall.
Frederick: George Washington, George Mercer.
Gloucester: Thomas Whiting, John Page.
Goochland: John Payne, Josias Payne.
Halifax: Nathaniel Terry, Robert Wade.
Hampshire: James Mercer, Thomas Rutherford.
Hanover: Nathaniel West Dandridge, John Syme.
Henrico: Bowler Cocke (an almanac has "Bowler Cocke, Jr."), Philip Mayo.
James City: Lewis Burwell, Philip Johnson.
Isle of Wight: James Bridger, Joseph Bridger.
King George: Charles Carter, Charles Carter, Jr.
King and Queen: John Pendleton, John Robinson, Speaker.
King William: Bernard Moore, Carter Braxton.
Lancaster: Charles Carter, Richard Mitchell.
Loudoun: Francis Lightfoot Lee, James Hamilton.
Louisa: William Johnson, Thomas Johnson.
Lunenburg: Henry Blagrave, Clement Reade [Jr], (in place of Clement Reade, deceased).
Middlesex: John Smith, Ralph Wormeley.
Nansemond: Willis Riddick, Lemuel Riddick.
New Kent: Burwell Bassett, Richard Adams.
Norfolk: William Bradley, Thomas Veal.
Northumberland: Richard Hull, Spencer Ball.
Northampton: John Harmanson, Thomas Dalby.
Orange: James Taylor, James Walker.
Prince Edward: Peter Legrand, Abner Nash.
Prince George: Richard Bland, Richard Bland, Jr.

Princess Anne: Edward Hack Moseley, Anthony Walke.
Prince William: John Baylis, Henry Lee.
Richmond: John Woodbridge, Landon Carter.
Southampton: Joseph Gray, Benjamin Symmons.
Spotsylvania: Fielding Lewis, Wm. Johnston.
Stafford: William Fitzhugh, Thos. L. Lee.
Surry: Hartwell Cocke, William Bailey.
Sussex: David Mason, John Edmunds.
Warwick: William Digges, William Harwood.
Westmoreland: Richard Henry Lee, Richard Lee.
York: Dudley Digges, Thomas Nelson, Jr.
College of William and Mary: Mann Page.
Jamestown: Edw'd Champion Travis.
Norfolk Borough: Joseph Hutchings.
Williamsburg: Mr. Attorney.

Session of January 12, 1764

Accomac: Thomas Parramore, Southey Simpson.
Albemarle: Thomas Walker, John Fry.
Amelia: David Greenhill, Thomas Tabb.
Augusta: Israel Christian, John Wilson.
Amherst: William Cabell, Cornelius Thomas.
Brunswick: William Thornton, Isaac Rowe Walton.
Bedford: William Callaway, John Talbot.
Buckingham: Robert Bolling, Jun., Joseph Cabell.
Caroline: John Baylor, Edmund Pendleton.
Charles City: Benjamin Harrison, William Kennon.
Chesterfield: Archibald Cary, Richard Eppes.
Culpeper: John Field, James Barbour.
Cumberland: George Carrington, John Fleming.
Dinwiddie: Robert Bolling, Leonard Claiborne, Jun.

Elizabeth City: George Wythe, William Wager.
Essex: John Lee, John Upshaw.
Fairfax: George Johnston, John West.
Fauquier: Thomas Harrison, Thomas Marshall.
Frederick: George Washington, George Mercer.
Goochland: John Payne, Josias Payne.
Gloucester: Thomas Whiting, John Page.
Halifax: Nathaniel Terry, Robert Wade.
Hampshire: James Mercer, Thomas Rutherford.
Hanover: Nathaniel West Dandridge, John Syme.
Henrico: Bowler Cocke, Philip Mayo.
James City: Lewis Burwell, Philip Johnson.
Isle of Wight: James Bridger, Dolphin Drew (in place of Joseph Bridger, who had accepted the office of sheriff).
King George: Charles Carter, Charles Carter, Jun.
King and Queen: John Pendleton, John Robinson, Speaker.
King William: Bernard Moore, Carter Braxton.
Lancaster: Charles Carter, Richard Mitchell.
Loudoun: Francis Lightfoot Lee, James Hamilton.
Louisa: William Johnson, Thomas Johnson.
Lunenburg: Henry Blagrave, Clement Reade, Jun.
Middlesex: John Smith, Ralph Wormeley.
Nansemond: Willis Riddick, Lemuel Riddick.
New Kent: Burwell Bassett, Richard Adams.
Norfolk: William Bradley, Thomas Veal.
Northumberland: Richard Hull, Spencer Ball.
Northampton: John Harmanson, Thomas Dalby.
Orange: James Taylor, James Walker.
Prince Edward: Peter Legrand, Abner Nash.
Prince George: Richard Bland, Richard Bland, Jun.
Princess Anne: Edward Hacke Moseley, Anthony Walke.

Prince William: John Baylis, Henry Lee.
Richmond: John Woodbridge, Landon Carter.
Southampton: Joseph Gray, Benjamin Symmons.
Spotsylvania: Fielding Lewis, William Johnston.
Stafford: William Fitzhugh, Thomas L. Lee.
Surry: Hartwell Cocke, William Bailey.
Sussex: David Mason, John Edmunds.
Warwick: William Digges, William Harwood.
Westmoreland: Richard Henry Lee, Richard Lee.
York: Dudley Digges, Thomas Nelson, Jun.
College of William and Mary: Mann Page.
Jamestown: Edward Champion Travis.
Norfolk Borough: Joseph Hutchings.
Williamsburg: Mr. Attorney.

Session of October 30, 1764

Accomac: Thomas Parramore, Southey Simpson.
Albemarle: Thomas Walker, Henry Fry (in place of John Fry, who had accepted the office of coroner).
Amelia: David Greenhill, Thomas Tabb.
Augusta: Israel Christian, John Wilson.
Amherst: William Cabell, Cornelius Thomas.
Brunswick: William Thornton, Isaac Rowe Walton.
Bedford: William Callaway, John Talbot.
Buckingham: Robert Bolling, Jr., Joseph Cabell.
Caroline: John Baylor, Edmund Pendleton.
Charles City: Benjamin Harrison, William Kennon.
Chesterfield: Archibald Cary, [probably Seth Ward] (in place of Richard Eppes, deceased).
Culpeper: John Field, James Barbour.
Cumberland: John Fleming, Thomas Prosser (in place of George Carrington, who had accepted the office of sheriff).

Dinwiddie: Robert Bolling, Leonard Claiborne, Jun.
Elizabeth City: George Wythe, William Wager.
Essex: John Lee, John Upshaw.
Fairfax: George Johnston, John West.
Fauquier: Thomas Harrison, Thomas Marshall.
Frederick: George Washington, George Mercer.
Gloucester: Thomas Whiting, John Page.
Goochland: John Payne, Josias Payne.
Halifax: Nathaniel Terry, Edward Booker (in place of Robert Wade, deceased).
Hampshire: James Mercer, Thomas Rutherford.
Hanover: James Littlepage, John Syme.
Henrico: Bowler Cocke, Philip Mayo.
James City: Lewis Burwell, Philip Johnson.
Isle of Wight: James Bridger, Dolphin Drew.
King George: Charles Carter, William Champe (in place of Charles Carter, Sr., deceased).
King and Queen: John Pendleton, John Robinson, Speaker.
King William: Bernard Moore, Carter Braxton.
Lancaster: Charles Carter, Richard Mitchell.
Loudoun: Francis Lightfoot Lee, James Hamilton.
Louisa: William Johnson, Thomas Johnson.
Lunenburg: Henry Blagrave, Clement Reade, Jun.
Middlesex: John Smith, ——— ——— (in place of Ralph Wormeley, who had accepted a place of profit).
Nansemond: Willis Riddick, Lemuel Riddick.
New Kent: Burwell Bassett, Richard Adams.
Norfolk: William Bradley, Thomas Veal.
Northumberland: Richard Hull, Spencer Ball.
Northampton: John Harmanson, Thomas Dalby.
Orange: James Taylor, James Walker.

Prince Edward: Peter Legrand, Abner Nash.
Prince George: Richard Bland, Richard Bland, Jun.
Princess Anne: Edward Hacke Moseley, Anthony Walke.
Prince William: John Baylis, Henry Lee.
Richmond: John Woodbridge, Landon Carter.
Southampton: Joseph Gray, Benjamin Symmons.
Spotsylvania: Fielding Lewis, William Johnston.
Stafford: William Fitzhugh, Thomas L. Lee.
Surry: Hartwell Cocke, William Bailey.
Sussex: David Mason, John Edmunds.
Warwick: William Digges, William Harwood.
Westmoreland: Richard Henry Lee, Richard Lee.
York: Dudley Digges, Thomas Nelson, Jun.
College of William and Mary: Mann Page.
Jamestown: Edward Champion Travis.
Norfolk Borough: Joseph Hutchings.
Williamsburg: Mr. Attorney.

Session of May 1, 1765 (By adjournment from previous session).

Accomac: Thomas Parramore, Southey Simpson.
Albemarle: Thomas Walker, Henry Fry.
Amelia: Thomas Tabb, —— —— (in place of David Greenhill, who had accepted the office of sheriff).
Augusta: Israel Christian, John Wilson.
Amherst: William Cabell, Cornelius Thomas.
Brunswick: William Thornton, Isaac Rowe Walton.
Bedford: William Callaway, John Talbot.
Buckingham: Robert Bolling, Jun., Joseph Cabell.
Caroline: John Baylor, Edmund Pendleton.
Charles City: Benjamin Harrison, William Kennon.

Chesterfield: Archibald Cary. (The name of the other Burgess is uncertain—probably Seth Ward).
Culpeper: John Field, James Barbour.
Cumberland: John Fleming, Thomas Prosser. (During this session Thomas Prosser was expelled from the House, and a new election ordered, but the name of his successor does not appear.)
Dinwiddie: Robert Bolling, Leonard Claiborne, Jun.
Elizabeth City: George Wythe, William Wager.
Essex: John Lee, John Upshaw.
Fairfax: George Johnston, John West.
Fauquier: Thomas Harrison, Thomas Marshall.
Frederick: George Washington, George Mercer.
Gloucester: Thomas Whiting, John Page.
Goochland: John Payne, Josias Payne.
Halifax: Edward Booker, —— —— (in place of Nat. Terry, who had accepted the office of sheriff).
Hampshire: James Mercer, Thomas Rutherford.
Hanover: James Littlepage, John Syme.
Henrico: Bowler Cocke, Philip Mayo.
James City: Lewis Burwell, Philip Johnson.
Isle of Wight: James Bridger, Dolphin Drew.
King George: Charles Carter, William Champe.
King and Queen: John Robinson, Speaker, John Pendleton.
King William: Bernard Moore, Carter Braxton.
Lancaster: Charles Carter, Richard Mitchell.
Loudoun: Francis Lightfoot Lee, James Hamilton.
Louisa: Thomas Johnson, Patrick Henry, Jun. (in place of William Johnson, who had accepted the office of coroner).
Lunenburg: Henry Blagrave, William Taylor (in place of Clement Reade, who had accepted the office of coroner).

Mecklenburg: Edmund Taylor, Robert Munford.
Middlesex: John Smith. (The name of the other Burgess is uncertain.)
Nansemond: Willis Riddick, Lemuel Riddick.
New Kent: Burwell Bassett, Richard Adams.
Norfolk: William Bradley, Thomas Veal.
Northumberland: Richard Hull, Spencer Ball.
Northampton: John Harmanson, Thomas Dalby.
Orange: James Taylor, James Walker.
Prince Edward: Peter Legrand, Abner Nash.
Prince George: Richard Bland, Richard Bland, Jun.
Princess Anne: Edward Hacke Moseley, Anthony Walke.
Prince William: John Baylis, Henry Lee.
Richmond: John Woodbridge, Landon Carter.
Southampton: Joseph Gray, Benjamin Symmons.
Spotsylvania: Fielding Lewis, William Johnston.
Stafford: William Fitzhugh, Thomas L. Lee.
Surry: Hartwell Cocke, William Bailey.
Sussex: David Mason, John Edmunds.
Warwick: William Digges, William Harwood.
Westmoreland: Richard Henry Lee, Richard Lee.
York: Dudley Digges, Thomas Nelson, Jun.
College of William and Mary: Mann Page.
Jamestown: Edward Champion Travis.
Norfolk Borough: Joseph Hutchings.
Williamsburg: Mr. Attorney.

Assembly of October 1765

Jameson's list makes no mention of this Assembly, nor is there known to be any journal of it extant. No newspaper of that date is known to the compilers, and therefore no information can be obtained from that source. But there was certainly a general election in July, 1765, and the Burgesses then elected appear to have met in October. Washington, in a letter dated August 2, 1765, states that he had been elected for Fairfax, instead of Frederick for which he had previously sat, and that on the 28th of July he had received notice of the prorogation. The records of Fairfax show that George Washington and John West were elected Burgesses on July 16. The records of Essex show that John Lee and Francis Waring were elected July 9, and the Va. Gazette (quoted in an interleaved almanac by John Randolph), states that on July 5, Attorney General Peyton Randolph was elected member for Williamsburg in the next Assembly. In Hening, Vol. 8, p. 69, the acts passed October, 1765, begin. See the note on that page.

In the Collection of the Virginia Historical Society is an interleaved almanac, formerly the property of John Randolph of Roanoke. On various pages he has made copies from the Virginia Gazette of 1765, and among them the following, imperfect, list of the members of the House of Burgesses elected that year:

Accomac: Thomas Parramore, Southey Simpson.
Albemarle: Thomas Walker, Edward Carter.
Amelia: Thomas Tabb, Robert Munford.
Augusta: John Wilson, William Preston.
Amherst: William Cabell, Cornelius Thomas.
Brunswick: William Thornton, Frederick Macklin.
Bedford: John Talbot, James Callaway.
Buckingham: Joseph Cabell, Samuel Jordan.
Caroline: Edmund Pendleton, Walker Taliaferro.
Charles City:
Charlotte: Clement Reade, Paul Carrington.

Chesterfield: Archibald Cary, Seth Ward.
Culpeper: John Field, Thomas Slaughter.
Cumberland: John Fleming, Alexander Trent.
Dinwiddie: Robert Bolling, John Banister.
Elizabeth City: George Wythe, Willson Miles Cary.
Essex: John Lee, Francis Waring.
Fairfax: George Washington, John West.
Fauquier: Thomas Harrison, Thomas Marshall.
Frederick:
Gloucester:
Goochland:
Halifax: Edward Booker, Walter Coles.
Hampshire:
Hanover:
Henrico: Richard Randolph, Bowler Cocke.
James City: Lewis Burwell, Robert Carter Nicholas.
Isle of Wight:
King George: William Champe, Charles Carter.
King and Queen: John Robinson, Speaker, George Brooke.
King William: Carter Braxton, Harry Gaines.
Lancaster: Charles Carter, Richard Mitchell.
Loudoun: Francis Lightfoot Lee, James Hamilton.
Louisa: Patrick Henry, Jr., Richard Anderson.
Lunenburg: William Taylor, Henry Blagrave.
Middlesex:
Mecklenburg: Henry Deloney, Robert Munford.
Nansemond: Lemuel Riddick, Willis Riddick.
New Kent:
Norfolk: Thomas Newton, Robert Tucker, Jun.
Northumberland:
Northampton:

Orange: James Walker, Zachariah Burnley.
Prince Edward: Peter Legrand, Nathaniel Venable.
Prince George: Richard Bland, Alexander Bolling.
Princess Anne:
Prince William: Henry Lee, Foushee Tebbs.
Richmond: John Woodbridge, Landon Carter.
Southampton: Joseph Gray, Benjamin Symmons.
Spotsylvania:
Stafford: John Alexander, Thompson Mason.
Surry:
Sussex: David Mason, John Edmunds.
Warwick: William Digges, William Harwood.
Westmoreland: Richard Henry Lee, Richard Lee.
York: Dudley Digges, Thomas Nelson.
College of William and Mary: John Blair.
Jamestown: John Ambler.
Norfolk Borough: Joseph Hutchings.
Williamsburg: Mr. Attorney.

Assembly of 1766-1768

[It is not known exactly when the elections for this Assembly were held, but there is a proclamation published in the Virginia Gazette reciting the fact that it had been called to meet on the first Tuesday in March, 1766, stating that there was no urgent reason why it should meet on that date, and proroguing it. There were several other prorogations until the actual assembling on November 5, 1766. The first session adjourned shortly before December 18, 1766.]

Session of November 6, 1766

Accomack: Thomas Parramore, Southey Simpson.
Albemarle: Thomas Walker, Edward Carter.

Amelia: Thomas Tabb, Robert Munford.
Augusta: John Wilson, William Preston.
Amherst: William Cabell, Jr., Cornelius Thomas.
Bedford: John Talbot, James Callaway.
Buckingham: Joseph Cabell, Samuel Jordan.
Caroline: Edmund Pendleton, Walker Taliaferro.
Charles City: Benjamin Harrison, William Acrill.
Chesterfield: Archibald Cary, Seth Ward.
Culpeper: John Field, Thomas Slaughter.
Cumberland: John Fleming, Alexander Trent.
Charlotte: Clement Read, Paul Carrington.
Dinwiddie: Robert Bolling, John Banister.
Elizabeth City: George Wythe, Wilson Miles Cary.
Essex: John Lee, Francis Waring.
Fairfax: George Johnston (died in summer of 1766); George Washington, John West (in place of Johnston, deceased.)
Fauquier: Thomas Harrison, Thomas Marshall.
Frederick: Robert Rutherford, James Wood.
Gloucester: John Page, Thomas Whiting.
Goochland: John Payne, John Bolling.
Halifax: Walter Coles, Edward Booker.
Hampshire: Thomas Rutherford, James Mercer.
Hanover: John Syme, James Littlepage (died in 1766); Samuel Meredith (in place of Littlepage, deceased).
Henrico: Richard Randolph, Bowler Cocke, Jr.
James City: Lewis Burwell, Robert C. Nicholas.
Isle of Wight: Dolphin Drew, James Bridger.
King George: Charles Carter, William Robinson.
King and Queen: John Robinson (died May, 1766), George Brooke, Richard Tunstall (in place of Robinson, deceased.)

King William: Carter Braxton, Henry Gaines.
Lancaster: Richard Mitchell, Charles Carter.
Loudoun: Francis L. Lee, James Hamilton.
Louisa: Patrick Henry, Jr., Richard Anderson.
Lunenburg: William Taylor, Henry Blagrave.
Middlesex: John Smith, Gawin Corbin.
Mecklenburg: Henry Delaney, Robert Munford.
Nansemond: Lemuel Riddick, Willis Riddick.
New Kent: Burwell Bassett, William Clayton.
Norfolk: Thomas Newton, Jr., Robert Tucker, Jr.
Northumberland: Spencer Ball, Thomas Gaskins.
Northampton: John Harmanson, Severn Eyre.
Orange: James Walker, Zachariah Burnley.
Prince Edward: Peter Le Grand, Nathaniel Venable.
Prince George: Richard Bland, Alexander Bolling.
Princess Anne: Edward Hack Moseley, Robt. Ballard.
Prince William: Henry Lee, Foushee Tebbs.
Richmond: John Woodbridge, Landon Carter.
Southampton: Joseph Gray, Benjamin Symmons.
Spotsylvania: Benjamin Grymes, Fielding Lewis.
Stafford: John Alexander, Thomson Mason.
Surry: Hartwell Cocke, Thomas Bailey.
Sussex: David Mason, John Edmunds.
Warwick: William Harwood, William Digges.
Westmoreland: R. H. Lee, Richard Lee.
York: Dudley Digges, Thomas Nelson, Jr.
College of William and Mary: John Blair.
Jamestown: John Ambler (died before meeting of Assembly), Edward Ambler (in place of Ambler, deceased.)
Norfolk: Joseph Hutchings.
Williamsburg: Peyton Randolph.
Sources: Virginia Almanac, 1767. Virginia Gazette.

Session of March 12, 1767
(By adjournment from last session.)

Accomack: Thomas Parramore, Southey Simpson.
Albemarle: Thomas Walker, Edward Carter.
Amelia: Thomas Tabb, Robert Munford.
Augusta: John Wilson, William Preston.
Amherst: William Cabell, Jr., Cornelius Thomas.
Bedford: John Talbot, James Callaway.
Buckingham: Joseph Cabell, Samuel Jordan.
Caroline: Edmund Pendleton, Walker Taliaferro.
Charles City: Benjamin Harrison, William Acrill.
Chesterfield: Archibald Cary, Seth Ward.
Culpeper: John Field, Thomas Slaughter.
Cumberland: John Fleming, Alexander Trent.
Charlotte: Clement Reade, Paul Carrington.
Dinwiddie: Robert Bolling, John Banister.
Elizabeth City: George Wythe, Wilson Miles Cary.
Essex: John Lee, Francis Waring.
Fairfax: George Washington, John West.
Fauquier: Thomas Harrison, Thomas Marshall.
Frederick: Robert Rutherford, James Wood.
Gloucester, John Page, Thomas Whiting.
Goochland: John Payne, John Bolling.
Halifax: Walter Coles, Edward Booker.
Hampshire: Thomas Rutherford, James Mercer.
Hanover: John Syme, Samuel Meredith.
Henrico: Richard Randolph, Bowler Cocke, Jr.
James City: Lewis Burwell, Rob't Carter Nicholas.
Isle of Wight: Dolphin Drew, James Bridger.
King George: Charles Carter, William Robinson.
King and Queen: George Brooke, Richard Tunstall.
King William: Carter Braxton, Henry Gaines.

Lancaster: Robert Mitchell, Charles Carter.
Loudoun: Francis L. Lee, James Hamilton.
Louisa: Patrick Henry, Jr., Richard Anderson.
Lunenburg: William Taylor, Henry Blagrave.
Middlesex: John Smith, Gawin Corbin.
Mecklenburg: Henry Delaney, Robert Munford.
Nansemond: Lemuel Riddick, Willis Riddick.
New Kent: Burwell Bassett, William Clayton.
Norfolk: Thomas Newton, Jr., Robert Tucker, Jr.
Northumberland: Spencer Ball, Thomas Gaskins.
Northampton: John Harmanson, Severn Eyre.
Orange: James Walker, Zachariah Burnley.
Prince Edward: Peter Le Grand, Nathaniel Venable.
Prince George: Richard Bland, Alexander Bolling.
Princess Anne: Edw'd Hack Moseley, Robert Ballard.
Prince William: Henry Lee, Foushee Tebbs.
Richmond: John Woodbridge, Landon Carter.
Southampton: Joseph Gray, Benjamin Symmons.
Spotsylvania: Benjamin Grymes, Fielding Lewis.
Stafford: John Alexander, Thomson Mason.
Surry: Hartwell Cocke, Thomas Bailey.
Sussex: David Mason, John Edmunds.
Warwick: William Harwood, William Digges.
Westmoreland: R. H. Lee, Richard Lee.
York: Dudley Digges, Thomas Nelson, Jr.
College of William and Mary: John Blair.
Jamestown: Edward Ambler.
Norfolk: Joseph Hutchings.
Williamsburg: Peyton Randolph.
(At the close of this session the Assembly was prorogued, and convened again on March 31, 1768.)
Sources: Virginia Almanacs of 1768. Virginia Gazette.

Session of March 31, 1768

Accomac: Thomas Parramore, Southey Simpson.
Albemarle: Thomas Walker, Edward Carter.
Amelia: Thomas Tabb, Robert Munford.
Augusta: John Wilson, William Preston.
Amherst: William Cabell, Jr., Cornelius Thomas.
Bedford: John Talbot, James Callaway.
Buckingham: Joseph Cabell, Samuel Jordan.
Caroline: Edmund Pendleton, Walker Taliaferro.
Charles City: Benjamin Harrison, William Acrill.
Chesterfield: Archibald Cary, Seth Ward.
Culpeper: John Field, Thomas Slaughter.
Cumberland: Alexander Trent, John Mayo (in place of John Fleming, deceased).
Charlotte: Clement Read, Paul Carrington.
Dinwiddie: Robert Bolling, John Banister.
Elizabeth City: George Wythe, Wilson Miles Cary.
Essex: John Lee, Francis Waring.
Fairfax: George Washington, John West.
Fauquier: Thomas Harrison, Thomas Marshall.
Frederick: Robert Rutherford, James Wood.
Gloucester: John Page, Thomas Whiting.
Goochland: John Payne, John Bolling.
Halifax: Walter Coles, Edward Booker.
Hampshire: Thomas Rutherford, James Mercer.
Hanover: John Syme, Samuel Meredith.
Henrico: Richard Randolph, Bowler Cocke, Jr.
James City: Lewis Burwell, Rob't C. Nicholas.
Isle of Wight: Dolphin Drew, Richard Baker (in place of Bridger, who had accepted the office of coroner).
King George: Charles Carter, William Robinson.
King and Queen: George Brooke, Richard Tunstall.

King William: Carter Braxton, Thomas Claiborne (in place of Gaines, deceased).
Lancaster: Robert Mitchell, Charles Carter.
Loudoun: Francis L. Lee, James Hamilton.
Louisa: Patrick Henry, Jr., Richard Anderson.
Lunenburg: William Taylor, Henry Blagrave.
Middlesex: John Smith, Gawin Corbin.
Mecklenburg: Henry Delaney, Robert Munford.
Nansemond: Lemuel Riddick, Willis Riddick.
New Kent: Burwell Bassett, William Clayton.
Norfolk: Thomas Newton, Jr., Robert Tucker, Jr.
Northumberland: Spencer Ball, Thomas Gaskins.
Northampton: John Harmanson, Severn Eyre.
Orange: Peter Le Grand, Nathaniel Venable.
Prince George: Richard Bland, Peter Poythress (in place of Bolling, deceased).
Princess Anne: Edward Hack Moseley, Robert Ballard.
Prince William: Henry Lee, Foushee Tebbs.
Richmond: John Woodbridge, Landon Carter.
Southampton: Joseph Gray, Benjamin Symmons.
Spotsylvania: Benjamin Grymes, Fielding Lewis.
Stafford: John Alexander, Thomson Mason.
Surry: Hartwell Cocke, Thomas Bailey.
Sussex: David Mason, John Edmunds.
Warwick: William Harwood, William Digges.
Westmoreland: R. H. Lee, Richard Lee.
York: Dudley Digges, Thos. Nelson, Jr.
College of William and Mary: John Blair.
Jamestown: Edward Ambler.
Norfolk: Joseph Hutchings.
Williamsburg: Peyton Randolph.
At the close of the session this Assembly was dissolved.

Source: The changes in membership as shown by the Virginia Gazette.

Assembly of May, 1769

[There was but one session of this Assembly which met on May 8, and was dissolved on May 17, 1769. On the preceding day the House of Burgesses adopted vigorous resolutions asserting colonial rights, and on the 17th the Governor, Lord Botetourt called them before him and said: " Mr. Speaker and Gentlemen of the House of Burgesses,— I have heard of your resolves and augur ill of their effects. You have made it my duty to dissolve you, and you are dissolved accordingly."]

Accomack: Southey Simpson, Thomas Parramore.
Albemarle: Thomas Jefferson, Thomas Walker.
Amelia: Thomas Tabb, Robert Munford.
Amherst: William Cabell, Jr., Cornelius Thomas.
Augusta: John Wilson, Gabriel Jones.
Bedford: John Talbot, Charles Lynch.
Buckingham: Joseph Cabell, Benjamin Howard.
Brunswick: Nathaniel Edwards, Jr., Frederic Maclin.
Caroline: Edmund Pendleton, Francis Coleman.
Charles City: Benjamin Harrison, William Acrill.
Charlotte: Paul Carrington, Isaac Read.
Chesterfield: Archibald Cary, Edward Osborne.
Culpeper: Henry Claiborne, John Green.
Cumberland: John Mayo, Alexander Trent.
Dinwiddie: Robert Bolling, Bolling Starke.
Elizabeth City: Wilson Miles Cary, James Wallace.
Essex: Francis Waring, William Roane.
Fairfax: George Washington, John West.
Fauquier: Thomas Harrison, James Scott.

Frederick: Robert Rutherford, James Wood.
Gloucester: Thomas Whiting, Lewis Burwell.
Goochland: John Woodson, Josias Payne.
Halifax: Nathaniel Terry, John Lewis.
Hampshire: James Mercer, Abraham Hite.
Hanover: William Macon, Jr., Patrick Henry, Jr.
Henrico: Richard Randolph, Richard Adams.
James City: Robt. Carter Nicholas, Lewis Burwell.
Isle of Wight: Richard Baker, James Bridger.
King and Queen: William Lyne, John Tayloe Corbin.
King George:
King William: Carter Braxton, Thomas Claiborne.
Lancaster: James Ball, Charles Carter.
Loudoun: Francis Peyton, James Hamilton.
Louisa: Richard Anderson, Thomas Johnson.
Lunenburg: Henry Blagrave, John Randolph (Att'y Genl.).
Mecklenburg: Robert Munford, Matthew Marrable.
Middlesex: Gawin Corbin, Philip Ludwell Grymes.
Nansemond: David Meade, Willis Riddick.
New Kent: Burwell Bassett, William Clayton.
Norfolk: John Wilson, Thomas Newton, Jr.
Northampton: Severn Eyre, John Harmanson.
Northumberland: Spencer Mottram Ball, George Ball.
Orange: James Walker, Thomas Barbour.
Pittsylvania: John Donelson, Hugh Innes.
Prince Edward: Thomas Scott, Peter Johnston.
Prince George: Richard Bland, Peter Paythress.
Princess Anne: John Ackiss, Edward H. Moseley, Jr.
Prince William: Foushee Tebbs, Henry Lee.
Richmond: John Woodbridge, Thomas Glasscock.
Southampton: Henry Taylor, Edwin Gray.

Spotsylvania: Benjamin Grymes, Peter Marye. (Late in the session the members for Spotsylvania were unseated, on petition, and a new election ordered.)
Stafford: Thomson Mason, John Alexander.
Surry: Thomas Bailey, Hartwell Cocke.
Sussex: David Mason, John Edmunds.
Warwick: William Harwood, William Digges.
Westmoreland: R. H. Lee, Richard Lee.
York: Dudley Digges, Thomas Nelson, Jr.
College of William and Mary: John Blair.
Jamestown: Champion Travis, Jr.
Norfolk Borough: Joseph Hutchings.
Williamsburg: Peyton Randolph.
Sources: A list of members published in the Va. Gazette of May 11, 1769 (Va. Historical Society Collection), supplemented in a few instances by the reports of elections in the Gazette of November 24, 1768, and succeeding dates, and by the journal of the session in the Congressional Library.

Assembly of 1769-1771

[This Assembly first met on November 7, 1769, and afterwards by successive adjournments and prorogations, on May 21, 1770, and July 11, 1771. On July 20 of the last named year it was prorogued to the fourth Thursday in October, but by proclamation of October 12, this Assembly was dissolved.]

Session of November 7, 1769

Accomack: Thomas Parramore, Southy Simpson.
Albemarle: Thomas Walker, Thomas Jefferson.

Amelia: Thomas Tabb (died during the session); John Winn.
Amherst: William Cabell, Jr., Cornelius Thomas.
Augusta: Gabriel Jones, John Wilson.
Botetourt: William Preston, John Bowyer.
Brunswick: Nathaniel Edwards, Jr., Thomas Stith.
Bedford: John Talbot, Charles Lynch.
Buckingham: Joseph Cabell, Benj. Howard.
Caroline: Edmund Pendleton, Walker Taliaferro.
Charles City, Benjamin Harrison, William Acrill.
Chesterfield: Archibald Cary, Edward Osborne.
Culpeper: Henry Pendleton, Henry Field, Jr.
Cumberland: John Mayo, Alexander Trent.
Charlotte: Isaac Read, Paul Carrington.
Dinwiddie: Bolling Starke, John Banister.
Elizabeth City: James Wallace, Wilson Miles Cary.
Essex: William Roane, James Edmondson.
Fairfax: George Washington, John West.
Fauquier: James Scott, Thomas Marshall.
Frederick: Robert Rutherford, James Wood.
Gloucester: Lewis Burwell, Thomas Whiting.
Goochland: John Woodson, Thomas Mann Randolph.
Halifax: Nathaniel Terry, Walter Coles.
Hampshire: Abram Hite, James Mercer.
Hanover: William Macon, Jr., Patrick Henry, Jr.
Henrico: Richard Randolph, Richard Adams.
James City: Lewis Burwell, Robert Carter Nicholas.
Isle of Wight: Richard Baker, James Bridger.
King George: Charles Carter, William Robinson.
King and Queen: William Lyne, John Tayloe Corbin.
King William: Carter Braxton, Bernard Moore.
Lancaster: Richard Mitchell, Charles Carter.

Loudoun: Francis Peyton, James Hamilton.
Louisa: Thomas Johnson, Richard Anderson.
Lunenburg: Thomas Pettus, Lodowick Farmer.
Middlesex: Philip Ludwell Grymes, Gawin Corbin.
Mecklenburg: Matthew Marrable, Robert Munford.
Nansemond: Lemuel Riddick, Benjamin Baker.
New Kent: William Bassett, William Clayton.
Norfolk: Thomas Newton, Jr., John Wilson.
Northumberland: Spencer M. Ball, Samuel Eskridge.
Northampton: John Burton, Severn Eyre.
Orange: James Walker, Thomas Barbour.
Pittsylvania: John Donelson, Hugh Innes.
Prince Edward: Thomas Scott, Paschall Greenhill.
Prince George: Richard Bland, Peter Poythress.
Princess Anne: Edward Hack Moseley, Jr., John Ackiss.
Prince William: Henry Lee, Foushee Tebbs.
Richmond: Rob't Wormeley Carter, Francis Lightfoot Lee.
Southampton: Edwin Gray, Henry Taylor.
Spotsylvania: Benjamin Grymes, Roger Dixon.
Stafford: John Alexander, Thomson Mason.
Surry: Hartwell Cocke, Thomas Bailey.
Sussex: David Mason, John Edmunds.
Warwick: William Harwood, William Digges.
Westmoreland: Rich'd Henry Lee, Richard Lee.
York: Dudley Digges, Thomas Nelson, Jr.
College of William and Mary: John Blair, Jr.
Jamestown: Champion Travis.
Norfolk: Joseph Hutchings.
Williamsburg: Peyton Randolph.

Sources: A list of members published in the Virginia Gazette, November 10, 1769. Journals of this session in the Virginia State and Congressional Libraries.

Session of May 21, 1770

Accomack: Thomas Parramore, Southey Simpson.
Albemarle: Thomas Walker, Thomas Jefferson.
Amelia: John Winn, Robert Munford (in place of Tabb, deceased).
Augusta: Gabriel Jones, John Wilson.
Amherst: William Cabell, Jr., Cornelius Thomas.
Botetourt: William Preston, John Bowyer.
Brunswick: Nathaniel Edwards, Jr., Thomas Stith.
Bedford: John Talbot, Charles Lynch.
Buckingham: Joseph Cabell, Benjamin Howard.
Caroline: Edmund Pendleton, Walker Taliaferro.
Charles City: Benjamin Harrison, William Acrill.
Chesterfield: Archibald Cary, Edward Osborne.
Culpeper: Henry Pendleton, Henry Field, Jr.
Cumberland: John Mayo, Alexander Trent.
Dinwiddie: Bolling Starke, John Banister.
Elizabeth City: James Wallace, Wilson Miles Cary.
Essex: William Roane, James Edmondson.
Fairfax: George Washington, John West.
Fauquier: James Scott, Thomas Marshall.
Frederick: Robert Rutherford, James Wood.
Gloucester: Lewis Burwell, Thomas Whiting.
Goochland: John Woodson, Thos. Mann Randolph.
Halifax: Nathaniel Terry, Walter Coles.
Hampshire: Abram Hite, James Mercer.
Hanover: William Macon, Jr., Patrick Henry, Jr.
Henrico: Rich'd Randolph, Richard Adams.
James City: Lewis Burwell, Robt. C. Nicholas.
Isle of Wight: Richard Baker, James Bridger.
King George: Charles Carter, William Robinson.
King and Queen: William Lyne, John T. Corbin.

King William: Carter Braxton, Bernard Moore.
Lancaster: Richard Mitchell, Charles Carter.
Loudoun: Francis Peyton, James Hamilton (who about June 13 vacated his seat by accepting the office of coroner).
Louisa: Thomas Johnson, Richard Anderson.
Lunenburg: Thomas Pettus, Lodowick Farmer.
Middlesex: Philip Ludwell Grymes, Gawin Corbin.
Mecklenburg: Matthew Marrable, Robert Munford.
Nansemond: Lemuel Riddick, Benjamin Baker.
New Kent: Burwell Bassett, William Clayton.
Norfolk: Thomas Newton, Jr., John Wilson.
Northumberland: Spencer M. Ball, Samuel Eskridge.
Northampton: John Burton, Severn Eyre.
Orange: James Walker, Thomas Barbour.
Pittsylvania: John Donelson, Hugh Innes.
Prince Edward: Thomas Scott, Paschall Greenhill.
Prince George: Richard Bland, Peter Poythress.
Princess Anne: Edward Hack Moseley, Jr., John Ackiss.
Prince William: Henry Lee, Foushee Tebbs.
Richmond: Robert Wormeley Carter, Francis Lightfoot Lee.
Southampton: Edwin Gray, Henry Taylor.
Spotsylvania: Benjamin Grymes, Roger Dixon.
Stafford: John Alexander, Thomas Mason.
Surry: Hartwell Cocke, Thomas Bailey.
Sussex: David Mason, James Bell (in place of Edmunds, deceased).
Warwick: William Harwood, William Digges.
Westmoreland: R. H. Lee, Richard Lee.
York: Dudley Digges, Thomas Nelson, Jr.
College of William and Mary: John Blair, Jr.

Jamestown: Champion Travis.
Norfolk Borough: Joseph Hutchings.
Williamsburg: Peyton Randolph.
Sources: There is no list of members at this session; but the Journal (Va. State Library) compared with the list of the first session shows the membership to have been as given above.

Session of July 11, 1771

Accomack: Southey Simpson, Thomas Parramore.
Albemarle: Thomas Walker, Thomas Jefferson.
Amelia: John Winn, Robert Munford.
Amherst: William Cabell, Jr., Cornelius Thomas.
Augusta: Gabriel Jones, John Wilson.
Bedford: John Talbot, Charles Lynch.
Brunswick: Thomas Stith. (During the session a new writ was asked for an election in Brunswick to fill the place of Nathaniel Edwards, Jr., deceased; but no records remain to show who was chosen. It was probably John Jones.)
Botetourt: William Preston, John Bowyer.
Buckingham: Joseph Cabell, Benjamin Howard.
Chesterfield: Archibald Cary, Edward Osborne.
Charles City: Benjamin Harrison, William Acrill.
Culpeper: Henry Pendleton, Henry Field, Jr.
Charlotte: Isaac Read. (During the session a new writ was asked for Charlotte to fill the place of Paul Carrington, who had vacated his seat by accepting the office of deputy king's attorney for the county. Who was chosen does not appear from any record, but probably Carrington was reëlected.)
Caroline: Edmund Pendleton, Walker Taliaferro.
Dinwiddie: Bolling Starke, John Banister.

Elizabeth City: Wilson Miles Cary, James Wallace.
Essex: James Edmondson, William Roane.
Fairfax: George Washington, John West.
Frederick: Robert Rutherford, James Wood.
Fauquier: Thomas Marshall, James Scott.
Gloucester: Thomas Whiting, Lewis Burwell.
Goochland: John Woodson, Thos. Mann Randolph.
Halifax: Nathaniel Terry, Walter Coles.
Hampshire: James Mercer, Abraham Hite.
Hanover: William Macon, Jr., Patrick Henry, Jr.
Henrico: Richard Randolph, Richard Adams.
James City: Robert C. Nicholas, Lewis Burwell.
Isle of Wight: Richard Baker, James Bridger.
King and Queen: William Lyne, John T. Corbin.
King William: Carter Braxton, Bernard Moore.
King George: Charles Carter, William Robinson.
Loudoun: Francis Peyton, Josias Clapham (in place of Hamilton, who had accepted the office of coroner).
Lancaster: Richard Mitchell, Charles Carter.
Lunenburg: Thomas Pettus, Lodowick Farmer.
Louisa: Thomas Johnson, Richard Anderson.
Mecklenburg: Robert Munford, Matthew Marrable.
Middlesex: Gawin Corbin, Edmund Berkeley (in place of Grymes, who had accepted the office of sheriff).
Nansemond: Lemuel Riddick, Willis Riddick (in place of Baker, who had accepted the office of coroner).
New Kent: Burwell Bassett, William Clayton.
Norfolk: John Wilson, Thomas Newton, Jr.
Northampton: Severn Eyre, John Burton.
Northumberland: Spencer Mottram Ball, Peter Presley Thornton (in place of Eskridge, deceased).
Orange: James Walker, Thomas Barbour.

Pittsylvania: John Donelson, Hugh Innes.
Princess Anne: Edward Hack Moseley, Jr., John Ackiss.
Prince Edward: Thomas Scott, Paschall Greenhill.
Prince George: Richard Bland, Peter Poythress.
Prince William: Henry Lee, Foushee Tebbs.
Richmond: Robt. W. Carter, F. L. Lee.
Spotsylvania: Roger Dixon, Benjamin Grymes.
Southampton: Edwin Gray, Henry Taylor.
Stafford: John Alexander, Thomson Mason.
Surry: Thomas Bailey, Hartwell Cocke.
Sussex: David Mason, James Bell.
Warwick: William Harwood, William Digges.
Westmoreland: R. H. Lee, Richard Lee.
York: Dudley Digges, Thos. Nelson, Jr.
Jamestown: Champion Travis.
Williamsburg: Peyton Randolph.
College of William and Mary: John Page (Rosewell) (in place of John Blair, Jr., appointed clerk of the Council).
Norfolk Borough: Joseph Hutchings.

Sources: Journal in Va. State Library. Va. Almanacs of 1772 in Congressional Library. It has been found on examination and comparison that the list of members given in this almanac is certainly that of the session of July 11, 1771, and not that of the new House which was elected towards the close of the year 1771.

Assembly of 1772-1774

[This Assembly first met on February 10, 1772, though the writs for election were dated October 31, 1771. It assembled afterwards, by various prorogations, on March 4, 1773, and May 5, 1774.]

Session of February 10, 1772

Accomack: Southey Simpson, James Henry.
Albemarle: John Walker, Thomas Jefferson.
Amelia: John Winn, John Tabb.
Amherst: William Cabell, Jr., Joseph Cabell.
Augusta: John Wilson, Samuel McDowell.
Bedford: John Talbot, Charles Lynch.
Berkeley: Robert Rutherford, Thomas Hite.
Brunswick: John Jones, Thomas Stith.
Botetourt: Andrew Lewis, John Bowyer.
Buckingham: Benjamin Howard (died before session began); Henry Bell, Charles May (in place of Howard, deceased).
Charles City: William Acrill, Benjamin Harrison.
Chesterfield: Archibald Cary, Benjamin Watkins.
Charlotte: Paul Carrington, James Speed.
Cumberland: William Fleming, John Mayo.
Caroline: Edmund Pendleton, Walker Taliaferro.
Culpeper: Henry Pendleton, Henry Field, Jr.
Dinwiddie: Robt. Bolling, John Banister.
Dunmore: Francis Slaughter, Joseph Watson.
Elizabeth City: Henry King, Worlich Westwood.
Essex: James Edmondson, William Roane.
Fairfax: George Washington, John West.
Frederick: Robt. Rutherford, James Wood.
Fauquier: Thomas Marshall, James Scott.
Gloucester: Thomas Whiting, Lewis Burwell.
Goochland: John Woodson, Thos. Mann Randolph.
Halifax: Nathaniel Terry, Isaac Coles.
Hampshire: James Mercer, Alexander White.
Hanover: Patrick Henry, Jr., John Smith.
Henrico: Richard Randolph and Richard Adams were

returned; but their seats were contested and on February 27, 1772, they were declared unduly elected and a new election was ordered. This was held about March 10, and Richard Adams and Samuel Duval were elected.

James City: Robert C. Nicholas, Lewis Burwell.

Isle of Wight: James Bridger, Richard Hardy.

King and Queen: George Brooke, John Tayloe Corbin.

King William: Philip Whitehead Claiborne (died before or during the session), William Aylett, Augustine Moore (in place of Claiborne, deceased).

King George: Joseph Jones, William Fitzhugh.

Loudoun: Thomson Mason, Francis Peyton.

Lancaster: Richard Mitchell, Charles Carter.

Lunenburg: Richard Claiborne. (Thomas Pettus was returned as one of the members; but on contest was unseated and Henry Blagrave was given his place. Later in the session Blagrave was declared unduly elected and a new election ordered to fill his seat. This time Thomas Pettus was duly elected).

Louisa: Richard Anderson, Dabney Carr.

Mecklenburg: Matthew Marrable, Robert Munford.

Middlesex: Edmund Berkeley, James Montague.

Nansemond: Benjamin Baker, Lemuel Riddick.

New Kent: Burwell Bassett, Bartholomew Dandridge.

Norfolk: Thomas Newton, Jr., James Holt.

Northampton: Severn Eyre, John Burton.

Northumberland: Peter Presley Thornton, Spencer Mottram Ball.

Orange: Zachariah Burnley, Thomas Barbour.

Pittsylvania: John Donelson, Hugh Innes.

Princess Anne: Edward H. Moseley, Jr., Christopher Wright.

Prince Edward: Peter Legrand, Paschall Greenhill.
Prince George: Richard Bland, Peter Poythress.
Prince William: Foushee Tebbs, Henry Lee.
Richmond: R. W. Carter, F. L. Lee.
Southampton: Edwin Gray, Henry Taylor.
Spotsylvania: George Stubblefield, Mann Page, Jr.
Stafford: John Alexander, Yelverton Peyton.
Surry: Allen Cocke, Hartwell Cocke.
Sussex: David Mason, Richard Blunt.
Warwick: William Harwood, William Langhorne.
Westmoreland: R. H. Lee, Richard Lee.
York: Dudley Digges, Thomas Nelson, Jr.
Jamestown: Champion Travis.
Williamsburg: Peyton Randolph.
Norfolk Borough: Joseph Hutchings.
The College: John Page (Rosewell).
Sources: Journal in Va. State Library. Va. Almanac 1773, Congressional Library. Virginia Gazette, 1772.

Session of March 4, 1773

Accomack: Southey Simpson, James Henry.
Albemarle: John Walker, Thomas Jefferson.
Amelia: John Winn, John Tabb.
Amherst: William Cabell, Jr., Joseph Cabell.
Augusta· Samuel McDowell, Charles Lewis (in place of Wilson, deceased).
Bedford: John Talbot, Charles Lynch.
Berkeley: Robert Rutherford (?), Thomas Hite.
Brunswick: Thomas Stith, John Jones.
Botetourt: Andrew Lewis, John Bowyer.
Buckingham: Henry Bell, Charles May.
Charles City: Benjamin Harrison, William Acrill.

Chesterfield: Archibald Cary, Benjamin Watkins.
Charlotte: James Speed, Paul Carrington.
Cumberland: William Fleming, John Mayo.
Caroline: Edmund Pendleton, Walker Taliaferro.
Culpeper: Henry Pendleton, Henry Field, Jr.
Dinwiddie: Robert Bolling, John Banister.
Dunmore: Francis Slaughter, Joseph Watson.
Elizabeth City: Henry King, Worlich Westwood.
Essex: James Edmondson, William Roane.
Fairfax: George Washington, John West.
Fincastle: William Christian, Robert Doak.
Frederick: James Wood, Isaac Zane (in place of Rutherford, who had accepted the office of coroner).
Fanquier: James Scott. (At this session a writ was issued for an election in Fanquier to fill the place of Thomas Marshall, who had accepted the office of clerk of the new County of Dunmore.)
Gloucester: Thomas Whiting, Lewis Burwell.
Goochland: John Woodson, T. M. Randolph.
Halifax: Nathaniel Terry, Isaac Coles.
Hampshire: James Mercer, Joseph Nevill (in place of White, who had accepted the office of Deputy King's Attorney).
Hanover: Patrick Henry, Jr., John Syme (in place of Smith, deceased).
Henrico: Richard Adams, Samuel Duval.
James City: R. C. Nicholas, Lewis Burwell.
Isle of Wight: James Bridger, Richard Hardy.
King and Queen: George Brooke, John Tayloe Corbin.
King William: William Aylett, Augustine Moore.
King George: Joseph Jones, William Fitzhugh.
Loudoun: Francis Peyton, Thomson Mason.

Lancaster: Richard Mitchell, Charles Carter.
Lunenburg: Richard Claiborne, Thomas Pettus.
Louisa: Richard Anderson, Dabney Carr.
Mecklenburg: Matthew Marrable, Robert Munford.
Middlesex: Edmund Berkeley, James Montague.
Nansemond: Benjamin Baker, Lemuel Riddick.
New Kent: Burwell Bassett, Bartholomew Dandridge.
Norfolk: Thomas Newton, Jr., James Holt.
Northampton: John Burton, John Bowdoin (in place of Eyre, deceased).
Northumberland: Peter P. Thornton, Rodham Kenner (in place of Ball, who had accepted the office of sheriff).
Orange: Zachariah Burnley, Thomas Barbour.
Pittsylvania: John Donelson, Hugh Innes.
Prince George: Richard Bland, Peter Poythress.
Princess Anne: Edward H. Moseley, Jr., Christopher Wright.
Prince Edward: Peter Legrand, Paschall Greenhill.
Prince William: Henry Lee, Foushee Tebbs.
Richmond: R. W. Carter, F. L. Lee.
Southampton: Edwin Gray, Henry Taylor.
Spotsylvania: George Stubblefield, Mann Page, Jr.
Stafford: John Alexander, Charles Carter (in place of Peyton, who had accepted the office of tobacco inspector).
Surry: Allen Cocke, Nicholas Faulcon, Jr. (in place of Hartwell Cocke, deceased).
Sussex: David Mason, Richard Blunt.
Warwick: William Harwood, William Langhorne.
Westmoreland: R. H. Lee, Richard Lee.
York: Dudley Digges, Thomas Nelson, Jr.
Jamestown: Champion Travis.
Williamsburg: Peyton Randolph.

Norfolk Borough: Joseph Hutchings.
The College: John Page (Burwell).

This session was so short, only extending from March 4 to 15, that it is not probable that many of the new members elected under writs to fill vacancies, actually sat. Probably some of the elections were held after the session closed. The members, however, so elected were present next year.

Sources: The journal in Va. State Library, compared with the Journal of 1774.

Session of May 5, 1774

Accomack: Southey Simpson, James Henry.
Albemarle: Thomas Jefferson, John Walker.
Amelia: John Tabb, John Winn.
Amherst: William Cabell, Jr., Joseph Cabell.
Augusta: Samuel McDowell, Charles Lewis.
Bedford: John Talbot, Charles Lynch.
Berkeley: Robert Rutherford (?), Thomas Hite.
Brunswick: Thomas Stith, ——— ——— (in place of John Jones, who had accepted the office of sheriff).
Botetourt: Andrew Lewis, John Bowyer.
Buckingham: Henry Bell, Charles May.
Charles City: Benjamin Harrison, William Acrill.
Chesterfield: Archibald Cary, Benjamin Watkins.
Charlotte: Paul Carrington, James Speed.
Cumberland: John Fleming, John Mayo.
Caroline: Edmund Pendleton, James Taylor (in place of Walker Taliaferro, who had accepted the office of sheriff).
Culpeper: Henry Pendleton, Henry Field, Jr.
Dinwiddie: Robert Bolling, John Banister.
Dunmore: Francis Slaughter, ——— ——— (in place of Joseph Watson, deceased).

Elizabeth City: Worlich Westwood, Henry King.
Essex: James Edmondson, William Roane.
Fairfax: George Washington, John West.
Fincastle: William Christian, Robert Doak (who on May 9 was unseated, because at the time of his election he held the office of deputy surveyor).
Frederic: James Wood, Isaac Zane.
Fauquier: James Scott.
Gloucester: Thomas Whiting, Lewis Burwell.
Goochland: T. M. Randolph, John Woodson.
Halifax: Nathaniel Terry, Isaac Coles.
Hampshire: James Mercer, Joseph Nevill.
Hanover: Patrick Henry, John Syme.
Henrico: Samuel Duval, Richard Adams.
Isle of Wight: Richard Hardy, James Bridger.
James City: Lewis Burwell, R. C. Nicholas.
King and Queen: George Brooke, J. T. Corbin.
King William: William Aylett, Augustine Moore.
King George: William Fitzhugh, Joseph Jones.
Loudoun: Francis Peyton, Thomson Mason.
Lancaster: Richard Mitchell, Charles Carter.
Lunenburg: Richard Claiborne, Thomas Pettus.
Louisa: Richard Anderson, Thomas Johnson (in place of Dabney Carr, deceased).
Mecklenburg: Robert Munford, Matthew Marrable.
Middlesex: Edmund Berkeley, James Montague.
Nansemond: Benjamin Baker, Lemuel Riddick.
New Kent: Burwell Bassett, Bartholomew Dandridge.
Norfolk: Thomas Newton, Jr., James Holt.
Northampton: John Burton, John Bowdoin.
Northumberland: Rodham Kenner, Peter P. Thornton.
Orange: Thos. Barbour, ———— ———— (in place of Burnley, who had accepted the office of sheriff).

Pittsylvania: Hugh Innes, John Donelson.
Prince George: Richard Bland, Peter Poythress.
Prince Edward: Peter Le Grand, Paschall Greenhill.
Prince William: Henry Lee, —— —— (in place of Tebbs, who had accepted the office of tobacco inspector.)
Princess Anne: E. H. Moseley, Jr., Christopher Wright.
Richmond: R. W. Carter, F. L. Lee.
Southampton: Edwin Gray, Henry Taylor.
Spotsylvania: George Stubblefield, Mann Page, Jr.
Stafford: John Alexander, Charles Carter.
Surry: Allen Cocke, Nicholas Faulcon, Jr.
Sussex: David Mason, —— —— (in place of Blunt, deceased).
Warwick: William Harwood, William Langhorne.
Westmoreland: R. H. Lee, Richard Lee.
York: Dudley Digges, Thomas Nelson, Jr.
Jamestown: Champion Travis.
Williamsburg: Peyton Randolph.
Norfolk Borough: Joseph Hutchings.
The College: Attorney General John Randolph (in place of Page, appointed to the Council).

Sources: Journal in Va. State Library. As the new Assembly was summoned to meet on August 11, 1774, an election was held prior to that time. It is probable that some of the vacancies of this session were not filled. The members of this House reassembled on August 1st, 1774, as members of the first Convention held in Virginia.

Assembly of 1775-1776

[This Assembly was summoned to meet on August 11, 1774; but its assembling was delayed by various prorogations and it did not actually convene until June 1, 1775.

On June 24 it adjourned until October 12th when thirty-seven members were present; but as there was no quorum no business was transacted, and there was another adjournment to the first Monday in March succeeding. On March 7, 1776, thirty-two members met, but there was again no quorum and they adjourned to the first Monday in May next. On that day (May 6th), the journal records that "several members met, but did neither proceed to business or adjourn." And below these words the clerk has written in heavy lettering, "Finis," and finally finished the record of the last of the Virginia Colonial Legislatures with an elaborate cork-screw like tail piece. Therefore, there was really only one session of this Assembly.]

Session of June 1, 1775

Accomack: Southey Simpson, Isaac Smith.
Albemarle: Thomas Jefferson, John Walker.
Amelia: John Tabb, John Winn.
Amherst: William Cabell, Jr., Joseph Cabell.
Augusta: Charles Lewis (killed in battle before the House met), Samuel McDowell, George Matthews (in place of Lewis, deceased).
Bedford: John Talbot, Charles Lynch.
Berkeley: Robert Rutherford, John Hite.
Brunswick: Frederick Maclin, Henry Tazewell.
Botetourt: Andrew Lewis, John Bowyer.
Buckingham: John Nicholas, Anthony Winston.
Charles City: Benjamin Harrison, William Acrill.
Chesterfield: Archibald Cary, Benjamin Watkins.
Charlotte: Paul Carrington, James Speed.
Culpeper: Henry Pendleton, Henry Field, Jr.
Cumberland: William Fleming, John Mayo.

Dinwiddie: John Banister, Robert Bolling (who died before the beginning of the session); —— —— (in place of Bolling, deceased).
Dunmore: Francis Slaughter, Abraham Bird.
Elizabeth City: Henry King, Worlich Westwood.
Essex: James Edmondson, Meriwether Smith.
Fairfax: George Washington, Charles Broadwater.
Fauquier: Thomas Marshall, James Scott.
Frederick: James Wood, Isaac Zane.
Fincastle: William Christian, Stephen Trigg.
Gloucester: Thomas Whiting, Lewis Burwell.
Goochland: John Woodson, Thomas M. Randolph.
Halifax: Nathaniel Terry, Micajah Watkins.
Hampshire: James Mercer, Joseph Neville.
Hanover: Patrick Henry, Jr., John Syme.
Henrico: Richard Adams, Samuel Du Val.
Isle of Wight: John S. Wills, John Day.
James City: Robert C. Nicholas, William Norvell.
King George: Joseph Jones, William Fitzhugh.
King and Queen: George Brooke, George Lyne.
King William: Carter Braxton, William Aylett.
Lancaster: James Selden, Charles Carter.
Loudoun: Francis Peyton, Josias Clapham.
Louisa: Thomas Johnson, Thomas Walker.
Lunenburg: Richard Claiborne, Thomas Pettus.
Middlesex: Edmund Berkeley, James Montague.
Mecklenburg: Robert Munford, Matthew Marrable.
Nansemond: Lemuel Riddick, Willis Riddick.
New Kent: Burwell Bassett, Bartholomew Dandridge.
Norfolk: Thos. Newton, Jr., James Holt.
Northampton: Adiel Milby (died before beginning of session), John Bowdoin, —— —— (in place of Milby, deceased).

Northumberland: Peter P. Thornton, Rodham Kenner.
Orange: Thomas Barbour, James Taylor.
Pittsylvania: Peter Perkins, Benjamin Lankford.
Prince Edward: Peter Legrand, William Bibb.
Prince George: Richard Bland, Peter Poythress.
Princess Anne: William Robinson, Christopher Wright.
Prince William: Henry Lee, Thomas Blackburn.
Richmond: Robt. W. Carter, F. L. Lee.
Southampton: Edwin Gray, Henry Taylor.
Spotsylvania: George Stubblefield, Mann Page, Jr.
Stafford: John Alexander (died before beginning of session), Charles Carter, —— —— (in place of Alexander, deceased).
Surry: Allen Cocke, Nicholas Faulcon, Jr.
Sussex: David Mason, Michael Blow.
Warwick: William Harwood, William Langhorne.
Westmoreland: R. H. Lee, Richard Lee.
York: Dudley Digges, Thomas Nelson, Jr.
College of William and Mary: Mr. Attorney General (John Randolph).
Jamestown: Champion Travis.
Norfolk Borough: Joseph Hutchings.
Williamsburg: Peyton Randolph.
Sources: List of members elected, in Va. Gazette, Va. State Library, and Almanacs of 1775 and 1776, Va. Hist. Society. Journals, Va. State Library. It is not probable that any of the vacancies indicated were ever filled.

CONVENTIONS OF 1775 AND 1776

Convention assembled March 20th, 1775

Williamsburg: Peyton Randolph, President.
Accomack: Isaac Smith.
Albemarle: Thomas Jefferson, John Walker.
Amelia: John Tabb, John Winn.
Amherst: William Cabell, Jr., Joseph Cabell.
Augusta: Thomas Lewis, Samuel McDowell.
West Augusta: John Nevill, John Harvie.
Bedford: John Talbot, Charles Lynch.
Botetourt: Andrew Lewis, John Bowyer.
Brunswick: Frederick Maclin, Henry Tazewell.
Buckingham: John Nicholas, Anthony Winston.
Berkeley: Robert Rutherford, Adam Stephen.
Caroline: Edmund Pendleton, James Taylor.
Charles City: Benjamin Harrison, William Acrill.
Charlotte: Paul Carrington, Isaac Read.
Chesterfield: Archibald Cary, Benjamin Watkins.
Culpeper: Henry Pendleton, Henry Field, Jr.
Cumberland: William Fleming, John Mayo.
Dinwiddie: John Banister, William Watkins.
Dunmore: Jonathan Clarke, Peter Muhlenburg.
Elizabeth City: Henry King, Worlich Westwood.
Essex: James Edmondson, Meriwether Smith.
Fairfax: George Washington, Charles Broadwater.
Fauquier: Thomas Marshall, James Scott.
Frederick: Isaac Zane, Charles Mynn Thruston.

Fincastle: William Christian.
Gloucester: Thomas Whiting, Lewis Burwell.
Goochland: John Woodson, Thomas Mann Randolph.
Halifax: Nathaniel Terry, Micajah Watkins.
Hampshire: James Mercer.
Hanover: Patrick Henry, Jr., John Syme.
Henrico: Richard Adams, Samuel Duval.
James City: Robert C. Nicholas, William Norvell.
Isle of Wight: John S. Wills, Josiah Parker.
King George: Joseph Jones, William Fitzhugh.
King and Queen: George Brooke, George Lyne.
King William: Carter Braxton, William Aylett.
Lancaster: James Selden, Charles Carter.
Loudoun: Francis Peyton, Josiah Clapham.
Louisa: Thomas Johnson, Thomas Walker.
Lunenburg: Richard Claiborne, David Garland.
Middlesex: Edmund Berkeley.
Mecklenburg: Robert Burton, Bennett Goode.
Nansemond: Lemuel Riddick, Willis Riddick.
New Kent: Burwell Bassett, Bartholomew Dandridge.
Norfolk County: Thomas Newton, Jr., James Holt.
Northampton: John Burton.
Northumberland: Rodham Kenner, Thomas Jones.
Orange: Thomas Barbour, James Taylor.
Pittsylvania: Peter Perkins, Benjamin Lankford.
Prince Edward: Robert Lawson, John Nash.
Prince George: Richard Bland, Peter Poythress.
Princess Anne: William Robinson, Christopher Wright.
Prince William: Henry Lee, Thomas Blackburn.
Richmond: Robert Wormeley Carter, Francis Lightfoot Lee.
Southampton: Edwin Gray, Henry Taylor.

Spotsylvania: George Stubblefield, Mann Page, Jr.
Stafford: John Alexander, Charles Carter.
Surry: Allen Cocke, Nicholas Faulcon, Jr.
Sussex: David Mason, Henry Gee.
Warwick: William Langhorne.
Westmoreland: Richard Henry Lee, Richard Lee.
York: Dudley Digges, Thomas Nelson, Jr.
Jamestown: Champion Travis.
Norfolk Borough: Joseph Hutchings.
Source: Printed Journal of the Convention.

Convention assembled July 17th, 1775

Williamsburg: Peyton Randolph, President. (Retired from office August 17, on account of bad health.)

Albemarle: John Walker, Charles Lewis (sat until August 9 as alternate for Thomas Jefferson); Thomas Jefferson (from August 9).

Amelia: John Tabb, John Winn.

Amherst: William Cabell, Jr., Joseph Cabell.

Augusta: Samuel McDowell, Thomas Lewis, John Harvie, George Roots.

Bedford: John Talbot, Charles Lynch.

Botetourt: John Bowyer.

Brunswick: Frederick Maclin, Henry Tazewell.

Buckingham: John Nicholas, Robert Bolling.

Berkeley: Robert Rutherford, Adam Stephen.

Caroline: James Taylor, William Woodford (sat until August 9 as alternate for Edmund Pendleton); Edmund Pendleton from August 9.

Charles City: William Arcill, Benjamin Harrison, Jr. (sat until August 9 as alternate for Benjamin Harrison); Benjamin Harrison from August 9.

Culpeper: Henry Field, Jr., Henry Pendleton.
Cumberland: William Fleming, John Mayo.
Dinwiddie: John Bannister, John Ruffin.
Dunmore: Jonathan Clarke.
Elizabeth City: Henry King, Worlich Westwood.
Essex: Meriwether Smith.
Fairfax: Charles Broadwater, George Mason.
Fauquier: Thomas Marshall, James Scott.
Frederick: Isaac Zane, Charles Mynn Thruston.
Fincastle: William Christian, Stephen Trigg.
Gloucester: Lewis Burwell.
Goochland: John Woodson, Thomas Mann Randolph.
Halifax: Micajah Watkins.
Hampshire: James Mercer.
Hanover: John Syme, Garland Anderson (sat until August 9 as alternate for Patrick Henry); Patrick Henry from August 9.
Henrico: Richard Adams, Richard Randolph.
James City: Robert C. Nicholas (elected President, August 7); William Norvell.
Isle of Wight: John S. Wills, Josiah Parker.
King George: Joseph Jones, William Fitzhugh.
King and Queen: George Brooke, George Lyne.
King William: Carter Braxton, William Aylett.
Lancaster: James Selden, Charles Carter.
Loudoun: Francis Peyton, Josiah Clapham.
Louisa: Thomas Johnson, Thomas Walker.
Lunenburg: David Garland, Thomas Tabb.
Middlesex: James Montague.
Mecklenburg: Robert Burton, Bennett Goode.
Nansemond: Andrew Meade, James Murdaugh.
New Kent: Burwell Bassett, Bartholomew Dandridge.

Norfolk County: Thomas Newton, James Holt.
Northumberland: Peter Presley Thornton, Rodham Kenner.
Orange: Thomas Barbour.
Prince Edward: Robert Lawson, William Bibb.
Prince George: Richard Bland, Peter Poythress.
Princess Anne: William Robinson.
Prince William: Henry Lee, Thomas Blackburn.
Richmond: Robert Wormeley Carter.
Southampton: Edwin Gray.
Spotsylvania: George Stubblefield, Mann Page, Jr.
Stafford: Charles Carter, Thomas Ludwell Lee.
Surry: Allen Cocke, Nicholas Faulcon.
Sussex: David Mason, Henry Gee.
Warwick: William Langhorne.
Westmoreland: Richard Lee, John A. Washington (sat as alternate for R. H. Lee until August 11); R. H. Lee from August 11.
York: Dudley Digges, Thomas Nelson.
Jamestown: Champion Travis.
Norfolk Borough: Joseph Hutchings.
Source: Printed Journal of the Convention.

Convention assembled December 1st, 1775

Albemarle: John Walker, Charles Lewis.
Amelia: John Tabb, John Winn.
Amherst: William Cabell, Jr., Joseph Cabell.
Augusta: Samuel McDowell, Thomas Lewis.
Bedford: John Talbot.
Botetourt: Andrew Lewis, John Bowyer.
Brunswick: Frederick Maclin, Henry Tazewell.
Buckingham: Thomas Pattesson.

Berkeley: Robert Rutherford, William Drew.
Caroline: Edmund Pendleton, President; James Taylor.
Charles City: William Acrill, Benjamin Harrison.
Charlotte: Paul Carrington, Isaac Read.
Chesterfield: Archibald Cary, Benjamin Watkins.
Culpeper: Henry Pendleton, Henry Field, Jr.
Cumberland: William Fleming, John Mayo.
Dinwiddie: John Banister, John Ruffin.
Dunmore: Jonathan Clark, Peter Muhlenburg.
Elizabeth City: Henry King, Worlich Westwood.
Essex: James Edmondson, Meriwether Smith.
Fairfax: Charles Broadwater.
Fanquier: James Scott.
Frederick: Rev. Charles M. Thruston.
Fincastle: George Rootes.
Gloucester: Thomas Whiting.
Goochland: John Woodson, Thomas M. Randolph.
Halifax: Nathaniel Terry, Micajah Watkins.
Hampshire: James Mercer, Joseph Neville.
Hanover: John Syme, Samuel Meredith.
Henrico: Richard Adams, Richard Randolph.
James City: Robert C. Nicholas, William Norvell.
Isle of Wight: John S. Wills, Josiah Parker.
King George: Joseph Jones, William Fitzhugh.
King and Queen: George Brooke.
King William: Carter Braxton, William Aylett.
Lancaster: James Selden, Charles Carter.
Loudoun: Francis Peyton, Josiah Clapham.
Louisa: Thomas Johnson, Thomas Walker.
Lunenburg: David Garland, Thomas Tabb.
Middlesex: Edmund Berkeley, James Montague.
Mecklenburg: Robert Burton, Bennet Goode.

Nansemond: James Murdaugh, Andrew Meade.
New Kent: Burwell Bassett, Bartholomew Dandridge.
Norfolk: Thomas Newton, James Holt.
Northampton: Michael Christian.
Northumberland: Peter P. Thornton, Rodham Kenner.
Orange: Thomas Barbour, James Taylor.
Pittsylvania: Peter Perkins, Benjamin Lankford.
Prince Edward: Robert Lawson, William Bibb.
Prince George: Richard Bland, Peter Poythress.
Princess Anne: Christopher Wright.
Prince William: Henry Lee, Thomas Blackburn.
Richmond County: Robert W. Carter, Walter Jones.
Southampton: Edwin Gray, Henry Taylor.
Spotsylvania: George Stubblefield, Mann Page.
Stafford: Charles Carter, Jr., Thomas Ludwell Lee.
Surry: Allen Cocke, Nicholas Faulcon.
Sussex: David Mason, Henry Gee.
Warwick: William Harwood, William Langhorne.
Westmoreland: Richard Lee, John A. Washington.
York: Dudley Digges, Hugh Nelson.
Jamestown: Champion Travis.
Williamsburg: Joseph Prentis.
Source: Printed Journal of the Convention.

Convention assembled May 6th, 1776

Accomac: Southey Simpson, Isaac Smith.
Albemarle: Charles Lewis, George Gilmer (alternate for Thomas Jefferson).
Amelia: John Tabb, John Winn.
Augusta: Thomas Lewis, Samuel McDowell.
West Augusta: Charles Simms, John Harvie.
Amherst: William Cabell, Gabriel Penn.

Bedford: John Talbot, Charles Lynch.
Botetourt: John Bowyer, Patrick Lockhart.
Brunswick: Frederick Maclin, Henry Tazewell.
Buckingham: Charles Pattesson, John Cabell.
Berkeley: Robert Rutherford, William Drew.
Caroline: Edmund Pendleton, President; James Taylor.
Charles City: William Acrill, Samuel Harwood (alternate for Benjamin Harrison).
Charlotte: Paul Carrington, Thomas Read.
Chesterfield: Archibald Cary, Benjamin Watkins.
Culpeper: Henry Field, French Strother.
Cumberland: John Mayo, William Fleming.
Dinwiddie: John Banister, Bolling Starke.
Dunmore: Abraham Bird, John Tipton.
Elizabeth City: Wilson Miles Cary, Henry King.
Essex: Meriwether Smith, James Edmondson.
Fairfax: John West, Jr., George Mason.
Fauquier: Martin Pickett, James Scott.
Frederick: James Wood, Isaac Zane.
Fincastle: Arthur Campbell, William Russell.
Gloucester: Thomas Whiting, Lewis Burwell.
Goochland: John Woodson, Thomas M. Randolph.
Halifax: Nathaniel Terry, Micajah Watkins.
Hampshire: James Mercer, Abraham Hite.
Hanover: Patrick Henry, John Syme.
Henrico: Nathaniel Wilkinson, Richard Adams
James City: Robert C. Nicholas, William Norvell.
Isle of Wight: John S. Wills, Charles Fulgham.
King George: Joseph Jones, William Fitzhugh.
King and Queen: George Brooke, William Lyne.
King William: William Aylett, Richard Squire Taylor.
Lancaster: James Selden, James Gordon.

Loudoun: Francis Peyton, Josias Clapham.
Louisa: George Meriwether, Thomas Johnson.
Lunenburg: David Garland, Lodowick Farmer.
Middlesex: Edmund Berkeley, James Montague.
Mecklenburg: Joseph Speed, Bennett Goode.
Nansemond: Willis Riddick, William Cowper.
New Kent: William Clayton, Bartholomew Dandridge.
Norfolk: James Holt, Thomas Newton.
Northumberland: Rodham Kenner, John Cralle.
Northampton: Nathaniel L. Savage, George Savage.
Orange: James Madison, William Moore.
Pittsylvania: Benjamin Lankford, Robert Williams.
Prince Edward: William Watts, William Booker.
Prince George: Richard Bland, Peter Poythress.
Princess Anne: William Robinson, John Thoroughgood.
Prince William: Cuthbert Bullitt, Henry Lee.
Richmond: Hudson Muse, Charles McCarty.
Southampton: Edwin Gray, Henry Taylor.
Spottsylvania: Mann Page, George Thornton.
Stafford: Thomas Ludwell Lee, William Brent.
Surry: Allen Cocke, Nicholas Faulcon.
Sussex: David Mason, Henry Gee.
Warwick: William Harwood, Richard Cary.
Westmoreland: Richard Lee, Richard Henry Lee, John A. Washington (alternate).
York: Dudley Digges, Thomas Nelson, Jr.; William Digges (alternate).
Jamestown: Champion Travis.
Williamsburg: Edmund Randolph (alternate for George Wythe).
Norfolk Borough: William Roscoe Wilson Curle.
College of William and Mary: John Blair.
Source: Printed Journal of the Convention.

ADDENDA

At the session of January 6, 1630, John Sidney and Henry Seawell were also members for Lower Norfolk.

At the session of January 12, 1641, John Sidney was also member for Lower Norfolk.

At the session of October 12, 1648, Cornelius Loyd was also member for Lower Norfolk.

At the session of October 12, 1649, Robert Eyres was also member for Lower Norfolk.

On November 15, 1650, the court of Lower Norfolk County ordered payments to John Hill and John Sidney, Burgesses.

At the session of March, 1651, John Hill and John Sidney were members instead of Thomas Lambert and John Martin.

At the session of April 26, 1652, John Martin was also member for Lower Norfolk.

AUTHORITY. — The records of Lower Norfolk copied by Mr. Edward Wilson James.

On p. 180 for Henry Claiborne (burgess for Culpeper) read Henry Pendleton.

On p. 181 for Paythress read Poythress.

On pp. 103 and 112 and 115 for Reddick read Riddick.

On p. 108 for Goockland read Goochland.

On p. 131 for Edwards read Edmunds.

On p. 179 insert Prince Edward before Peter Legrand and Nathaniel Venable, and after Orange insert J. Walker and Z. Burnley.

On. p. 185 insert Charlotte: Isaac Read, Paul Carrington.

INDEX.

NOTE. It should be remembered that no matter how many times a name may appear upon a page of the text, there is only one reference to such name and page in the Index; therefore, readers in searching for a name should examine the entire page referred to.
Variations in forms of surnames are indicated in the Index, the modern form appearing first. Variations found in the records believed to be misspellings or clerical errors are given in parentheses.

A.

Abrahall, Abrell: 71, 75.
Accomac, 56, 57, 58.
Accomac, Accomack County: 42, 59, 61, 78, 79, 84, 86, 88, 91, 94, 100, 102, 103, 104, 105, 108, 110, 111, 114, 115, 117, 119, 120, 122, 124, 126, 128, 130, 132, 134, 135, 138, 140, 142, 144, 146, 150, 152, 154, 156, 158, 160, 162, 164, 166, 168, 171, 173, 176, 178, 180, 182, 185, 187, 190, 192, 195, 198, 201, 207.
Ackiss: 181, 184, 186, 189.
Acrill: 108, 174, 176, 178, 180, 183, 185, 187, 190, 192, 195, 198, 201, 203, 206, 208.
Adams: 53, 127, 129, 131, 133, 135, 137, 139, 141, 143, 145, 147, 149, 151, 155, 157, 161, 163, 165, 167, 170, 181, 183, 185, 188, 190, 191, 193, 196, 199, 202, 204, 206, 208.

Albemarle County: 117, 119, 120, 122, 124, 126, 128, 132, 134, 135, 138, 140, 142, 144, 146, 150, 154, 156, 158, 160, 162, 164, 166, 168, 171, 173, 176, 178, 180, 185, 187, 190, 192, 195, 198, 201, 203, 205, 207.
Albemarle, Earl of: 19.
Alexander: 126, 128, 130, 132, 134, 136, 138, 173, 175, 177, 179, 184, 186, 189, 192, 194, 197, 200, 203.
Allen: 51, 54, 83, 85, 86, 111, 122, 124, 126, 128, 140, 142, 144, 146, 149, 150, 151, 152.
Allerton: 42, 79, 80, 81, 82, 91, 98, 100.
Allonby: 86.
Ambler: 9, 152, 154, 173, 175, 177, 179.
Amherst County: 154, 156, 158, 160, 162, 164, 166, 168, 171, 174, 176, 178, 180, 183,

185, 187, 192, 195, 198, 201, 205, 207.
Amherst, Governor: 20.
Amelia County: 108, 110, 111, 112, 116, 117, 119, 120, 122, 124, 126, 128, 130, 132, 134, 135, 138, 140, 142, 144, 146, 150, 152, 154, 156, 158, 160, 162, 164, 166, 171, 178, 180, 183, 185, 187, 190, 192, 195, 198, 201, 203, 205, 207.
Anderson: 85, 86, 130–139, 141, 143, 145, 147, 149, 151, 172, 175, 177, 179, 181, 184, 186, 188, 194, 196, 204.
Andrews: 78, 114.
Andros: 17.
Annapolis, Md.: 18.
Antigua: 43.
Appleton: 81.
Applewhaite, Applewhite, Applethwaite: 84, 86, 94, 105, 106.
Archer: 21, 27.
Archer's Hope: 54, 55, 56.
Archer's Hope and Glebe Land: 58.
Archer's Hope and Martin's Hundred, Plantations between: 54.
Argall: 14, 28.
Argall's Gift: 52.
"Arlington:" 41, 43, 46.
Arrowhattocks, Neck of Land, and Curles: 56, 57, 58.
Armistead: 42, 84, 88, 91, 94, 98, 100, 103, 106, 155, 157, 159, 161.
Arundel: 59.
Ashton: 72, 76, 96, 101.
Aston: 55, 56, 57, 58, 61, 63, Attorney General, Office of: 8.
Attorney Generals, List of: 25.
Atchison: 150, 152, 154.
Atkins: 56.
Aubrey: 86.
Auditor General, Office of: 7.
Auditor Generals, List of: 22.
Augusta County: 122, 124, 126, 128, 130, 132, 134, 135, 137, 138, 140, 142, 144, 146, 152, 154, 156, 158, 160, 164, 166, 168, 171, 174, 178, 180, 183, 185, 187, 190, 192, 195, 198, 201, 203, 205, 207.
Aylett: 105, 106, 109, 110, 111, 112, 191, 193, 196, 199, 202, 204, 206, 208.

B.

Bacon: 17, 22, 37, 40, 72, 74, 75, 81.
Bacon's Rebellion: 81.
Bagnall: 66, 71.

Bagwell: 54, 56, 58.
Bahamas: 50.
Baker: 79, 80, 81, 88, 105, 106, 115, 117, 118, 120, 121, 178, 181, 183, 184, 185, 186, 188, 194, 196.
Bailey: 162, 164, 166, 168, 170, 175, 177, 179, 182, 186, 189.
Baldridge: 68.
Baldry: 75.
Ball: 66, 79, 80, 81, 82, 83, 84, 86, 87, 89, 92, 94, 95, 96, 97, 98, 99, 100, 101, 102, 103, 105, 106, 108, 109, 110, 112, 123, 125, 127, 129, 130, 131, 132, 133, 134, 135, 136, 137, 138, 139, 141, 143, 145, 147, 149, 151, 156, 157, 159, 161, 163, 165, 167, 170, 175, 177, 179, 181, 184, 186, 188, 191, 194.
Ballard: 39, 57, 78, 84, 88, 91, 95, 175, 177, 179.
Baltimore, Md.: 49.
"Baltrope:" 40.
Banister: 172, 174, 176, 178, 183, 185, 187, 193, 195, 199, 201, 204, 206, 208.
Barber: 77, 78, 85, 86, 95, 100, 102, 103, 105, 106.
Barbour: 155, 157, 159, 160, 162, 164, 166, 169, 181, 184, 186, 188, 191, 194, 196, 200, 202, 205, 207.

Barham: 55.
Barker: 65.
"Barn Elms:" 45.
Barnes: 56.
Barnett (Bernard): 57, 61.
Barradall (Attorney Gen'l): 25, 111, 112, 115, 117.
Barret, Barrett: 64, 66, 67, 115, 116, 118, 120, 121, 123, 125, 141, 143, 145.
Barrington: 55.
Basse: 31, 53, 54.
Bassett: 44, 88, 90, 93, 94, 115, 117, 161, 163, 165, 167, 170, 175, 177, 179, 181, 184, 186, 188, 191, 194, 196, 199, 202, 204, 207.
Bates: 128, 130, 132, 134, 136, 138, 141, 143, 145.
Battaile: 88, 91, 92.
Batte, Batt: 71, 74, 85.
Baylor: 88, 102, 114, 116, 118, 119, 120, 122, 124, 140, 142, 144, 146, 150, 152, 155, 156, 158, 160, 162, 164, 166, 168.
Baylis: 156, 158, 160, 162, 164, 166, 168, 170.
Bayly: 62, 88, 91.
Baynham: 72.
Baugh: 61, 64.
Beale: 38.
Beazley: 72.
Bedford County: 132, 134, 135, 136, 140, 142, 144, 146, 150, 152, 154, 156, 158, 160,

162, 164, 166, 168, 171, 174,
176, 178, 180, 183, 185, 187,
190, 192, 195, 198, 201, 203,
205, 208.
"Belfield:" 36, 43, 46.
Bell: 141, 143, 145, 152, 186,
189, 190, 192, 195.
"Belvidere:" 41.
"Belvoir:" 47.
Benn: 90.
Bennett: 15, 34, 54, 57, 64,
65.
Bentley: 54.
Berkeley: 15, 16, 30, 45, 78,
109, 110, 112, 188, 191, 192,
194, 196, 199, 202, 206, 209.
Berkeley County: 190, 195,
198, 203, 208.
Berkeley Hundred: 29, 30.
Bermuda: 28, 29.
Bernard (see Barnett): 35, 62,
63, 64, 65.
Beverley: 22, 24, 26, 40, 48,
51, 81, 85, 94, 97, 100, 103,
109, 110, 111, 112, 113, 114,
116, 118, 119, 121, 123, 124.
Bibb: 200, 205, 207.
Bigge: 53.
Bird: 96, 100, 199, 208.
Bishop: 64, 68, 70.
Blackburn: 118, 120, 121, 200,
202, 205, 207.
Blacke: 74.
Blackwell: 113, 115, 117, 118,
120, 121, 123, 125, 127, 129,
131, 133, 135, 137, 139.
Blacky: 73.
Blagrave: 151, 155, 157, 159,
163, 165, 167, 169, 172, 175,
177, 179, 181, 191.
Blair: 19, 20, 22, 42, 47, 102,
103, 105, 106, 107, 109, 111,
112, 173, 175, 177, 182, 184,
186, 189, 209.
Blake: 72, 79.
Bland: 20, 39, 51, 60, 75, 93,
94, 98, 115, 117, 120, 121,
123, 125, 127, 129, 131, 133,
135, 137, 139, 141, 143, 145,
147, 149, 156, 158, 160, 161,
163, 165, 168, 170, 173, 175,
177, 179, 181, 184, 186, 189,
192, 194, 197, 200, 202, 205,
207.
"Blandfield:" 48.
Blaney: 31, 53.
Blewitt: 29.
Blow: 200.
Blunt: 192, 194, 197.
Bohun: 30.
Bolling: 96, 98, 100, 101, 105,
106, 107, 114, 116, 118, 119,
121, 123, 124, 126, 130, 132,
134, 136, 138, 140, 141, 142,
143, 144, 145, 147, 149, 151,
154, 155, 156, 157, 158, 159,
160, 162, 164, 166, 167, 168,
169, 172, 173, 174, 175, 176,

177, 178, 179, 180, 190, 193, 195, 199, 203.
Bond: 71, 72, 73, 74, 75.
Booker: 108, 110, 111, 114, 116, 117, 120, 140, 142, 144, 146, 150, 152, 167, 169, 172, 174, 176, 178, 209.
Booth: 70, 71.
Borne, Bourue: 74.
Borough: 90.
Botetourt County: 183, 185, 187, 189, 192, 195, 198, 203, 205, 208.
Botetourt, Lord: 20, 180.
Boucher: 70.
Boughan, Baughan: 92, 95, 96, 98.
Boush: 98, 99, 100, 101, 102, 103, 105, 106, 109, 110, 112, 115, 117, 118, 120, 121, 127, 129, 131.
Bowden: 25.
Bowdoin: 109, 110, 112, 194, 196, 199.
Bowler: 40.
Bowyer: 183, 185, 187, 190, 195, 198, 201, 203, 205, 208.
Boys, Boyse: 52, 53, 54, 55, 57.
Bradley: 151, 159, 161, 163, 165, 167, 170.
Branch: 60, 61, 63.
"Brandon," Middlesex County: 39, 46, 48.

Brasseur: 85, 91.
Braxton: 20, 102, 103, 105, 106, 107, 115, 116, 118, 119, 121, 123, 124, 147, 149, 155, 157, 159, 161, 163, 165, 167, 169, 172, 175, 176, 179, 181, 183, 186, 188, 199, 202, 204, 206.
Bray: 39, 86, 94.
Brereton: 83.
Breman: 71.
Brent: 86, 209.
Brewer: 32, 55, 73.
Brewster: 54, 55, 58.
Bridger: 39, 73, 77, 79, 100, 101, 103, 141, 143, 145, 149, 151, 155, 157, 159, 161, 163, 165, 167, 169, 174, 176, 178, 181, 183, 185, 188, 191, 193, 196.
Briggs: 131, 135, 137, 139, 141, 144, 145.
British Public Record Office: 5.
Broadhurst: 70.
Broadwater: 199, 201, 204.
Brocas: 33.
Brodnax: 102, 103, 105, 106, 122, 124.
Brooke: 172, 174, 176, 178, 191, 193, 196, 199, 202, 204, 206, 208.
Browne: 33, 34, 54, 75, 78, 80, 82, 83, 156, 158, 160, 162.

Browning: 55, 57.
Brunswick County: 108, 110, 111, 114, 116, 117, 119, 120, 122, 124, 126, 128, 130, 132, 134, 136, 138, 140, 142, 144, 146, 150, 151, 154, 156, 158, 160, 162, 164, 166, 168, 171, 180, 183, 185, 187, 189, 192, 195, 198, 201, 203, 205, 208.
Bryan: 143.
Buckingham County: 154, 156, 158, 160, 162, 164, 166, 168, 171, 174, 176, 178, 180, 183, 185, 187, 189, 192, 195, 198, 201, 203, 205, 208.
Buckner: 26, 100, 102, 109, 111, 112, 116, 118.
Bullitt: 209.
Bullock: 32.
Burgess: 56, 107, 108.
Burnham: 63, 65, 68, 81.
Burnley: 146, 150, 152, 173, 175, 177, 191, 194, 196.
Burroughs, Burrowes: 64, 65, 69, 92.
Burton: 184, 186, 188, 191, 194, 196, 202, 204, 206.
Burwell: 19, 44, 48, 50, 98, 102, 103, 108, 110, 112, 114, 116, 118, 119, 121, 123, 124, 127, 128, 129, 130, 131, 132, 134, 136, 138, 141, 143, 145, 147, 149, 151, 155, 157, 159, 161, 163, 165, 167, 169, 172, 174, 176, 178, 181, 183, 185, 188, 190, 191, 193, 195, 196, 199, 202, 204, 208.
"Bushy Park:" 44.
Bushrod: 74, 75, 120, 122, 123, 125, 127, 129, 131, 133, 135, 137, 139.
Butler: 61, 62, 70, 73.
Butt: 93.
Byrd: 22, 23, 41, 45, 49, 82, 83, 90, 91, 93, 127, 129, 131, 133, 134.

C.

Cabell: 20, 140, 142, 144, 146, 150, 152, 154, 156, 158, 160, 162, 164, 166, 168, 171, 174, 176, 178, 180, 183, 185, 187, 190, 192, 195, 198, 201, 203, 205, 207, 208.
Callaway: 132, 134, 135, 138, 140, 142, 144, 154, 156, 158, 160, 162, 164, 166, 168, 171, 174, 176, 178.
Calthorpe, Caulthropp, Caultropp: 63, 64, 65, 70, 75.
Camm: 50.
Campbell: 116, 118, 119, 121, 208.
Canfield, Cawfield: 73, 74, 75, 81.
Cant: 76, 88, 89.
Cape Merchant: 24.
Capp, Capps: 31, 52.

Cargill: 115, 117.
Caroline County: 107, 108, 109, 111, 114, 116, 118, 119, 120, 122, 124, 126, 128, 130, 134, 136, 138, 140, 142, 144, 146, 150, 152, 155, 156, 158, 160, 162, 164, 168, 171, 176, 178, 180, 183, 185, 187, 190, 193, 195, 203, 206, 208.
Carr: 191, 194, 196.
Carrington: 20, 103, 118, 121, 123, 124, 126, 130, 132, 134, 136, 138, 140, 142, 144, 146, 150, 152, 155, 157, 159, 160, 162, 164, 166, 171, 174, 176, 178, 180, 183, 187, 190, 193, 195, 198, 201, 206, 208.
Carter: 18, 21, 24, 37, 38, 43, 46, 49, 51, 61, 63, 67, 71, 73, 74, 76, 87, 91, 92, 109, 110, 115, 116, 118, 119, 121, 123, 124, 127, 129, 130, 131, 133, 134, 135, 136, 137, 138, 139, 141, 143, 147, 149, 151, 155, 156, 157, 158, 159, 160, 161, 162, 163, 164, 165, 166, 167, 168, 169, 170, 171, 172, 173, 174, 175, 176, 177, 178, 179, 181, 183, 184, 185, 186, 188, 189, 191, 192, 194, 196, 197, 199, 200, 202, 203, 204, 205, 206, 207.
'Carter's Creek:" 44, 48.
Carthagena: 18.
Carver: 78, 79.

Cary: 26, 39, 75, 86, 88, 89, 93, 95, 96, 97, 98, 112, 113, 123, 124, 140, 142, 144, 146, 152, 155, 157, 158, 160, 162, 164, 166, 169, 172, 174, 176, 178, 180, 183, 185, 187, 188, 190, 193, 195, 198, 201, 206, 208, 209.
Catlett: 89, 90, 93, 94.
Catchmaie: 75.
Causy: 53.
Cave: 127, 129, 131, 133, 135, 137, 139, 141, 143, 145, 147, 149, 151.
Ceely: 54, 60.
Champe: 167, 169, 172.
Chandler: 65, 66, 67.
Chaplaine's Choice: 55.
Chaplin: 53.
Charles City: 52, 60.
Charles City County: 32, 33, 34, 35, 36, 39, 41, 42, 45, 46, 47, 49, 61, 63, 64, 65, 66, 67, 68, 69, 70, 71, 72, 73, 74, 75, 77, 78, 84, 86, 88, 91, 93, 94, 96, 97, 100, 101, 103, 104, 105, 108, 110, 111, 114, 116, 118, 119, 120, 122, 124, 126, 128, 130, 132, 134, 136, 139, 140, 142, 144, 146, 150, 152, 155, 157, 160, 162, 164, 166, 168, 171, 174, 176, 178, 180, 183, 185, 187, 190, 192, 195, 198, 201, 203, 206, 208.
Charles River: 60.

Charles River County: 61.
Charlotte County: 171, 174, 176, 178, 180, 183, 187, 190, 193, 195, 198, 201, 206, 208.
Charlton: 64, 70.
"Chatsworth:" 48.
Chisman, Cheesman: 36, 63. 85.
Chesterfield County: 125, 126, 128, 130, 132, 134, 136, 138, 140, 142, 144, 146, 150, 152, 155, 157, 158, 160, 162, 164, 166, 169, 172, 174, 176, 178, 180, 183, 185, 187, 189, 193, 195, 198, 201, 206, 208.
Chew: 53, 54, 63, 105, 106.
Chicheley: 16, 39, 72.
Chickahominy: 57.
Chickahominy Parish, or The Upper Chippokes and Smith's Fork: 60.
Chiles: 36, 61, 62, 63, 64, 65. 67, 70, 74, 77, 105.
Chilton: 25.
Chinn: 123, 124, 127, 129, 130.
Chippokes (Lower), Hog Island, Lawn Creek: 60.
Chiswell: 114, 116, 118, 119, 123, 124, 127, 128, 130, 132, 134, 136, 138, 144.
Christian: 146, 152, 154, 156, 158, 160, 162, 164, 166, 168, 193, 196, 199, 202, 204, 207.
Churchill: 44, 87, 96.

Church: 81, 94.
Clack: 122, 124, 150, 152.
Claiborne, Clayborne: 21, 24, 26, 31, 77, 78, 109, 110, 112, 123, 125, 127, 129, 131, 146, 150, 152, 155, 157, 159, 160, 162, 164, 167, 169, 179, 180, 181, 191, 194, 196, 199, 202.
Clapham: 188, 199, 202, 204, 206, 209.
Clarke, Clark: 201, 204, 206.
Clause: 54, 57.
Clayton: 25, 103, 105, 106, 107, 175, 177, 179, 181, 184, 186, 188, 209.
Clement, Clements: 61, 88.
Clinch: 141, 143.
Cobbs: 114, 116, 117, 119, 120, 124.
Cocke: 21, 45, 71, 64, 66, 82, 90, 91, 92, 93, 94, 114, 116, 117, 118, 119, 120, 121, 127, 128, 130, 132, 134, 136, 138, 141, 143, 145, 147, 149, 151, 155, 156, 157, 158, 159, 160, 161, 162, 163, 164, 165, 166, 167, 168, 169, 170, 172, 174, 175, 176, 177, 178, 179, 182, 184, 186, 189, 192, 194, 197, 200, 203, 205, 207, 209.
Cockeram: 77.
Codd: 82, 83.
Cole: 21, 40, 54, 102, 103, 104, 106.
Coleman: 180.

Coles: 172, 174, 176, 178, 183, 185, 188, 190, 193, 196.
Collclough: 75.
College: 55.
College, Plantation at: 54.
Colston: 88, 92.
Colville: 117, 118, 120, 121.
Committee of Safety, Members of: 20.
Coney; 55, 57, 58.
Congressional Library: 11.
Conway: 99, 100, 102, 105, 106, 107, 108, 109, 110, 112, 115, 116, 118, 120, 121, 123, 124, 127, 129, 130, 132, 134, 136, 138.
Conventions of 1775 and 1776: 201-209.
Cooke, Cook: 90, 94, 100, 104, 105, 106.
Cooper: 87, 92, 93.
Corbin: 23, 38, 48, 50, 74, 76, 94, 96, 102, 103, 109, 110, 112. 115, 117, 125, 175, 179, 181, 183, 184, 185, 186, 188, 191, 193, 196.
Corker: 57, 58, 64, 73.
"Corotoman:" 37, 43.
Corprew: 141, 143, 145.
Council (The), functions of: 8.
Council (The), list of members: 27-50.
Covington: 95.
Cowlinge: 32.
Cowper: 209.
Coxe: 57.
Cralle: 209.
Crawford, Craford: 86, 90, 100, 101, 102, 103, 105, 106, 109, 110, 112, 115, 117, 118, 120, 121.
Crew: 60, 63, 65, 66.
Crip, Cripps: 54, 58, 60.
Croshaw, Crowshaw: 53, 72, 74, 75.
Crump: 56, 57.
Culpeper: 26.
Culpeper County: 125, 126, 128, 130, 132, 134, 136, 138, 142, 144, 146, 150, 155, 157, 159, 160, 162, 164, 166, 169, 172, 174, 178, 180, 183, 185, 187, 189, 195, 198, 201, 204, 206, 208.
Culpeper, Lord: 17.
Cumberland County: 125, 126, 128, 130, 132, 134, 136, 138, 140, 142, 144, 146, 150, 152, 155, 157, 159, 160, 162, 164, 166, 169, 172, 174, 176, 178, 180, 183, 185, 190, 193, 195, 198, 201, 204, 206, 208.
Cunningham: 114.
Curle: 98, 209.
Currie: 128.
"Curles:" 40.
Curtis: 76, 109, 111, 123, 125,

127, 129, 131, 133, 135, 137, 139.
Custis: 41, 43, 46, 85, 89, 91, 102.

D.

Dacker: 62.
Dalby: 156, 158, 159, 161, 163, 165, 167, 170.
Dale: 13, 82, 83.
Dandridge: 46, 144, 147, 149, 151, 155, 159, 161, 163, 165, 191, 194, 196, 199, 202, 207, 209.
Dangerfield, Daingerfield: 102, 104, 106, 107, 123, 124, 130, 132, 134, 136, 138, 140, 142, 144.
Davenaut: 36.
Davis: 52, 63, 66, 72, 74.
Davison: 21, 31.
Dawson: 48, 49.
Day: 199.
Death: 63.
Delaney, Deloney: 172, 175, 177, 179.
Delaware, Lord: 5.
Denbigh, Denby: 56, 58.
Denbigh and Water's Creek: 57.
Denson: 75.
Dew: 37, 51, 62, 69, 70, 71.
Dewey: 127, 129, 131, 133, 135, 137, 139.

Digges: 15, 22, 23, 36, 43, 46, 91, 102, 108, 109, 111, 112, 115, 117, 119, 120, 122, 124, 125, 127, 129, 131, 133, 135, 137, 139, 142, 145, 150, 151, 152, 154, 156, 157, 158, 160, 162, 164, 166, 168, 170, 173, 175, 177, 179, 182, 184, 186, 189, 192, 194, 197, 200, 203, 205, 207, 209. ,
Dilke: 53, 58.
Dinwiddie: 19, 47.
Dinwiddie County: 128, 130, 132, 134, 136, 138, 140, 142, 144, 146, 150, 152, 155, 159, 160, 162, 164, 167, 169, 172, 174, 176, 178, 180, 183, 185, 187, 190, 193, 195, 199, 201, 204, 206, 208.
Dipnall: 71.
Dixon: 184, 186, 189.
Doak: 193, 196.
Doe: 54.
Donelson: 181, 184, 186, 189, 191, 194, 197.
Donne: 33.
Downes: 58, 115.
Downing: 89.
Downman: 55.
Douglas: 63, 66, 114, 115, 117, 119, 120, 126, 130, 132, 134, 135, 138.
Dowse: 52.
"Drayton:" 32.

Drew: 165, 167, 169, 174, 176, 178, 206, 208.
Drummond: 100.
Drysdale: 18.
Dudley: 85, 86, 91, 98.
Duke: 44, 88, 91.
Dunmore County: 190, 193, 195, 199, 201, 204, 206, 208.
Dunmore, Earl of: 20.
Dunston: 67.
Duval, Du Val: 191, 193, 196, 199, 202.

E.

"Eagle's Nest:" 45.
Earle: 114, 116, 118, 119, 121.
Eastern Shore: 55.
East Indies: 27, 28.
Eaton: 108, 110, 112.
Edloe, Edlowe: 54, 74.
Edmondson: 89, 91, 92, 93, 94, 183, 185, 188, 190, 193, 196, 199, 201, 206, 208.
Edmunds: 109, 111, 112, 131, 133, 135, 137, 139, 141, 144, 145, 149, 151, 156, 158, 160, 162, 164, 166, 168, 170, 173, 175, 177, 179, 182, 186.
Edwards: 69, 70, 95, 96, 97, 131, 180, 183, 185, 187.
Effingham, Lord: 17.
Embry: 108, 110, 111, 123, 125, 133, 134, 136, 139, 141, 143, 145.

Emerson: 58.
Elizabeth City County: 31, 32, 33, 35, 37, 61, 63, 64, 65, 66, 67, 69, 70, 71, 72, 74, 75, 77, 79, 84, 86, 88, 91, 94, 98, 100, 102, 103, 105, 106, 108, 110, 111, 114, 116, 118, 119, 121, 123, 124, 126, 128, 130, 132, 134, 136, 138, 140, 142, 144, 146, 150, 152, 157, 159, 161, 163, 165, 167, 169, 172, 174, 176, 178, 180, 183, 185, 188, 190, 193, 196, 199, 201, 204, 206, 208.
Elizabeth City, Lower Parish of: 56.
Elizabeth City, Lower Parts of: 59.
Elizabeth City, Upper Part of: 56, 59.
Elizabeth City, Upper Parish of: 58.
Elligood: 109, 110, 112, 115, 117, 120, 121, 123, 125.
Elliott: 37, 66, 73.
Ellyson, Ellison: 72, 75, 77.
"Eltham:" 44.
English: 55, 58, 59, 74.
Eppes, Epes: 34, 56, 60, 65, 87, 89, 96, 100, 109, 110, 112, 115, 117, 120, 121, 123, 125, 126, 128, 130, 132, 134, 136, 138, 146, 150, 152, 155, 157, 158, 160, 162, 164, 166,

Eskridge : 97, 100, 102, 104, 105, 106, 108, 184, 186, 188.

Essex County : 46, 48, 88, 89, 90, 91, 92, 93, 94, 95, 96, 97, 98, 99, 102, 103, 106, 107, 108, 110, 111, 114, 116, 118, 119, 121, 123, 124, 126, 128, 130, 134, 136, 138, 140, 142, 144, 146, 150, 152, 155, 157, 159, 161, 163, 165, 167, 169, 171, 172, 174, 176, 178, 180, 183, 185, 188, 190, 193, 196, 199, 201, 204, 206, 208.

Evelyn : 26, 34.

Ewell : 102, 103.

Eyre, Eyres : 66, 67, 211.

Eyre : 115, 117, 120, 121, 123, 125, 127, 129, 131, 133, 135, 137, 139, 141, 143, 145, 147, 149, 151, 175, 177, 179, 181, 184, 186, 188, 191, 194.

F.

Fairfax : 47, 50, 113, 115, 117, 126, 128, 130, 132, 134, 136, 138, 142, 144, 161, 169, 174, 190.

Fairfax County : 47, 50, 114, 118, 119, 121, 123, 124, 126, 128, 130, 132, 134, 136, 138, 140, 142, 144, 146, 150, 152, 155, 156, 159, 163, 165, 167, 171, 172, 176, 178, 180, 183, 185, 188, 193, 196, 199, 201, 204, 206.

Fallows : 62.

Farley, Farloe : 55, 56.

Farloe's Neck to Waroe's Ponds : 60.

Farmer : 55, 184, 186, 188, 209.

Farrar : 31, 75, 77, 78, 82, 83, 94.

Faulcon : 194, 197, 200, 203, 205, 207, 209.

Fauntleroy : 63, 64, 66, 68, 70, 72, 74, 75, 109, 111, 112, 115, 117, 118, 120, 121, 123, 125.

Fauquier County : 152, 155, 157, 159, 161, 163, 165, 167, 172, 174, 176, 178, 180, 183, 185, 188, 190, 193, 196, 199, 201, 204, 206, 208.

Fauquier, Governor : 19,

Fawcett, Fossett : 54, 55, 60.

Fawdon, Fawdoune, Fowden : 66, 70.

Feild, Field : 86, 88.

Field : 140, 142, 144, 155, 157, 159, 160, 162, 164, 166, 169, 172, 174, 176, 178, 183, 187, 190, 193, 195, 198, 201, 204, 206, 208.

Felgate, Fellgate : 54, 55.

Filmer : 63.

Fincastle County : 193, 196, 199, 202, 204, 206, 208.

Finch : 32.

Fitzhugh : 45, 82, 83, 94, 100

102, 107, 109, 111, 112, 115, 117, 123, 125, 127, 129, 131, 133, 135, 137, 139, 141, 143, 145, 156, 158, 160, 162, 164, 166, 168, 191, 196, 199, 202, 204, 206, 208.
Fitzwilliam: 46.
Fleet: 70.
Fleming: 108, 110, 136, 138, 140, 142, 144, 146, 150, 152, 155, 157, 159, 160, 162, 164, 166, 169, 172, 174, 176, 178, 190, 193, 195, 198, 201, 204, 206, 208.
Fletcher: 69.
Flint: 54, 55, 56, 57, 58, 60, 63, 66, 89.
Flood, Fludd, 55, 56, 57, 63, 64, 68, 72.
Flowerdieu, Hundred: 52, 54, 55.
Floyd: 100, 102.
Follis: 61.
Ford: 75.
Fosaker: 95.
Foster: 72, 86, 94.
Fowke, Foulke: 74, 76, 77.
Fowler: 25, 61, 62.
Fox: 82, 84, 89, 94.
Francis: 73.
Franklin: 61, 62.
Frederick County: 114, 116, 118, 119, 121, 123, 124, 126, 128, 130, 132, 134, 136, 138, 140, 142, 144, 147, 150, 152, 155, 157, 159, 161, 163, 165, 167, 169, 171, 174, 176, 178, 181, 183, 185, 188, 190, 193, 196, 199, 201, 204, 206, 208.
Freeman: 35, 55, 57.
Fry: 117, 119, 120, 122, 124, 126, 128, 130, 132, 154, 156, 158, 160, 162, 164, 166, 168,
Fulgham: 208.
Fulford: 61.

G.

Gaines: 147, 149, 151, 172, 175, 176.
Gale: 127, 129, 130, 132, 134, 136, 138.
Garland: 202, 204, 206, 209.
Garnett: 113, 114, 116, 118, 119, 121.
Gaskins: 175, 177, 179.
Gates: 5, 13, 28.
Gee: 203, 205, 209.
General Assembly: 7, 8.
General Court: 8.
George: 66, 68.
Gibbes: 52.
Gibson: 108, 109, 110, 111.
Giles; 90, 94.
Gill: 70.
Gilmer: 207.
Glascock: 181.

Glebeland: 55.
Glebeland and Archer's Hope: 57.
Gloucester County: 38, 39, 41, 42, 43, 44, 45, 48, 50, 69, 70, 71, 72, 73, 75, 76, 77, 79, 84, 88, 90, 94, 97, 98, 100, 102, 103, 104, 105, 106, 107, 108, 110, 114, 116, 118, 119, 121: 123, 124, 126, 128, 130, 132, 134, 136, 138, 140, 143, 144, 147, 150, 152, 155, 157, 159, 161, 163, 165, 167, 169, 174, 176, 178, 181, 183, 185, 188, 190, 193, 196, 199, 202, 204, 206, 208.
Godfrey: 93, 94.
Godwin: 51, 71, 74, 100, 105, 106.
Gooch, Gouge: 19, 37, 70, 71.
Goochland County: 107, 108, 110, 111, 114, 116, 118, 119, 121, 123, 124, 126, 128, 130, 132, 134, 136, 138, 140, 144, 147, 150, 152, 155, 157, 159, 161, 163, 165, 167, 169, 174, 176, 178, 181, 183, 185, 188, 190, 193, 196, 199, 202, 204, 208.
Goode: 202, 204, 206, 209.
Goodrich: 91, 100, 101, 103, 136, 138, 140, 142, 144, 146, 150.
Goodwin: 74, 105.
Gookin (Coogan): 60, 61.
Gordon: 208.
Gough: 62.
Gouldman: 97, 99, 100.
Gourgainy: 52.
Governors, List of: 13, 20.
Governor, Office of: 5.
Gower: 82.
Graves: 52, 56, 58.
Gray: 77, 98, 99, 100, 101, 105, 106, 108, 110, 112, 114, 115, 116, 117, 118, 119, 120, 121, 123, 124, 131, 133, 135, 139, 141, 143, 145, 156, 158, 160, 162, 164, 166, 168, 170, 173, 175, 177, 179, 181, 184, 186, 189, 192, 194, 197, 200, 202, 205, 207, 209.
Green: 109, 110, 112, 126, 128, 130, 132, 134, 136, 146, 150, 152, 180.
Greenhill: 154, 156, 158, 160, 162, 164, 166, 168, 184, 186, 189, 192, 194, 197.
"Greenspring:" 40, 44, 49.
Griffin: 102, 105, 106.
Griffith: 75, 77.
Grindon: 58.
Grymes: 22, 23, 46, 48, 101, 102, 103, 107, 123, 156, 158, 160, 162, 175, 177, 179, 181, 182, 184, 186, 188, 189.
Gwyn, Gwinne: 60, 66, 69, 70, 96.

H.

Hack: 97, 103,
Hackett: 70.
Hairston: 146, 150, 152.
Halifax County: 128, 130, 132, 136, 138, 141, 144, 147, 150, 155, 157, 159, 161, 163, 165, 167, 169, 172, 174, 176, 178, 181, 183, 185, 188, 190, 193, 196, 199, 202, 204, 206, 208.
Hall: 101.
Ham: 74.
Hamilton: 147, 149, 150, 151, 155, 157, 159, 161, 163, 167, 168, 169, 172, 175, 177, 179, 181, 184, 186, 188.
Hamlin: 71, 100, 103,
Hammond; 38, 75.
Hamor: 21, 28.
Hampshire County: 132, 138, 141, 143, 147, 148, 149, 150, 155, 156, 159, 161, 163, 165, 167, 169, 174, 176, 178, 181, 183, 185, 188, 190, 193, 196, 199, 202, 204, 206, 208.
Hanover County: 104, 105, 106, 107, 108, 109, 110, 111, 114, 116, 118, 119, 121, 123, 124, 127, 128, 130, 132, 134, 136, 138, 140, 143, 144, 147, 149, 151, 155, 156, 159, 161, 163, 165, 167, 169, 174, 176, 178, 181, 183, 185, 188, 190, 193, 196, 199, 202, 204, 208.
Hardage, Hardige (Hardinge): 85, 86, 89.
Hardiman: 101.
Hardy, Hardie (Hardin): 61, 62, 63, 64, 65, 67, 68, 191, 193, 196.
Harlowe: 74.
Harmanson: 86, 103, 104, 105, 106, 109, 110, 112, 115, 117, 120, 121, 123, 125, 156, 158, 159, 161, 163, 165, 167, 170, 175, 177, 179, 181.
Harmer: 34, 51, 58, 64, 65, 115, 117, 119, 120, 122,
Harris: 53, 54, 55, 60, 67, 69, 71, 72, 73, 95, 96, 97, 105, 106, 109, 110, 111, 114, 116, 128, 130, 132, 134, 136, 138, 141, 143, 145.
Harrison: 22, 24, 25, 43, 45, 46, 52, 62, 82, 83, 87, 91, 92, 93, 94, 95, 96, 97, 101, 103, 105, 106, 107, 108, 109, 110, 111, 113, 114, 115, 116, 117, 118, 123, 124, 125, 126, 127, 128, 129, 130, 131, 132, 133, 134, 135, 136, 137, 138, 139, 140, 141, 142, 143; 144, 145, 146, 150, 152, 155, 157, 158, 159, 160, 161, 162, 163, 164, 165, 166, 167, 168, 169, 172, 174, 176, 178, 180, 183, 185, 187, 190, 192, 195, 198, 201, 203, 208.
Harrop: 30, 55.

Harrop and to Martin's Hundred: 58.
Hartwell: 42.
Harvey: 14, 15, 31, 59.
Harvie: 201, 203, 207.
Harwood: 20, 29, 51, 54, 55, 56, 57, 58, 60, 62, 64, 67, 85, 89, 100, 103, 104, 105, 115, 117, 119, 121, 123, 125, 127, 129, 131, 133, 135, 137, 139, 142, 144, 145, 150, 151, 160, 162, 164, 166, 168, 170, 173, 175, 177, 179, 182, 184, 186, 189, 192, 194, 197, 200, 207, 208, 209.
Hatcher: 65, 67, 68, 74.
Hawkins: 58, 98, 100, 102, 103.
Hawley: 24, 33.
Hay: 74.
Haynes: 111, 112.
Haynie (Haney): 74, 89, 90, 91, 92, 95, 96, 97.
Hayward: 71, 85, 86.
Heale: 89, 91, 149, 151.
Hedgman: 109, 111, 112, 115, 117, 119, 120, 121, 123, 125, 127, 129, 131, 133, 135, 137, 139, 141, 143, 145.
Henrico County: 31, 40, 41, 46, 48, 60, 61, 62, 64, 65, 66, 67, 68, 69, 71, 72, 73, 74, 75, 77, 78, 81, 82, 83, 84, 86, 87, 88, 89, 90, 91, 92, 93, 94, 95, 96, 97, 100, 101, 103, 105, 106, 108, 110, 112, 114, 116, 118, 119, 121, 123, 124, 127, 128, 130, 132, 134, 136, 138, 141, 145, 147, 149, 151, 155, 159, 161, 163, 165, 169, 172, 174, 178, 181, 183, 185, 188, 190, 193, 196, 199, 202, 204, 206, 208.
Henricus, City of: 52.
Henry: 154, 169, 172, 175, 177, 179, 181, 183, 185, 188, 190, 192, 195, 196, 199, 202, 208.
"Hewick:" 42.
Heyrick: 56, 63, 64.
Higginson: 35.
Hill; 24, 25, 36, 42, 51, 60, 61, 62, 64, 65, 66, 67, 68, 71, 74, 75, 77, 79, 96, 97, 211.
Hinton: 33.
Hite: 181, 183, 185, 188, 190, 192, 195, 198, 208.
Hobbs: 71.
Hobson: 33, 93, 94, 95.
Hockaday: 70, 123, 125.
Hodges: 90, 91.
Hodin, Hoddin: 63.
Hog Island: 54, 55, 57.
Hoggard: 104.
Holland: 28, 53, 72.
Holladay: 88, 127, 129, 131, 133, 135, 136, 139.

Holloway: 24, 52, 99, 100, 104, 105, 106.
Holman: 108, 110, 111.
Holmewood: 72.
Holt: 72, 92, 93, 191, 194, 196, 199, 202, 205, 207, 209.
Hone: 70, 79.
Hooe: 58, 64, 65, 66, 95.
Hooke: 33.
Horrocks: 49.
Horsey: 70.
Horsmanden: 37, 73, 74.
Hoskins: 67, 68, 69, 71, 72.
Hough: 59.
House of Burgesses: 8, 9.
House of Burgesses, Members of: 52.
Howard: 126, 128, 130, 132, 134, 135, 138, 146, 150, 152, 180, 183, 185, 187, 190.
Howe: 57, 58, 59.
Hubbard: 91.
Hull: 63, 157, 159, 161, 163, 165, 167, 170.
Hunter: 18, 123, 125.
Hutchings: 111, 115, 117, 119, 120, 122, 128, 129, 131, 133, 135, 137, 139, 146, 156, 158, 160, 162, 164, 166, 168, 170, 173, 175, 177, 179, 182, 184, 187, 189, 192, 195, 200, 203, 205.
Hutchinson: 57, 61, 63, 64, 66.

I.

Isle of Wight County; 39, 50, 61, 63, 64, 65, 66, 67, 68, 69, 70, 71, 72, 73, 74, 75, 77, 79, 84, 86, 88, 90, 94, 100, 101, 102, 105, 106, 108, 110, 112, 114, 116, 118, 119, 121, 123, 124, 127, 129, 130, 132, 134, 136, 138, 141, 143, 145, 147, 149, 151, 155, 156, 159, 161, 163, 165, 167, 169, 174, 176, 178, 181, 183, 185, 188, 191, 193, 196, 199, 202, 204, 206, 208.
Indians: 27, 29, 30.
Innes: 181, 184, 186, 189, 191, 194, 197.
Ireland: 38.
Iversonn: 70.

J.

Jackson: 52, 57, 61.
Jacquelin: 100.
Jameson's List of Journals of the House of Burgesses: 83, 84, 86, 87, etc.
James City County: 30, 32, 33, 34, 35, 36, 38, 40, 42, 44, 47, 49, 61, 63, 64, 65, 66, 67, 68, 69, 70, 71, 72, 73, 74, 75, 77, 78, 79, 84, 86, 88, 91, 100, 102, 103, 105, 106, 107, 108, 110, 112, 114, 115, 116, 118, 121, 123, 124, 127, 128,

130, 132, 134, 136, 138, 141,
143, 145, 147, 149, 151, 155,
156, 159, 161, 163, 165, 167,
169, 172, 174, 176, 178, 181,
183, 185, 187, 191, 193, 196,
199, 202, 204, 205, 206, 208.

Jamestown, James City, James City Island: 9, 30, 52, 54, 55, 56, 57, 60, 91, 100, 102, 103, 105, 106, 108, 110, 112, 115, 117, 119, 120, 122, 124, 125, 128, 129, 131, 133, 135, 137, 139, 142, 144, 146, 150, 152, 154, 156, 158, 160, 162, 166, 170, 173, 175, 177, 179, 182, 189, 192, 194, 197, 200, 203, 207, 209.

James City, Chickahominy and Pashbehay: 58.

Jarrell: 127, 129.

Jefferson: 52, 132, 134, 135, 138, 180, 182, 185, 187, 190, 192, 195, 198, 201, 203, 207.

Jeffreys: 16.

Jenings: 18, 21, 25, 39, 43, 76, 77, 79, 95.

Jenkins: 84, 91, 97, 102.

Johnson: 43, 60, 62, 65, 66, 69, 70, 71, 88, 94, 102, 103, 104, 105, 106, 109, 111, 112, 127, 129, 130, 132, 134, 136, 138, 141, 143, 145, 147, 149, 150, 151, 155, 157, 159, 161, 163, 165, 167, 169, 181, 184, 186, 188, 190, 196, 199, 202, 204, 206, 209.

Johnson's Neck, Archers Hope and the Neck of Land: 60.

Johnston: 146, 152, 155, 157, 161, 163, 164, 165, 166, 167, 168, 169, 170, 174, 181.

Jones: 20, 61, 63, 69, 75, 89, 100, 102, 103, 104, 106, 108, 110, 111, 122, 123, 124, 125, 126, 127, 128, 129, 130, 131, 132, 133, 134, 135, 136, 137, 138, 139, 140, 142, 147, 149, 150, 180, 183, 185, 187, 190, 191, 192, 193, 195, 196, 199, 202, 204, 206, 207, 208.

Jordan: 25, 52, 54, 56, 57, 63, 66, 74, 80, 81, 91, 171, 174, 176.

Jordan's Journey: 54, 55.

Justice: 128, 130, 132, 134, 135, 138, 140, 142, 144.

K.

Keeling: 141, 143, 145.

Keith: 155, 157, 159, 161.

Kethe's Creek to Mulberry Island and Saxon's Goal: 56.

Kemp: 15, 21, 32, 41, 51, 56, 85, 88, 89, 91, 105, 106, 107, 122.

Kendall: 27, 74, 78, 79, 84,

86, 89, 127, 129, 131, 133,
135, 137, 139, 141, 143, 145,
147, 149, 151.
Kenner: 86, 87, 89, 91, 92,
93, 94, 95, 194, 196, 200,
202, 205, 207, 209.
Kennon: 84, 110, 111, 114,
116, 118, 119, 120, 122, 124,
126, 128, 130, 132, 134, 136,
138, 146, 150, 152, 155, 157,
158, 160, 162, 164, 166, 168.
Key: 56.
Kicoughtan: 52.
King: 190, 193, 196, 199, 201,
204, 206, 208.
King and Queen County:
43, 48, 49, 89, 90, 93, 94, 96,
97, 99, 100, 102, 103, 104,
105, 106, 107, 109, 110, 112,
115, 116, 118, 119, 121, 123,
124, 127, 129, 130, 132, 134,
136, 138, 141, 143, 145, 147,
149, 151, 155, 157, 159, 161,
163, 165, 167, 169, 172, 174,
176, 178, 181, 183, 185, 188,
191, 193, 196, 199, 202, 204,
206, 208.
King George County: 104,
105, 106, 109, 110, 112, 115,
116, 118, 119, 121, 123, 124,
127, 129, 130, 134, 136, 141,
143, 145, 147, 149, 151, 156,
159, 161, 163, 165, 167, 169,
172, 174, 176, 178, 181, 183,
185, 188, 191, 193, 196, 199,
202, 204, 206, 208.
"King's Creek:" 44.
Kingsmill, Kingsmell: 53, 54.
Kingston: 54, 60.
King William County: 94,
98, 100, 102, 103, 105, 106,
109, 110, 112, 115, 116, 118,
120, 121, 123, 124, 127, 129,
130, 132, 134, 136, 138, 141,
143, 145, 147, 149, 151, 155,
157, 159, 161, 163, 165, 167,
169, 172, 175, 176, 179, 181,
183, 186, 188, 191, 193, 196,
199, 202, 204, 206, 208.
Kiskyacke: 58, 59.
Kiskyacke and the Isle of
Kent: 57.
Knight: 74, 76, 83, 85.

L.

Lambert: 67, 68, 69, 72, 211.
"Laneville:" 48.
Langhome: 123, 125, 192,
194, 197, 200, 203, 205, 207.
Langley: 72, 101.
Lapworth: 30.
Lawne: 52.
Lawne's Plantation: 52.
Lancaster County: 33, 35, 37,
38, 39, 43, 68, 70, 71, 72, 73,
74, 76, 77, 78, 79, 80, 81, 82,
83, 84, 86, 87, 89, 91, 92, 94,
95, 96, 97, 98, 99, 100, 101,

102, 103, 105, 106, 107, 108,
110, 112, 115, 116, 118, 120,
121, 123, 124, 127, 129, 130,
132, 134, 136, 138, 141, 143,
145, 147, 149, 151, 155, 157,
159, 161, 163, 165, 167, 169,
172, 175, 177, 179, 181, 183,
186, 188, 191, 194, 196, 199,
202, 204, 206, 208.
Lane: 89.
Lankford: 200, 202, 207, 209.
Lawson: 86, 202, 205, 207.
Lear: 41, 79, 85, 86, 88, 102, 103.
Lee: 19, 20, 21, 25, 36, 40, 47, 49, 66, 68, 69, 80, 81, 86, 89, 92, 104, 106, 107, 108, 114, 117, 119, 120, 122, 123, 125, 141, 142, 145, 147, 149, 150, 151, 152, 155, 156, 157, 158, 159, 160, 161, 162, 163, 164, 165, 166, 167, 168, 169, 170, 171, 172, 174, 175, 176, 177, 178, 179, 181, 182, 184, 186, 189, 192, 194, 197, 200, 202, 203, 205, 207, 209.
Leech: 30.
Legrand, Le Grand: 147, 149, 151, 156, 158, 159, 161, 163, 165, 168, 170, 173, 175, 177, 179, 192, 194, 197, 200.
Leigh: 40, 89, 90, 93, 94, 96.
Lewis: 44, 48, 116, 118, 120, 143, 147, 149, 156, 158, 160,

162, 164, 166, 168, 170, 175, 177, 179, 181, 190, 192, 195, 198, 201, 203, 205, 207.
Lightfoot: 42, 47, 140, 142, 144.
Lister: 97.
Littlepage: 85, 167, 169, 174.
Littleton: 35.
Llewellin, Luellin: 62, 64, 66, 69, 72.
Lloyd, Loyd: 63, 64, 65, 66, 68, 69, 70, 85, 92, 211.
Lobb: 72.
Lockhart: 208.
Lomax: 114, 116, 118, 119, 120, 122, 124, 126, 128, 130, 134, 136, 138.
Loudoun County: 147, 149, 151, 155, 157, 159, 161, 163, 165, 167, 169, 172, 175, 177, 179, 181, 184, 186, 188, 191, 193, 196, 199, 202, 204, 206, 209.
Loudoun, Earl of: 19.
Louisa County: 115, 116, 118, 120, 121, 123, 125, 127, 129, 130, 132, 134, 136, 138, 141, 143, 145, 147, 149, 151, 155, 157, 159, 161, 163, 165, 167, 169, 172, 175, 177, 179, 181, 184, 186, 188, 191, 194, 196, 199, 202, 204, 206, 209.
Loving: 26, 63, 73.
Lower Norfolk County: 33,

34, 60, 61, 63, 64, 65, 66, 67, 68, 69, 70, 71, 72, 73, 74, 75, 77, 78, 79, 81, 82, 85, 86, 211.
Lucas: 73, 77, 79.
Ludlow: 35, 61.
Luddington: 66.
Ludwell: 21, 22, 38, 40, 44, 49, 86, 91, 115, 117, 119, 120, 122, 124, 125.
Ludwell's List of Sessions of the General Assembly: 87, etc.
Lunenburg County: 123, 125, 127, 129, 131, 133, 134, 136, 139, 141, 143, 145, 147, 149, 151, 155, 157, 159, 161, 163, 165, 167, 169, 172, 175, 177, 179, 181, 184, 186, 188, 191, 194, 196, 199, 202, 204, 206, 209.
Lunsford: 36.
Lyddall: 88.
Lyde: 109, 110.
Lyggon: 72.
Lynch: 122, 124, 180, 183, 185, 187, 190, 192, 195, 198, 201, 203, 208.
Lyne: 181, 183, 185, 188, 199, 202, 204, 208.

M.

Maclin: 171, 180, 198, 201, 203, 205, 208.

Macock; 29.
Macon: 90, 109, 110, 181, 183, 185.
Madison: 31, 122, 124, 126, 128, 130, 132, 209.
Major: 51, 65, 66, 69, 70.
Mansell, Mansfield: 58, 60, 68.
Marrable: 94, 100, 102, 108, 110, 112, 134, 136, 139, 147, 149, 151, 153, 184, 186, 188, 191, 194, 196, 201.
Marshall: 106, 155, 157, 159, 161, 163, 165, 167, 169, 172, 174, 176, 178, 183, 185, 188, 190, 193, 204.
Martian: 53, 57, 58, 59.
Martin: 27, 68, 110, 111, 127, 129, 130, 132, 134, 136, 138, 141, 145, 147, 150, 152, 201.
Martin-Brandon: 52.
Martin's Hundred: 52, 54, 55, 57, 58.
Martin's Hundred to Kethe's Creek: 60.
Marye: 182.
Maryland; 33.
Mason: 20, 71, 72, 73, 74, 75, 77, 81, 83, 85, 86, 87, 88, 89, 91, 94, 95, 102, 103, 105, 106, 112, 146, 147, 150, 151, 152, 156, 157, 158, 160, 162, 164, 166, 168, 170, 173, 175, 177, 179, 182, 184, 186, 188,

189, 191, 192, 193, 194, 196,
197, 200, 203, 204, 205, 208,
209.
Massachusetts: 42.
Massie, Massey: 104, 105,
106, 123, 125.
Mathew: 81.
Matthews: 16, 31, 36, 69, 70,
71, 198.
"Matthews Mount:" 31.
May: 190, 192, 195.
Mayo: 159, 161, 163, 165,
167, 169, 178, 180, 183, 185,
190, 193, 195, 198, 201, 204,
206, 208.
McCarty: 52, 97, 101, 102,
104, 105, 109, 111, 112, 115,
117, 209.
McDowell: 190, 192, 195,
198, 201, 203, 205, 207.
Meade: 181, 204, 207.
Meares: 64, 66.
Mecklenburg County: 170,
172, 175, 177, 179, 181, 184,
186, 188, 191, 194, 196, 199,
202, 204, 206, 209.
Meese: 41, 79.
Mellin 70.
Mellings: 74.
Menifee: 33, 54.
Mercer: 20, 155, 157, 159,
161, 163, 165, 167, 169, 174,
176, 178, 181, 183, 185, 188,

190, 193, 196, 199, 202, 204,
206, 208.
Meredith: 174, 176, 178, 206.
Meriwether: 97, 98, 99, 100,
102, 103, 104, 105, 106, 107,
109, 110, 111, 116, 118, 119,
121, 123, 124, 209.
Middlesex County; 33, 35,
37, 38, 39, 40, 41, 42, 44, 45,
46, 48, 50, 80, 81, 82, 85, 86,
87, 88, 89, 91, 94, 96, 98, 99,
100, 102, 103, 105, 106, 107,
109, 110, 112, 115, 116, 117,
118, 120, 121, 123, 125, 127,
129, 131, 133, 135, 136, 139,
141, 143, 145, 147, 149, 151,
155, 157, 159, 161, 163, 165,
167, 170, 175, 177, 179, 181,
184, 186, 188, 191, 194, 196,
199, 202, 204, 206, 209.
Michell: 74.
Middleton: 29.
Milby: 199.
Milner: 51, 86, 88, 94.
Mitchell: 115, 118, 120, 121,
155, 157, 159, 161, 163, 165,
167, 169, 172, 175, 177, 179,
183, 186, 188, 191, 194, 196.
Monroe: 113, 115, 117, 119.
Montague: 69, 70, 73, 191,
194, 196, 199, 206, 209.
Moone: 61, 68, 71.
Moore: 116, 118, 120, 121,

123, 124, 127, 129, 130, 132,
134, 136, 138, 141, 143, 145,
155, 157, 159, 161, 163, 165,
167, 169, 183, 186, 188, 191,
193, 196, 209.
Morgan : 66, 69, 70.
Morlatt : 53.
Morley : 75.
Morton : 141, 143, 145.
Morrison, Moryson : 16, 35, 51.
Moseley : 81, 90, 95, 127, 129, 131, 133, 135, 137, 139, 156, 158, 160, 164, 165, 168, 170, 175, 177, 179, 181, 184, 186, 189, 191, 194, 197.
Mottram (Matrum) : 65, 69.
" Mt. Airy : " 47, 49.
Mounts Bay : 57.
" Mt. Pleasant : " 40.
Moyse, Moyses : 54, 55.
Muhlenberg : 201, 206.
Mulberry Island : 55, 57, 58.
Munford : 103, 109, 110, 112, 170, 171, 172, 174, 176, 177, 179, 180, 181, 184, 185, 186, 187, 188, 191, 194, 196.
Murdaugh : 204, 207.
Muscoe (Muscow) : 108, 110, 111.
Muse : 209.

N.

Nansemond : 34, 35, 37, 38, 41, 66, 67, 69, 70, 71, 72, 77, 79, 85, 86, 88, 91, 94, 96, 100, 102, 103, 105, 106, 109, 110, 112, 115, 117, 118, 120, 121, 123, 125, 127, 129, 131, 133, 135, 136, 139, 141, 143, 145, 147, 149, 151, 155, 157, 161, 163, 165, 167, 170, 172, 175, 177, 179, 181, 184, 186, 188, 191, 196, 199, 202, 204, 207, 209.
Nash : 131, 133, 135, 137, 139, 141, 143, 145, 156, 158, 159, 161, 163, 165, 168, 170, 202.
Neale : 61, 85, 97, 98, 99, 100, 101, 102.
Neck of Land : 54, 55, 57, 58.
Nelson : 20, 21, 48, 115, 117, 119, 121, 122, 124, 125, 158, 160, 162, 164, 166, 168, 170, 173, 175, 177, 179, 182, 184, 186, 189, 192, 194, 197, 200, 205, 207, 209.
Neville : 193, 196, 199, 201, 206.
" Newbottle : " 45.
Newce : 29, 30.
Newton : 99, 100, 105, 106, 172, 175, 177, 179, 181, 184, 186, 188, 191, 194, 196, 199, 202, 205, 207, 209.
New Kent County : 31, 42, 44, 71, 73, 74, 75, 77, 78, 85, 86,

88, 90, 93, 94, 98, 100, 102,
103, 104, 105, 106, 109, 110,
112, 115, 117, 118, 120, 121,
123, 125, 127, 129, 131, 135,
133, 137, 139, 141, 143, 145,
147, 149, 151, 155, 156, 157,
159, 161, 163, 165, 167, 170,
175, 177, 179, 181, 184, 186,
188, 191, 194, 196, 199, 202,
204, 207, 209.

Newman: 91.

Newport: 27.

Nicholas: 24, 140, 142, 144,
145, 150, 154, 172, 174, 176,
178, 181, 183, 185, 188, 191,
193, 198, 199, 201, 202, 203,
204, 206, 208.

Nicholson: 17.

Norfolk County: 88, 89, 90,
91, 92, 93, 94, 98, 99, 100,
101, 102, 103, 105, 106, 109,
110, 112, 115, 117, 118, 120,
121, 123, 125, 127, 129, 131,
133, 135, 137, 139, 141, 143,
145, 147, 149, 151, 155, 157,
159, 161, 163, 165, 167, 170,
172, 175, 177, 179, 181, 184,
186, 188, 191, 194, 196, 199,
202, 205, 207, 209.

Norfolk Borough: 9, 111, 112,
115, 117, 119, 120, 122, 124,
125, 128, 129, 131, 133, 135,
137, 139, 142, 144, 146, 150,
152, 154, 158, 160, 162, 166,
168, 170, 173, 177, 179, 182,

187, 189, 192, 195, 200, 203,
205, 209.

Northampton County: 34, 37,
41, 43, 46, 63, 64, 65, 66, 67,
69, 71, 72, 74, 75, 78, 79, 85,
86, 89, 91, 95, 100, 102, 103,
104, 105, 106, 109, 110, 112,
115, 117, 118, 120, 121, 123,
125, 127, 129, 131, 133, 135,
137, 139, 141, 143, 145, 147,
149, 156, 158, 159, 161, 165,
167, 170, 175, 177, 179, 181,
184, 186, 191, 194, 196, 199,
200, 202, 207.

Northumberland County: 36,
49, 65, 67, 68, 69, 70, 71, 72,
74, 75, 76, 77, 78, 79, 80, 81,
82, 83, 85, 86, 87, 89, 90, 91,
92, 93, 94, 95, 96, 97, 99,
100, 101, 103, 105, 106, 107,
109, 110, 112, 115, 117, 118,
120, 121, 123, 125, 127, 129,
131, 135, 137, 139, 141, 143,
145, 147, 149, 150, 156, 157,
159, 161, 163, 165, 167, 170,
175, 177, 179, 181, 184, 186,
188, 191, 194, 196, 202, 205,
207, 209.

"Northumberland House:"
49.

Norton: 125, 127, 129, 131,
133, 135, 137, 139.

Norvell: 199, 202, 204, 206,
208.

Norwood: 24.

"North End:" 50.
Norsworthy: 60.
Nott: 18.
"Nominy Hall:" 49.
Nutmeg Quarter: 54, 56, 59.

O.

Oldis: 61.
Oporto, Portugal: 49.
Orkney, Earl of: 18.
Orange County: 109, 110, 112, 115, 121, 123, 125, 127, 129, 131, 133, 135, 137, 139, 141, 143, 145, 147, 149, 151, 156, 158, 159, 161, 163, 165, 167, 170, 173, 175, 177, 179, 181, 184, 186, 187, 188, 191, 194, 196, 200, 202, 205, 207, 209.
Osborne: 54, 55, 56, 57, 58, 109, 123, 124, 180, 183, 185.
Other side of the water: 54, 55.
Ouldsworth: 30.
Ousley: 88.
Over the water against James City: 57.

P.

Pace's Paines: 54, 55.
Page: 20, 41, 43, 45, 50, 72, 86, 128, 130, 132, 134, 136, 138, 140, 143, 144, 147, 150, 152, 155, 156, 157, 158, 159, 160, 161, 162, 163, 164, 165, 166, 167, 168, 169, 170, 174, 176, 178, 189, 192, 194, 195, 197, 200, 203, 205, 207, 209.
Pagett: 54.
Paine; Peene: 53, 74.
Palmer: 54, 55.
Parke: 21, 39, 43, 78, 88.
Parker: 108, 110, 132, 138, 202, 204, 206.
Parramore: 122, 124, 146, 150, 152, 154, 156, 160, 162, 164, 166, 168, 171, 173, 176, 178, 180, 182, 185, 187.
Pashbehay: 54, 55, 57.
Pate: 39, 70.
Patteson: 205, 208.
Patton: 132, 134, 135, 137.
Paulett: Pawlett: 30, 35, 52, 58, 60.
Payne: 61, 126, 128, 130, 132, 136, 138, 140, 143, 144, 147, 150, 152, 155, 157, 159, 161, 163, 165, 167, 169, 174, 176, 178, 181.
Pendleton: 20, 126, 128, 130, 134, 136, 138, 140, 142, 144, 146, 150, 152, 155, 156, 157, 158, 159, 160, 161, 162, 163, 164, 165, 166, 167, 168, 169, 171, 174, 176, 178, 180, 183, 185, 189, 190, 193, 195, 198, 201, 203, 204, 206, 208.
Penn: 207.

Percy: 13, 28.
Perkins: 132, 136, 138, 200, 202, 207.
Perrott: 81, 82.
Perry: 32, 36, 54, 55, 56, 69, 71.
Perry's (Captain) Downwards to Hog Island: 56.
Pettus: 35, 184, 186, 188, 191, 194, 196, 199.
Peyton: 109, 111, 112, 143, 145, 147, 149, 151, 181, 184, 186, 188, 191, 192, 193, 194, 196, 199, 202, 204, 206, 209.
Phelps: 132, 134, 135, 138.
Phenny: 47.
Pickett: 208.
Pierce: 32.
Piercey: Persey: 24, 34.
Pinkard: 86.
"Piscataway:" 46.
Pitt: 67, 68, 70, 71, 74, 75.
Pittsylvania County: 181, 184, 186, 191, 194, 197, 200, 202, 207, 209.
Place: 40.
Pleasants: 88.
Polentine: 52.
Pollington: 53.
Poole: 66.
Popkton: 54.
Porteus: 45.
Portlock: 123, 125.
Pory: 29, 51.

Pott: 14, 30.
Pountis: 29.
Powell: 14, 29, 52, 57, 74, 75, 77, 79, 95.
Power: 115, 116, 118, 120, 121, 127, 129, 131, 133, 135, 137, 139, 141, 143, 145.
Poythress; Poythers: 64, 66, 68, 105, 106, 179, 181, 184, 186, 189, 192, 194, 197, 200, 205, 207, 209.
Prentis: 207.
Presley: 67, 68, 76, 77, 78, 79, 80, 81, 82, 83, 87, 98, 99, 101, 102, 103, 105, 106, 107, 109, 110, 112, 113, 115, 117, 118, 120, 121.
Preston: 171, 174, 176, 178, 183, 185, 187.
Price: 54, 55, 64, 65, 109, 110, 112, 147, 149, 151.
Prince: 64, 65.
Prince Edward County: 131, 133, 135, 137, 139, 141, 143, 145, 147, 149, 151, 156, 158, 159, 161, 163, 165, 168, 170, 173, 175, 177, 181, 184, 186, 189, 192, 197, 200, 202, 205, 207, 209.
Prince George County: 37, 96, 98, 100, 101, 103, 105, 106, 107, 109, 110, 112, 115, 117, 118, 121, 123, 125, 129, 131, 133, 135, 137, 139, 141,

143, 145, 147, 149, 151, 156, 158, 160, 161, 163, 165, 168, 170, 173, 175, 177, 179, 181, 184, 186, 189, 192, 194, 197, 200, 202, 205, 207, 209.
Princess Anne County: 33, 88, 90, 94, 95, 98, 99, 100, 101, 102, 103, 105, 106, 109, 110, 112, 115, 117, 118, 120, 121, 125, 127, 129, 131, 133, 135, 137, 139, 141, 143, 145, 147, 149, 151, 156, 158, 160, 162, 164, 165, 168, 170, 177, 179, 181, 184, 186, 189, 191, 194, 197, 200, 202, 205, 209.
Prince William County: 109, 111, 112, 115, 117, 118, 120, 121, 123, 125, 127, 129, 131, 133, 135, 137, 139, 141, 143, 145, 147, 149, 151, 156, 158, 160, 162, 164, 166, 168, 170, 173, 177, 179, 181, 184, 186, 189, 192, 194, 197, 200, 202, 205, 207, 209.
Prosser: 166, 169.
Pugh: 109, 110, 112.
Purefoy (Purfrey, etc.,): 56.
Pyland: 74.

Q.

Quarry: 44.
"Queen's Creek:" 37.

R.

Ramsey: 72, 73, 77, 78.

Ramshawe: 56.
Randolph: 24, 25, 48, 51, 52, 73, 83, 84, 86, 87, 88, 89, 90, 91, 92, 93, 96, 97, 98, 101, 103, 105, 106, 107, 108, 109, 110, 111, 112, 114, 116, 117, 118, 119, 120, 121, 122, 123, 124, 125, 127, 128, 130, 131, 132, 133, 134, 135, 136, 137, 138, 139, 141, 143, 145, 147, 149, 151, 155, 157, 171, 172, 174, 175, 176, 177, 178, 179, 181, 182, 183, 184, 185, 187, 188, 189, 190, 192, 193, 194, 196, 197, 199, 200, 201, 203, 204, 206, 208, 209.
Randolph (see "Attorney General"): 124, 125, 128, 129, 142, 144, 146, 150, 152, 154, 156, 158, 162, 164, 166, 168, 170, 173.
Ransom, Ranson: 69, 70, 88, 90, 91.
Rappahannock County: 36, 37, 40, 46, 73, 74, 75, 77, 85, 86.
Ratcliffe: 13, 27.
Ravenscroft: The *Virginia Gazette*, in Jan., 1736, announced the death "lately, Col. Thomas Ravenscroft, lately Burgess for Prince George Co." As the exact session at which he was a member is not known, his

name does not appear in the text.

Reade, Read: 38, 72, 123, 125, 127, 129, 133, 147, 151, 155, 157, 159, 161, 163, 165, 167, 169, 171, 174, 176, 178, 180, 183, 187, 201, 206, 208.

Receiver General, Office of: 7.

Receiver Generals, List of: 23.

Revell: 74.

Reynolds: 69.

Richards: 56, 57, 61.

Richardson: 88.

Richmond County: 47, 49, 88, 91, 92, 93, 94, 95, 96, 97, 98, 99, 100, 101, 102, 103, 105, 106, 107, 109, 111, 112, 112, 115, 117, 118, 120, 121, 123, 125, 127, 129, 131, 133, 135, 137, 139, 141, 143, 145, 147, 149, 151, 156, 158, 160, 162, 164, 166, 170, 173, 175, 177, 179, 181, 184, 186, 189, 192, 194, 197, 200, 202, 205, 207, 209.

"Rich Neck:" 40.

Ricketts: 103, 105.

Riddick: 102, 103, 109, 110, 112, 115, 117, 118, 120, 121, 123, 125, 127, 129, 131, 133, 135, 136, 139, 141, 143, 145, 147, 149, 151, 157, 159, 161, 163, 165, 167, 168, 170, 172, 175, 177, 179, 181, 184, 186, 188, 191, 194, 196, 199, 202, 209.

Ridley: 64, 66.

"Ripon Hall:" 43.

Roane: 180, 183, 185, 188, 190, 193, 196.

Robins: 37, 56, 61, 62, 63, 66, 67, 69, 70.

Robinson: 21, 24, 42, 46, 49, 52, 60, 85, 86, 87, 94, 96, 97, 98, 99, 100, 102, 103, 104, 105, 106, 107, 109, 110, 112, 115, 116, 118, 119, 121, 123, 124, 127, 128, 129, 130, 131, 132, 133, 134, 135, 136, 138, 139, 140, 141, 143, 145, 147, 149, 151, 155, 157, 159, 161, 163, 165, 167, 169, 172, 174, 176, 178, 183, 185, 188, 200, 202, 205, 209.

Rogers: 64.

Rolfe: 21, 28.

Rootes: 203, 206.

Roscoe, Roscow: 23, 103, 105, 106, 109, 111, 112.

"Rosegill:" 35, 39, 41, 50.

"Rosewell:" 45, 50, 52, 55.

Rowlston: 58, 59.

Ruffin: 111, 112, 115, 117, 119, 120, 121, 131, 133, 135, 137, 139, 146, 150, 152, 204, 206.

Russell: 208.
Rutherford: 155, 159, 161, 163, 165, 167, 169, 174, 176, 178, 181, 183, 185, 188, 190, 192, 193, 195, 198, 201, 203, 206, 208.

S.

Sadler: 63.
Salmon: 61.
Sandford: 88.
"Sandy Point:" 47.
Sandys: 24, 30.
Saunders: 59.
Savage: 79, 209.
Savin: 54, 56, 59.
Sawyer: 88.
Sayres: 89.
Scarborough, Scarburgh: 26, 42, 51, 56, 57, 59, 63, 65, 67, 69, 72, 75, 79, 86, 104, 105, 108, 110, 111, 114, 115, 116.
Scarlett: 88.
Scotchmore: 55, 57, 58.
Scotland: 42, 47.
Scott: 108, 110, 114, 126, 130, 132, 134, 136, 180, 181, 183, 184, 185, 186, 188, 189, 190, 193, 196, 199, 201, 204, 206, 208.
Scrivenor: 27.
Seawell: 58, 211.
Secretary of State, office of: 6.
Secretaries: 21.

Seely: 56.
Selden: 141, 143, 145, 199, 202, 204, 206, 208.
Seward: 65.
Sparpe: 52, 54.
Shelley: 52.
Sheppard, Shepherd: 59, 63, 66, 69, 71.
Sherman: 88, 91.
Sherwood: 25, 86, 91.
"Shirley:" 36, 42, 46.
Shirley Hundred Island: 54, 55, 57, 58.
Shirley Hundred Main: 54, 55.
Shirley Hundred Main and Cawsey's Cave: 57, 58.
Shirley Hundreds (Both), Mr. Farrars and Chaplains: 56.
Sibsey, Sipsey (Shipsie): 33, 58, 59, 60, 61.
Sidney: 63, 66, 72, 73, 74, 75, 211.
Simmons, Symmons: 98, 99, 100, 101, 103, 108, 112, 114, 116, 118, 119, 121, 123, 124, 147, 149, 151, 156, 158, 160, 162, 164, 166, 168, 170, 173, 175, 177, 179.
Simms: 207.
Simpson: 154, 156, 158, 160, 162, 164, 166, 168, 171, 173, 176, 178, 180, 182, 185, 187, 190, 192, 195, 198, 207.
Skelton: 147, 150.

Slaughter: 115, 140, 142, 144, 146, 150, 172, 174, 176, 178, 190, 193, 195, 199.

Smith: 13, 27, 30, 39, 44, 51, 54, 57, 63, 64, 67, 72, 74, 75, 84, 85, 86, 101, 103, 104, 105, 106, 108, 110, 111, 126, 128, 130, 132, 134, 136, 138, 140, 142, 143, 144, 150, 152, 155, 157, 159, 161, 163, 165, 167, 170, 175, 177, 179, 190, 198, 199, 201, 204, 206, 207, 208.

Smythe's Hundred: 52.

Smythe's Mount: 55.

Smythe's Mount and Perry's Point: 57.

Smythe's Mount, the other side of the water and Hog Island: 58.

Soane: 51, 68, 69, 70, 71, 73, 75, 89, 90, 100.

Somers: 28.

Southampton County: 125, 127, 129, 131, 133, 135, 137, 139, 141, 143, 145, 147, 149, 151, 156, 158, 160, 162, 164, 166, 168, 171, 173, 175, 177, 179, 181, 184, 186, 189, 192, 194, 197, 200, 202, 205, 207, 209.

Southerne: 53, 55, 56.

Southcoat: 78.

Span: 89.

Sparrow: 65, 67, 69, 75.

Speakers of the House of Burgesses, List of: 51, 52.

Speare: 91.

Speed: 190, 193, 195, 198, 209.

Speke: 68.

Spence, Spense: 52, 94, 95.

Spencer: 17, 21, 40, 58, 79.

Spicer: 85, 86, 88.

Spotsylvania County: 105, 106, 109, 111, 112, 115, 117, 119, 120, 121, 123, 125, 127, 129, 131, 133, 135, 137, 139, 141, 143, 145, 147, 149, 151, 156, 158, 160, 162, 164, 166, 168, 170, 175, 177, 179, 182, 184, 186, 189, 192, 194, 197, 200, 203, 205, 207, 209.

Spotswood: 18, 123, 125, 126, 128, 130, 132, 134, 136, 138, 141, 143, 145.

Sprat, Spratt: 105, 106.

Stacey: 52.

Stafford County: 45, 79, 81, 82, 83, 85, 86, 88, 91, 94, 95, 100, 102, 103, 105, 106, 107, 109, 110, 112, 115, 117, 119, 120, 121, 123, 125, 127, 129, 131, 133, 135, 137, 139, 141, 143, 145, 147, 149, 151, 158, 162, 164, 166, 168, 170, 173, 175, 177, 179, 184, 186, 188, 189, 192, 194, 197, 200, 203, 206, 207, 209.

Stanley Hundred: 57, 58.
Stanhope, Stanup: 100, 102, 103, 104.
Starke: 180, 183, 185, 187, 208.
Stegg: 22, 35, 39, 51. 63.
Stephen: 201, 203.
Stephens: 32, 53, 64, 68, 69.
Stith: 84, 88, 101, 103, 104, 105, 122, 124, 126, 128, 130, 132, 134, 136, 138, 140, 142, 144, 183, 185, 187, 190, 192, 195.
Stokes: 54, 56.
Stoner: 33.
Story: 90.
Stoughton: 66, 71.
Strachey: 21, 28.
Strafferton: 61.
"Stratford:" 47, 49.
Stratton: 56, 57.
Streeter: 72.
Stretchley: 89.
Stringer: 75.
Strother: 208.
Stubblefield: 192, 194, 197, 200, 203, 205, 207.
Studley: 24.
Sullivan: 94.
Surry County: 33, 34, 38, 43, 45, 46, 69, 70, 71, 73, 74, 75, 77, 79, 80, 81, 82, 83, 85, 86, 87, 88, 89, 90, 91, 92, 93, 94, 95, 96, 97, 98, 99, 100, 101, 103, 105, 106, 107, 109, 111, 112, 115, 117, 119, 120, 121, 123, 125, 127, 129, 131, 133, 135, 137, 139, 141, 143, 145, 149, 151, 156, 158, 160, 162, 164, 166, 170, 175, 177, 179, 182 184, 186, 189, 192, 194, 197, 200, 203, 205, 207, 209.
Surveyor General, Office of: 8,
Surveyor Generals, List of: 26.
Sussex County: 131, 133, 135, 137, 139, 141, 144, 145, 149, 151, 156, 158, 160, 162, 164, 166, 168, 170, 173, 175, 177, 179, 182, 184, 186, 189, 192, 197, 200, 203, 205, 207, 209.
Swan, Swann: 38, 64, 67, 73, 82, 83, 85, 86, 88, 89, 90, 92, 96.
"Swann's Point:" 38.
Swearingen: 140, 142, 144.
Sweny: 108, 110, 111, 114, 116, 118, 119, 121.
Syme: 104, 127, 140, 143, 144, 147, 149, 151, 155, 157, 159, 161, 163, 165, 167, 169, 174, 176, 178, 193, 196, 199, 202, 204, 208.

T.

Tabb: 20, 106, 122, 123, 124, 126, 128, 130, 132, 134, 135, 136, 138, 140, 142, 144, 146, 150, 154, 156, 158, 160, 162,

164, 166, 168, 171, 174, 176,
180, 183, 185, 190, 192, 195,
198, 201, 203, 204, 205, 206,
209.
Tabenor: 73.
Talbot: 154, 156, 158, 160,
162, 164, 166, 168, 171, 174,
176, 178, 180, 183, 185, 187,
190, 192, 195, 198, 201, 203,
205, 208.
Tangier, Africa: 18.
Tayloe (In early records written Taylor, but the Virginia Historical Society possesses a deed signed by the early councillor which signature is distinctly written William Tayloe): 36, 37, 49, 66, 93, 94, 95, 97, 107.
Taylor: 63, 66, 88, 91, 93, 94, 95, 121, 123, 125, 127, 129, 131, 135, 137, 139, 141, 143, 145, 151, 156, 158, 159, 161, 163, 165, 167, 170, 172, 175, 177, 179, 181, 184, 186, 189, 192, 194, 195, 197, 200, 201, 202, 203, 206, 207, 208, 209.
Taliaferro: 92, 147, 149, 151, 171, 174, 178, 183, 185, 187, 190, 193, 195.
"T. M.:" 81.
Tatem: 147, 149, 151.
Tarpley: 98, 99.
Tapewell: 198, 201, 203, 205, 208.

Teackle: 103.
Tebbs: 173, 175, 177, 179, 181, 182, 186, 189, 192, 194, 197.
Terry: 147, 150, 152, 155, 157, 159, 161, 163, 165, 167, 169, 181, 183, 185, 188, 190, 193, 196, 199, 202, 206, 208.
Thacker: 94, 96, 105, 106.
Thomas: 69, 72, 88, 154, 156, 158, 160, 162, 164, 166, 168, 171, 174, 176, 178, 180, 183, 185, 187.
Thompson: 54, 88, 89, 90, 91, 93, 94, 95, 101.
Thomson: 25.
Thornbury: 71.
Thornton: 49, 99, 100, 104, 105, 106, 115, 117, 119, 120, 121, 123, 125, 127, 129, 131, 133, 135, 137, 139, 140, 141, 142, 143, 144, 145, 146, 147, 149, 150, 151, 152, 154, 156, 157, 158, 160, 162, 164, 166, 168, 171, 188, 191, 194, 196, 200, 205, 207, 209.
Thoroughgood, Thorowgood: 33, 55, 56, 58, 78, 79, 90, 92, 95, 209.
Thorpe: 30.
Throckmorton's Plantation: 54.
Thruston: 201, 204, 206.
"Timberneck:" 43.
Tipton: 208.
Todd: 124, 125.

245

Townsend: 34, 54, 61, 62.
Tracy: 29.
Trahorne: 55.
Travers: 51, 68, 76, 78, 79, 80.
Travis: 9, 63, 116, 128, 129, 131, 135, 139, 144, 146, 150, 152, 156, 158, 160, 162, 164, 166, 168, 170, 182, 184, 187, 189, 192, 194, 197, 200, 203, 205, 207, 209.
Treasurers, List of: 24.
Treasurer, Office of: 7.
Tree: 54, 57.
Trent: 172, 174, 176, 178, 180, 183, 185.
Trigg: 199, 204.
Trussell: 68, 71, 72.
Tucker: 24, 29, 31, 52, 53, 127, 129, 131, 133, 135, 137, 172, 175, 177, 179.
Tuke: 61.
Tunstall: 60, 174, 176, 178.
Turberville: 95, 96.
"Turkey Island:" 46.
Turner: 109, 110, 115, 116, 118, 119, 121, 123, 124, 127, 129, 130, 134, 138, 139.

U.

Underwood: 70.
Upper Norfolk County: 60, 61, 63, 64, 65, 66, 73, 74, 75.
Upshaw: 146, 150, 152, 155, 157, 159, 161, 163, 165, 167, 169.

Upton: 56, 59, 61, 62, 65, 66.
Utie: 32, 53, 54, 55.
"Utimaria": 32.

V.

Vaulx: 127, 129, 131, 133.
Veal, Veale: 141, 143, 145, 147, 149, 151, 161, 163, 165, 167, 170.
Venable: 115, 116, 123, 126, 127, 129, 130, 132, 134, 135, 138, 173, 175, 177, 179.
Virginia Company: 5.
Virginia Historical Society: 5.
Virginia State Library: 5.

W.

Wade; 72, 147, 150, 152, 155, 157, 159, 161, 163, 165, 167.
Wager: 146, 150, 152, 155, 157, 159, 161, 163, 165, 167, 169.
"Wakefield:" 43, 45.
Waldoe: 27.
Walke: 100, 103, 109, 110, 112, 115, 117, 120, 121, 123, 125, 127, 129, 131, 133, 135, 137, 139, 141, 143, 145, 147, 149, 151, 156, 158, 160, 162, 164, 165, 168, 170.
Walker: 20, 37, 63, 65, 66, 67, 71, 79, 131, 127, 129, 143, 145, 147, 149, 150, 154, 156, 158, 159, 160, 161, 162, 163, 164, 165, 166, 167, 168, 170,

171, 173, 175, 176, 177, 178,
180, 181, 182, 184, 185, 186,
187, 188, 190, 192, 195, 198,
199, 201, 202, 204, 205, 206.
Wall: 108, 110, 111, 114, 116,
117, 119, 120.
Wallace: 180, 183, 185, 188.
Waller: 100, 103, 115, 116,
117, 118, 119, 120, 121, 123,
124, 125, 127, 128, 129, 130,
132, 134, 136, 141, 143, 145,
147, 149, 151.
Wallinge: 77.
Walton: 154, 156, 158, 160,
162, 164, 166, 168.
Ward: 52, 166, 169, 172, 174,
176, 178.
Ward's Plantation : 52.
Wareham : 57, 58.
Waring: 108, 110, 111, 126,
128, 130, 146, 150, 152, 171,
172, 174, 176, 178, 180.
Warne: 64.
Warner: 38, 41, 51, 69, 75, 77.
"Warner Hall:" 38, 41, 44,
48.
Warren : 63, 74, 79.
Warwick County : 29, 31, 32,
36, 39, 40, 63, 65, 66, 67, 69,
70, 71, 72, 74, 75, 77, 85, 86,
89, 91, 93, 95, 96, 97, 98, 100,
102, 103, 104, 105, 106, 109,
111, 112, 115, 117, 119, 120,
121, 123, 125, 127, 129, 131,

133, 135, 137, 139, 142, 144,
145, 150, 151, 156, 158, 160,
162, 164, 166, 168, 170, 173,
175, 177, 179, 182, 184, 186,
189, 194, 197, 200, 203, 205,
207, 209.
Warwick River: 54, 55, 56,
60.
Warwick River County: 61,
63, 64, 69.
Washer: 52.
Washburn : 91.
Washington : 79, 81, 114, 116,
118, 119, 121, 123, 124, 133,
135, 137, 139, 141, 142, 144,
145, 147, 150, 152, 155, 157,
159, 161, 163, 165, 167, 169,
171, 174, 176, 178, 180, 183,
185, 188, 190, 193, 196, 199,
201, 205, 207, 209.
Waters : 71, 75, 91, 95, 100,
102, 103.
Waters Creek and the Upper
Parish of Elizabeth City,
56.
Waters Creek (From) to Marie's Mount: 57.
Watkins: 53, 190, 193, 195,
198, 199, 201, 202, 204, 206,
208.
Warrosquoyacke, Worrosqueake: 54, 56, 57, 59.
Watson: 69, 70, 71, 190, 193,
195.

Watts: 209:
Waugh: 100, 117, 119, 120, 121.
Weale: 62.
Webb: 63, 71, 73, 74, 75, 147, 149, 151.
Webster: 57, 73.
Weekes: 81, 82.
Welburn: 94.
Wells: 65.
West: 14, 15, 28, 32, 54, 55, 85, 86, 94, 115, 116, 123, 124, 126, 128, 130, 132, 134, 136, 138, 140, 141, 142, 143, 144, 145, 155, 157, 159, 161, 163, 165, 167, 169, 171, 174, 176, 178, 180, 183, 185, 188, 190, 193, 196, 208.
West, Lord Delaware: 13.
West Augusta County: 201, 207.
Westcombe: 94, 95.
West Indies: 30.
Westmoreland County: 36, 40, 42, 47, 49, 72, 76, 77, 79, 80, 81, 85, 86, 89, 91, 94, 95, 96, 97, 98, 100, 101, 102, 104, 105, 106, 107, 108, 109, 111, 112, 115, 117, 118, 119, 120, 121, 122, 123, 125, 127, 129, 131, 133, 135, 137, 139, 142, 144, 145, 150, 152, 158, 160, 162, 164, 166, 168, 170, 173, 175, 179, 182, 184, 186, 189, 192, 194, 197, 200, 203, 205, 207, 209.
"Westover:" 35, 39, 45, 49, 54, 55.
Westover and Flowerdien Hundred: 57, 58.
Westropp: 64.
Westwood: 110, 111, 114, 116, 119, 123, 124, 126, 128, 130, 132, 134, 136, 138, 140, 142, 144, 190, 193, 196, 199, 201, 204, 206.
Wetherell, Weatherall: 64, 68, 69.
Weyanoke: 55, 57, 58.
Weye, Weyre: 74, 75, 77, 79.
Weynman: 28.
Whitaker: 38, 53, 67, 68, 69, 70, 71, 72, 74, 80, 81, 85, 86, 91.
Whitby: 51, 61, 69, 70, 71.
White: 61, 190, 193.
Whitehead: 106.
Whiting: 24, 42, 111, 114, 116, 118, 119, 121, 123, 124, 126, 128, 130, 132, 134, 136, 138, 140, 143, 144, 147, 150, 152, 155, 157, 159, 161, 163, 165, 167, 169, 174, 176, 178, 181, 183, 185, 188, 190, 193, 196, 199, 202, 206, 208.
"Whitemarsh:" 39.
Wickham: 29.
Wilcox: 53, 72, 74.

Wilford: 68.
Wilkins: 61.
Wilkinson: 59, 208.
William and Mary College: 8, 9, 26, 102, 103, 109, 111, 112, 115, 117, 118, 120, 122, 124, 125, 128, 129, 131, 133, 135, 137, 139, 142, 144, 146, 150, 152, 154, 156, 158, 160, 162, 164, 166, 168, 170, 173, 175, 177, 179, 182, 184, 186, 189, 192, 195, 197, 200, 209.
Williams: 209.
Williamsburg: 9, 45, 47, 48, 50, 105, 106, 109, 111, 112, 115, 117, 119, 120, 122, 124, 125, 128, 129, 131, 133, 135, 137, 139, 142, 144, 146, 150, 152, 154, 156, 158, 160, 162, 166, 168, 170, 171, 173, 175, 177, 182, 184, 187, 189, 192, 194, 197, 200, 201, 203, 207, 209.
Williamson: 79.
Willis: 38, 69, 70, 72, 75, 76, 79, 102, 103, 105, 106, 107, 108, 110, 111, 112, 118, 119, 121, 123, 124, 126, 128, 130, 132, 134, 136.
Willoughby: 34, 56, 58, 131, 133, 135, 137, 139.
Wills: 100, 199, 202, 204, 206.
Wilson: 84, 86, 88, 91, 94, 95, 102, 103, 122, 123, 124, 125, 126, 128, 130, 134, 135, 138, 140, 144, 146, 152, 154, 156, 158, 160, 162, 164, 166, 168, 171, 174, 176, 178, 180, 181, 183, 184, 185, 186, 188, 192.
"Wilton:" 47.
Windham: 62, 63.
Wingate: 24, 34.
Wingfield: 13, 27.
Winn: 152, 183, 185, 187, 190, 192, 195, 198, 201, 203, 205, 207.
Winston: 198, 201.
Withers: 91.
Wood: 37, 56, 57, 64, 65, 66, 69, 71, 72, 174, 176, 181, 183, 185, 188, 190, 193, 196, 199, 208.
Woodbridge: 101, 102, 103, 109, 111, 112, 115, 117, 118, 120, 121, 123, 125, 127, 129, 131, 133, 135, 137, 139, 141, 143, 145, 147, 149, 151, 156, 158, 160, 162, 164, 166, 168, 170, 173, 175, 177, 179, 181.
Woodford: 203.
Woodhouse: 66, 69, 102.
Woodlife: 69.
Woodson: 181, 183, 185, 188, 190, 193, 196, 199, 202, 204, 206, 208.
Woodward: 54.
Worleigh: 61, 62.
Wooldridge, Worlich, (Worbrigh): 63, 67, 71, 74, 75.
Wormeley: 21, 34, 35, 41, 42,

50, 68, 80, 87, 115, 117, 118,
120, 121, 123, 125, 127, 129,
131, 133, 135, 136, 139, 141,
143, 145, 147, 149, 151, 155,
157, 159, 161, 163, 165, 167.
Wright: 72, 100, 191, 194,
197, 200, 202, 207.
Wyatt: 14, 15, 35, 65, 72.
Wynne: 28, 51, 73, 75, 77, 78, 94.
Wythe: 102, 105, 106, 116,
135, 137, 139, 150, 152, 154,
155, 157, 159, 161, 163, 165,
167, 169, 172, 174, 176, 178,
209.

Y.

Yeardley, Yardley: 13, 14, 28, 34, 70.
Yeo: 64, 65, 77, 78, 79.
York: 58, 59.

York County: 32, 33, 34, 35,
36, 37, 38, 39, 41, 43, 44, 46,
63, 65, 66, 68, 69, 70, 71, 72,
74, 75, 77, 78, 84, 85, 86, 88,
91, 95, 100, 102, 104, 105,
106, 109, 111, 112, 115, 117,
119, 120, 122, 124, 125, 127,
129, 131, 133, 135, 137, 139,
142, 144, 145, 150, 152, 154,
156, 158, 160, 162, 164, 166,
168, 170, 173, 175, 177, 179,
182, 184, 186, 189, 192, 194,
197, 200, 203, 205, 207, 209.
Yorkshire, Eng.: 40.
Yorktown: 48.
Yowell: 86, 89.

Z.

Zane: 193, 196, 199, 201, 204, 208.

www.ingramcontent.com/pod-product-compliance
Lightning Source LLC
Chambersburg PA
CBHW050138170426
43197CB00011B/1877